STANLEY CAVELL, RELIGION,
AND
CONTINENTAL PHILOSOPHY

INDIANA SERIES IN THE PHILOSOPHY OF RELIGION

Merold Westphal, *editor*

STANLEY CAVELL, RELIGION, AND CONTINENTAL PHILOSOPHY

ESPEN DAHL

Indiana University Press
Bloomington and Indianapolis

This book is a publication of

INDIANA UNIVERSITY PRESS
Office of Scholarly Publishing
Herman B Wells Library 350
1320 East 10th Street
Bloomington, Indiana 47405 USA

www.iupress.indiana.edu

Telephone 800-842-6796
Fax   812-855-7931

♾ The paper used in this publication meets the minimum requirements
of the American National Standard for Information Sciences—Permanence
of Paper for Printed Library Materials, ANSI Z39.48-1992.

Manufactured in the United States of America

Cataloging information is available from the Library of Congress
ISBN 978-0-253-01202-9 (cloth)
ISBN 978-0-253-01206-7 (paperback)

1 2 3   4 5   18 17 16 15 14

CONTENTS

Acknowledgments   vii

List of Abbreviations   ix

Introduction   1

1. Modernism and Religion   16

2. The Ordinary Sublime   33

3. Acknowledging God   47

4. Skepticism, Finitude, and Sin   66

5. The Tragic Dimension of the Ordinary   81

6. The Other and Violence   102

7. Forgiveness and Passivity   121

Conclusion: The Last Question:
Self-redemption or Divine Redemption?   139

Notes   147

Bibliography   163

Index   171

ACKNOWLEDGMENTS

I am grateful for instructive comments and responses to drafts of various chapters in this book. My thanks go to Stephen Mulhall, Ståle Finke, Jan Olav Henriksen, Elisabeth Løvlie, Marius Mjaaland, Stine Holte, and Jonas Jakobsen. The writing of major parts of the book was made possible thanks to the funding of the Ethics Programme at the University of Oslo, where I also profited from participating in colloquial groups. The Faculty of Theology at the University of Oslo as well as the Department of History and Religious Studies at the University of Tromsø have provided me with good working conditions while writing the book.

Several chapters grew out of previously published articles, and I would like to thank the respective publishers for permission to draw on that material: Chapter 2: "The Ordinary Sublime after Stanley Cavell and Cora Diamond," *Transfiguration: Nordic Journal of Religion and the Arts* (2010–2011): 51–68; permission granted by Museum Tusculanum Press. Chapter 3: "On Acknowledgement and Cavell's Unacknowledged Theological Voice," *Heythrop Journal* 51 (2010): 931–945; permission granted by the Trustees for Roman Catholic Purposes Registered and by Blackwell Publishing. Introduction and chapter 4: "Finitude and Original Sin: Cavell's Contribution to Theology," *Modern Theology* 27 (2011): 497–515; permission granted by Wiley-Blackwell.

ABBREVIATIONS

CHU   Stanley Cavell, *Conditions Handsome and Unhandsome: The Constitution of Emersonian Perfectionism* (Chicago: University of Chicago Press, 1990)

CR   Stanley Cavell, *The Claim of Reason: Wittgenstein, Skepticism, Morality, and Tragedy* (New York: Oxford University Press, 1979)

CT   Stanley Cavell, *Contesting Tears: The Hollywood Melodrama of the Unknown Woman* (Chicago: University of Chicago Press, 1996)

CW   Stanley Cavell, *Cities of Words: Pedagogical Letters on a Register of the Moral Life* (Cambridge, Mass.: Belknap Press of Harvard University Press, 2004)

DK   Stanley Cavell, *Disowning Knowledge in Seven Plays of Shakespeare*, updated edition (Cambridge: Cambridge University Press, 2003)

HDTW   J. L. Austin, *How to Do Things with Words*, 2nd ed., ed. J. O Urmson and M. Sbisa (Cambridge, Mass.: Harvard University Press, 1975)

IQO   Stanley Cavell, *In Quest of the Ordinary: Lines of Skepticism and Romanticism* (Chicago: University of Chicago Press, 1988)

LK   Stanley Cavell, *Little Did I Know: Excerpts from Memory* (Stanford, Calif.: Stanford University Press, 2010)

LI   Jacques Derrida, *Limited Inc*, trans. S. Weber (Evanston, Ill.: Northwestern University Press, 2008)

MWM   Stanley Cavell, *Must We Mean What We Say? A Book of Essays* (Cambridge: Cambridge University Press, 1976)

NYUA   Stanley Cavell, *This New Yet Unapproachable America: Lectures after Emerson after Wittgenstein* (Albuquerque: Living Batch Press, 1989)

OB   Emmanuel Levinas, *Otherwise than Being or Beyond Essence*, trans. A. Lingis (Pittsburgh, Pa.: Duquesne University Press, 1998)

PAL   Stanley Cavell, Cora Diamond, John McDowell, Ian Hacking, and Cary Wolfe, *Philosophy and Animal Life* (New York: Columbia University Press, 2008)

PDT   Stanley Cavell, *Philosophy the Day after Tomorrow* (Cambridge, Mass.: Belknap Press of Harvard University Press, 2005)

PH   Stanley Cavell, *Pursuits of Happiness: The Hollywood Comedy of Remarriage* (Cambridge, Mass.: Harvard University Press, 1981)

PI   Ludwig Wittgenstein, *Philosophical Investigations*, trans.
          G. E. M. Anscombe, P. M. S. Hacker, and J. Schulte (Oxford:
          Wiley-Blackwell, 2009)
PP   Stanley Cavell, *Philosophical Passages: Wittgenstein, Emerson, Austin,
          Derrida* (Cambridge Mass.: Blackwell, 1995)
PoP   Stanley Cavell, *A Pitch of Philosophy: Autobiographical Exercises*
          (Cambridge, Mass.: Harvard University Press, 1994)
SW   Stanley Cavell, *Senses of Walden*, expanded edition (Chicago:
          University of Chicago Press, 1981)
TI   Emmanuel Levinas, *Totality and Infinity: An Essay on Exteriority*,
          trans. A. Lingis (Pittsburgh, Pa.: Duquesne University Press, 1969)
TS   Stanley Cavell, *Themes Out of School* (San Francisco: North Point
          Press, 1984)
WV   Stanley Cavell, *The World Viewed*, enlarged edition (Cambridge,
          Mass.: Harvard University Press, 1979)

STANLEY CAVELL, RELIGION,
AND
CONTINENTAL PHILOSOPHY

INTRODUCTION

"Why are the most unlikely people, including myself, suddenly talking about God?" Terry Eagleton asks, referring to the return of religion among intellectuals, in affirmation as well as criticism of it.[1] Stanley Cavell also has quite a bit to say about God, as attested by the very existence of this book. But since religion is notably not one of the topics on which Cavell's fame as a thinker rests, it seems reasonable to count Cavell among the "unlikely people" Eagleton has in mind. Nonetheless, such a characteristic would be misleading. Cavell has not "suddenly" or recently started "talking about God"; beginning with his very first publication, religious themes have continued to find their way into his thinking and writing. Admittedly, Cavell often merely alludes to such themes rather than treats them explicitly; scattered observations and comments are frequently composed as parenthetical remarks or offered as examples *en passant*, "as if," one of Cavell's finest commentators puts it, "being overlooked was the condition to which they aspired."[2]

Given only a superficial impression of the cultural, intellectual, and spiritual breadth of his enterprise, it would in fact be more "unlikely" were Cavell among those who have nothing to say concerning religion. But since his approach to religion is far from straightforward, the question remains: Exactly why does Cavell continue to invoke religious tropes and topics? This book is my attempt not only to answer that question but also to show how the wider philosophical context of the ordinary, finitude, skepticism, acknowledgment, modernism, and other of Cavell's principal occupations can shed light on the significance of the explicit religious tropes and topics. Moreover, the philosophical context, worked out in Cavell's rich and profound analyses and readings, carry religious implications of their own, which will be equally significant here. Starting out as a proponent of a highly original extension of ordinary language philosophy in the aftermath of J. L. Austin and the late Wittgenstein, Cavell has carved out the implications of his thinking in numerous contexts and on numerous topics, including music, film, Shakespeare, American transcendentalism, and romantic poetry. Despite his uncontested interest in religious themes along with his occasionally expressed unwillingness to subscribe to religious faith, Cavell has not worked out his complicated relation to religion in any detail. Nevertheless, he refers frequently to the Bible, Augustine, Luther, Pascal, Milton, Kierkegaard, and, more recently, Benjamin and Levinas, suggesting that he has an affirmative relation to religious topics; in regard to Cavell's critical or rival take on religion, Nietzsche and Emerson play prevalent roles. Apart from their particular usage by Cavell, one does not have to be a theologian to perceive that his key concepts, such as confession, return, conversation, transfiguration, redemption, and praise, indicate a profound affinity to Christianity.

One already understands from such lists of names and concepts that Cavell's stance toward religion calls for a differentiated interpretation. Despite his own intimations, and even the high regard he can express for Christianity, Cavell at times levels harsh criticism at it, even contending that religion is beyond contemporary sensibility;[3] for instance, he writes that "[r]espectable further theologizing of the world has, I gather, ceased" (DK, 36 n3). Yet, in other passages he can write that the Christian outlook is something that he is "not in a position to share, but admire[s] and rejoice[s] in" (CHU, 131). Leaving aside the question of how, or whether at all, such utterances can be reconciled, they at least bear witness to the inherent complexity and tension found at almost every juncture of Cavell's treatment of religious ideas. Such complexity is by no means lessened when one takes into account that Cavell is not a Christian but a Jew, indeed a more or less secular Jew. When asked by an interviewer how he conceives of the relation between Christianity and Judaism, he replies:

> To choose between Judaism and Christianity is, I suppose, still a live issue for me. I don't mean that I would convert to either. I grew up as a Jew and I believe in Martin Buber about these things. You don't have to convert to being a Jew . . . For me to say that the figure of Christ is an obsessive figure for a Jewish intellectual is hardly news.[4]

Perhaps the issue at stake is a matter of feeling drawn to both Christianity as well as to the Jewish tradition to which he already belongs, while simultaneously resisting them both.

In that interview, Cavell reflects on the relation between the American and the Jewish tradition, especially as he sometimes feels that Emerson and Thoreau have suggested ways to bring them together for him. Referring to his book on Thoreau's Walden and his essays on Emerson, Cavell says that "I made Thoreau write a scripture that is as much old testament, and I made Emerson into the philosopher of immigrancy."[5] Since he was the only son of an immigrant Jew, this latter theme strikes a significant chord in Cavell's autobiography. And since biography and philosophy are for him inextricably connected, this bears on his efforts to think through the conditions of philosophy, not least of American philosophy. Immigrancy, Cavell suggests, has to do with the theme of abandonment in Emerson, which, in Cavell's hands, draws both on the sense of Exodus and on the disciples' readiness for departure when the Master calls. Moreover, immigrancy suggests another undercurrent in Cavell's writing, namely the feeling of being a stranger—not only to others, but first and foremost to oneself (*PoP*, xv). Such inherent alienation entails a sense of diaspora, which also offers an intelligible backdrop to Cavell's recurrent occupation with separation and partiality, with exile and a longing for a homecoming of words.

This position of not being religious yet feeling indebted to religion, of moving between confessions and rejections, of being a secular Jew yet fascinated with Christianity is certainly composite, complex, and indeed ambivalent—but precisely therefore fascinating and open.[6] If philosophy is supposed to awaken us to the perplexity of what we otherwise take for granted, such a position seems a highly promising starting point for an exploration of religion. The intriguing problem in regard to Cavell's religious register is that it is in no way clear which way one shall proceed from Cavell, and it is therefore not at all surprising that the growing body of literature on this topic reaches in manifold directions.

Since the rest of this book discusses what I hold to be the most significant receptions of Cavell and religion, here I will sketch a threefold typology. In brief, there are, first, those who read Cavell as an emphatically secular and atheist philosopher and who also sympathetically affirm this stance. On the background of my constructive purpose, I will call this a negative reading. Such readers typically downplay the inherent weight in Cavell's frequent use of religious vocabulary, figures, and ideas, and instead emphasize the way in which Cavell can be taken as working through a sense of finitude in the aftermath of the death of God.[7] The second type of Cavell readers concurs on the whole with the negative reading that the overall orientation of his thought moves against Christianity, but they normatively hold this against Cavell since such readers are sympathetic to the Christian inheritance. Such critical reading tends to emphasize that Cavell's insistence on the autonomy of the self or the metaphysical independence of the finite world collides with its Christian alternative.[8] Finally, the third, affirmative reading emphasizes the affinity between Cavell's philosophical concerns and theological concepts. This position contends that despite the ambiguities in Cavell's writing, it must be regarded as essentially open to theology or religion more generally. According to such readers, not only Cavell's religious vocabulary, but also the structure of thought entailed in such key notions as skepticism, sin, acknowledgment, and redemption overlap so significantly with theological concerns as to invite further elaboration along those lines.[9]

Although I maintain the conversation with the negative as well as the critical readings, this book as a whole will follow the outlines of the third, affirmative approach. That said, I strive not to neglect or be insensitive to Cavell's negative stance toward religion; indeed, paying heed to such a stance as one side of Cavell's (at least) two-sided relation to religion is the very issue of the first chapter. In accordance with the second, critical reading, I also endeavor not to deny that there are points where theology parts from Cavell's thought, as becomes clear in the final pages of this book. However, those concerns should not foreclose any inquiry into Cavell's possible contributions as if they were irreconcilable with religion or even Christian theology. I hope to cultivate a sense of patience: a patience to await whatever there is of religious insights contained in his writing, and a patience that willingly faces his moments of open reluctance. I attempt to identify, respond to, and expand on Cavell's rich writings with their overlaps, allusions, and employment of religious ideas that allow for further philosophical and theological thought along the suggested lines. Nonetheless, my aim is not primarily to provide an exegesis of Cavell's thinking on religion, but rather to expand on his valuable intuitions, in a way that is perhaps more Cavellian than Cavell, following him so to speak more according to his spirit than according to his words. In doing so, I elaborate his thoughts in two directions invited by the conversations with theology and continental philosophy.

Theology and Philosophy, Analytic and Continental

The question, then, is where this approach leaves this book: should it be shelved as theology or philosophy, or perhaps philosophy of religion? Cavell himself hesitates when it comes to the presupposition often required by philosophy of religion, namely that religion can be singled out and studied as a specialized discipline within philosophy. Cavell regards ethics and religion as integral to at least Wittgenstein's practice—they are constitutive parts of the practice's spiritual fervor, bound enigmatically up with Wittgenstein's attention to what seems almost too trivial to mention, sometimes thought of as prophecy (NYUA, 75). Hence, as far as I am guided by Cavell and as far as one grants that what he is doing counts as philosophy, then what I present in this book should also be thought of as philosophy (with its spiritual pretension kept intact). There is no way to steer clear of theology, however, if only for the reason that Cavell himself invokes it at key stages. Additionally, theology furnishes, at least to some degree, the perspective from which I read Cavell, and thus theology—especially Protestant theology— will inform this work. That theology matters to Cavell's philosophy is partly because theological writings are among the most influential ways the Judeo-Christian tradition is handed down and has flown into the Western cultural conceptual repertoire. If philosophy's virtue, as Cavell understands it, is primarily responsiveness, it must respond to texts, myths, film, and art—whatever there is in the culture that demands attention and thought. He accordingly speaks of philosophy's principal task as that of "confront[ing] the culture with itself" (CR,

125). Because theology has unmistakably left its mark on our culture, to engage in philosophy means also to confront the culture with its own, albeit potentially suppressed, theological inheritance. Hence philosophy should engage in a conversation with theology, despite its tendency to shun it.

Although they are at times contested, theology and philosophy are nonetheless academic disciplines. However critical Cavell is of the professionalization of philosophy, it remains an integral part of those disciplines' task—whether within or outside of academia—to discover and to test their own conditions, indebtedness, and autonomy with regard both to their own past and to bordering disciplines. Cavell has repeatedly drawn on film and literature and yet insisted that such preoccupations do not turn his work into film studies or literary theory; and likewise, to the extent that it opens itself toward religion, neither does his philosophy become theology. It is obvious that, for Cavell, the secular cultural state in which he unfolds his thought can no longer take God for granted as its given point of departure. Perhaps we can say that philosophy comprises human existence turning reflectively upon itself, restricted to the way that reflection unfolds within its finite resources. By contrast, theology presupposes that God has spoken first and that we are addressed from beyond ourselves, an address to which it replies with continual, questioning afterthought. Hence, even if philosophy and theology find mutual interest in the human world and in its origins and meaning, their sources and perspectives differ.

Even Paul Ricoeur, who is open about his willingness to listen to theology, insists that as a philosopher and a responsible thinker, he cannot start out with theological answers—he must instead remain a beginner, suspended between faith and atheism.[10] As beginners, philosophers assume the position of the child who questions everything, a position that, moreover, is echoed in Cavell's statement that philosophy is education for grown-ups (*CR*, 125). This seems like a promising way to proceed, since it does not exclude the conversation between theology and philosophy while at the same time respecting their difference. For such reasons, and like Heidegger before him, Cavell does not want to undo the separation between theology and philosophy: "[Heidegger] is careful to deny that philosophy and religion are the same, presumably on the ground that philosophy cannot acknowledge religion as letting—the way religion works to let—truth happen, say by authority or by revelation" (*TNUA*, 3). As for Heidegger, philosophy's separation from theology does not preclude a fruitful interaction, but is rather taken as the presupposition of their mutual acknowledgment.[11]

Perhaps the best way to think of this relation is to conceive Cavell's philosophy as in *competition* with religion. Cavell himself explicitly reads the Shakespearian corpus in such a manner, adding that "I suppose this is why the idea of Shakespeare as producing a 'secular scripture' does not quite satisfy me" (*DK*, 18).

I take Cavell's description of his reading of Shakespeare to indicate his general stance toward religion and theology. "Competing" does not mean "ruling out," because that would amount to a secular reading that would dissatisfy Cavell. On the contrary, in the same book Cavell claims that "the reason a reader like Santayana claimed to find everything in Shakespeare but religion was that religion is Shakespeare's pervasive, hence invisible, business" (*DK*, 218). Although "competition" can imply an attempt to overcome and succeed or renew religion, I take Cavell's statement about Shakespeare's pervasive business to imply that competition means that religion also enters into drama or philosophy, perhaps as the mutual informing and mutual rivalry of different voices—hence as a conversation. Cavell has detected such an internal conversation in both Emerson and Heidegger and thinks of them as "internalizing the unending quarrel between philosophy and theology" (*SW*, 131). Such a juxtaposition makes the two disciplines cast new light on each other according to their shifting constellations, yet without diminishing their separateness. As Jürgen Habermas has suggested, theology should regard its exposure to secular outlooks, and vice versa, as a dialectical learning process.[12] Such a recommendation comes close to the conversation I take Cavell to invite. Something can be gained by taking a detour through the dialectics between theology and philosophy. However, a lack of mutual exchange has too often been the rule, and in 2010 Cavell notes his regret of the loss of that conversation, especially when it comes to reflecting on what he understands as skepticism or sin. "In this, philosophy has suffered from the way it has put distance between itself and theology. Theology is drenched in fallen worlds, the only ones there are, anyway the only ones that contain philosophy (or theology)" (*LK*, 446). Consequently, I want neither to extricate Cavell's philosophy from theology nor establish a forced unity, but rather to think of his philosophy and theology as a fruitful companionship. But exactly how far such companionship can go remains in question: there are points where Cavell cannot follow theology, and conversely, there are aspects of Cavell's thinking that seem highly problematic from a theological point of view. But as I hope to demonstrate, the companionship between the two still carries us remarkably far.

Given my wish to emphasize and elaborate on Cavell's relation with not only theology but also what is generally known as continental philosophy, I should briefly comment on another divide that has occupied Cavell, namely the divide between Anglophone, analytic philosophy and continental philosophy. Cavell was attracted by continental philosophy's characteristic style and broad historical and cultural scope, while analytic philosophy offered a sharp eye for philosophical puzzles and problems, particularly having to do with our conceptual presuppositions in thinking. Despite the undeniable presence of the analytical philosophical inheritance in Cavell's oeuvre, as influenced by Wittgenstein and Austin, in the following chapters I focus as much on Cavell's responses to thinkers who tend to be grouped under the heading of continental philosophy, such as Kierkegaard, Nietzsche, Derrida, and Levinas. From his earliest publication, with the telling title "Existential and Analytic Philosophy," Cavell has been torn between those two philosophical traditions. In the preface to *The Claim of Reason*, Cavell speaks of his writing as witnessing the loss of that separation and as taking on the aspiration of healing the rift (*CR*, xiii). Cavell elaborates on the acute sense of how philosophical problems arise within our language, central to Anglophone philosophy, in a manner and breadth that brings it into touch with continental thought. "Existential and Analytic Philosophy" most extensively deals with Kierkegaard, which suggests that healing the split between the analytic and continental traditions can also prove fruitful for the other split—that between reason and faith, between philosophy and theology. But, as Cavell has noted, the other way also holds true: the presence of German theology in the United States during the years of his philosophical maturation, represented by Paul Tillich, Reinhold Niebuhr, and Karl Barth, ensured that the continental tradition could not be erased entirely under the pressure of logical positivism (*LK*, 456–457).

The Ordinary

A sharper picture of what Cavell calls the ordinary or the everyday is needed before we investigate his religious register. Clarifying these notions poses some initial problems, however, for as Heidegger has pointed out, what is nearest to us is also most distant from our apprehension—far from obvious, as it first appears, the everyday is instead most enigmatic.[13] Wittgenstein expresses a similar insight thus: "We want to *understand* something that is already in plain view. For *this* is what we seem in some sense not to understand" (*PI*, § 89). To make matters worse, according to Cavell there is no "approach" to the ordinary, or at least not what Wittgenstein depicts as the ordinary; for an approach implies that we start out at a distance. But we are in fact already immersed in the ordinary as we attempt to find some philosophical orientation (*CR*, 6)—so how, then, can we even begin to come to grips with the ordinary? That is Cavell's problem, or philosophy's problem, which can only make progress by the experience of the ordinary as problematic—when we are lost to it and thus already at some distance from it. My present problem is more restricted, since I provide here essentially an account of Cavell's writing on the ordinary.

One way to come to grips with Cavell's pervasive and perplexing notion is to follow how different aspects of the ordinary surface at different stages of his evolving authorship. At the risk of oversimplification, I suggest three decisive strands as signposts for readers of this study. The first, and most formative strand, is connected to Cavell's highly original way of receiving and elaborating ordinary language philosophy; the second strand is connected to his interpretation of romanticism; and the third strand concerns what Cavell has called moral perfectionism. Although these different strands come to the fore at different stages of his authorship, they do not eclipse one another; rather, later strands preserve the former and add new dimensions to a constantly developing and increasingly enriched notion of the everyday.

Must We Mean What We Say? (1969), Cavell's first book of essays, bears witness to the impact brought about by J. L. Austin's and, later, by Wittgenstein's attention to the language of the ordinary. These two philosophers undertook in distinct ways the patient and laborious work of tracing how we use words under shifting circumstances; they brought out "what we should say when" and what we mean by what we say, that is, what the implications are in the relevant contexts (*MWM*, 20). An appeal to this perception—that what we normally say and mean deeply controls what we can philosophically say and mean—seems hopelessly weak compared to the past metaphysical aspirations of philosophy; to the logical positivism that held sway in the 1940s and 1950s, it seemed to shatter all hopes for logical precision and the progress of knowledge. Actually, the philosophical appeal to ordinary language was accused of being overly conservative—despite the fact that its protagonists regarded it as revolutionary. Indeed, this is how Cavell saw it: the encounter with the writings of Austin and Wittgenstein exacts nothing short of a conversion, where what before appeared trivial now takes on great importance (*CR*, xvii). Apart from the religious overtones, such a conversion does not so much provide new, previously hidden information as redirect our vision of our relation toward what we already somehow know. All that ordinary language philosophers have to go on is the appeal to our willingness to find ourselves captured in the representative exposition of what we say when. Voicing such an inclusive "we" as the source of philosophical authority is doomed to hit a note between arrogance and humility—arrogance insofar as the philosopher claims to speak representatively of the human condition; humility insofar as such voicing must subject itself to the demands of our mutual acceptance of the ordinary and common as the laws of intelligibility (*PoP*, 8).

So what does the adherence to ordinary language offer philosophy? On the face of it, not much. It provides neither theses nor any testing against empirical facts; it is essentially armchair philosophy insofar as its only source of authority is our willingness to agree on what we can say when. In this sense, "philosophy concerns those necessities we cannot, being human, fail to know" (*MWM*, 96). Competent speakers cannot fail to know what we call a chair, what it means to be expecting someone, why someone might find it difficult to point to a color on an object, and the like. It demands no expertise since everyone is in the position of recognizing what philosophy wants to know. So it seems that ordinary language philosophy is a way of defending common sense. But Cavell denies this also, for however widespread some opinions might be, they can always be disputed. Nonetheless, the very fact that an opinion can be disputed is important, because it requires that we agree on the use of words that express the opinions in question. The existence of such agreement and the way it influences what we can say and mean reveals the conditions of possibility for our intelligibility as speaking animals. Hence, what is articulated in ordinary language philosophy is what Kant would call transcendental knowledge—knowledge about ourselves, our conditions, and our limitations (*MWM*, 65).

But the question remains: why would such an agreement in what we say and do be important to elucidate? The question can only gain importance because the agreement is all too easily lost, in philosophy as in life. At this point, Cavell's otherwise relatively orthodox version of ordinary language philosophy stands apart: whereas ordinary language philosophers will typically claim that the loss is due to the misuse of words or conventions or the transgression of constitutive rules, Cavell thinks that stance drastically underrates the linguistic competence of competing philosophers. Cavell suggests instead that when we fail to recognize necessities we cannot fail to know, it is due not to unintended misuse of words but to denial: we *willfully* avoid the meaning of what we should say when, as if casting ourselves out of the garden of meaning. For some reason, we, or the skeptic in us, continue to utter words that cannot really interest us—words uttered without any point, placed outside language games.

In Cavell's depiction, it seems as though humans long for something absolutely certain and metaphysically assured. Such certainty must be established apart from my reliance on and participation in the notoriously unreliable ordinary language, for example, by means of sense perceptions that are in principle indubitable. But if such aspirations are ultimately frustrated, the craving for certainty easily turns into its skeptical counterpart—we have no knowledge of, say, other's minds or of the external world at all. Both the craving for absolute certainty and its rejection attests to an underlying nostalgia for the presence of the world, which again attests to the lurking sense of being at a distance from the world (*WV*, 41). This is a typical condition for modern subjectivity, according to Cavell, but its skeptical resolution can be devastating. At the heart of skepticism Cavell detects a wish to escape the fact that our meaning is conditioned by our form of life with words. Skepticism displays the human wish to transcend the human condition, whether called the drive to inhumanity or, in a religious register, sin. What we truly need is not more information or new discoveries, but to be brought back in touch with what is right in front of us. Wittgenstein famously writes, "What *we* do is to bring words back from their metaphysical to their everyday use" (*PI*, § 116). This everyday use is in turn upheld by the constant participation in "the whirl of organism Wittgenstein calls 'forms of life'" (*MWM*, 52). Without having explicitly agreed on conventions or without relying on metaphysical support, we are still so profoundly and so systematically attuned to one another in that form of life as to provide meaningful exchange. To acknowledge such perception without despair is an achievement to which Cavell aspires.

Cavell diverges from the more traditional interpretation of Wittgenstein in shifting the emphasis from rules toward Wittgenstein's notion of criteria. Criteria are the means by which we regulate our application of concepts, and hence they manifest our mutual agreement in meaning.[14] But since criteria rest on nothing more than our continued capability and willingness to participate in a shared form of life, they can also be dismissed or repudiated. And to be sure, out of disappointment with our vulnerable intelligibility so conceived, we seize this opportunity—either in terms of metaphysical speculation or skeptical denial. Yoking metaphysics and skeptical denials together under the notion of skepticism, Cavell repeatedly underlines that skepticism is something that a philosophy committed to ordinary language should not and cannot refute. Criteria's vulnerability to skeptical denial is essential to language being *ours*—that it depends on us and that we are responsible for its continued existence (*IQO*, 5). Taking skepticism seriously and as internal to the ordinary, Cavell has spent most of his career pondering this strange and yet relentless human drive to repudiate or repress our very conditions that make us intelligible creatures.

The second strand of Cavell's notion of the ordinary relates to his reception of (particularly Anglo-American) romanticism. Fragments of romantic themes found their way into part 6 of *The Claim of Reason* (1979), but romanticism was only in the subsequent years picked up and treated separately in a more sustained way (especially in *In Quest of the Ordinary*). Cavell takes his cue from Wordsworth's foreword to *Lyrical Ballads*, where romantic poetry is supposed to make "the incidents of common life interesting" (quoted in *IQO*, 6). Broadly speaking, Cavell locates not only romanticism but also Wittgenstein's and Austin's work in this evolving tradition. Emerson and Thoreau can be considered as America's belated romantics, and their foreshadowing of occupations central to ordinary language philosophy is indispensable for Cavell's understanding of the ordinary. Cavell writes: "[T]he sense of the ordinary that my work derives from the practice of the later Wittgenstein and from J. L. Austin, in their attention to the language of ordinary or everyday life, is underwritten by Emerson and Thoreau in their devotion to the thing they call the common, the familiar, the near, the low" (*IQO*, 4).

According to Cavell, romanticism not only challenges the professionalized division between literature and philosophy, but it does so by way of its incessant occupation with our intimacy with the world and the loss of that intimacy. According to romanticism, this loss is tantamount to death: it is motivated by a fear that not only words but along with it the world tend to becomes dead for us; it is nourished by the conviction that philosophy has participated in deadening it, emblematically expressed in Kant's securing of knowledge by renouncing the thing itself (*IQO*, 53). The romantic poetic-philosophical task then becomes one of bringing the world back to life. Such lost and regained intimacy with the world is what romanticism adds to the depiction of the ordinary—it adds something that Austin and Wittgenstein were never able to find a satisfactory expression of (*NYUA*, 81). One way in which Cavell thinks romanticism helps us understand the ordinary concerns how this intimacy comes to expression by means of an acute attentiveness to the ordinary. However, such attentiveness must be gained or regained against the odds: the intimacy and familiarity with ordinary life makes it almost invisible and often not regarded as worthy of attention. Still, what Emerson demands of his students is precisely the attention to such things as "[t]he meal in the firkin; the milk in the pan; the ballad in the street; the news of the boat; the glance of the eye; the form and gait of the body" (*PH*, 15). Cavell claims that this list epitomizes "what we may call the physiognomy of the ordinary, a form of what Kierkegaard calls the perception of the sublime in the everyday" (*PH*, 15). Whatever the surprising invocation of Kierkegaard and the sublime implies—a question that is the topic of chapter 2—suffice it here to point out that it invests the apparently trivial and dispensable with philosophical importance.

The task of calling attention to the physiognomy of the ordinary betrays that we have already lost interest in the ordinary. Cavell contends that Wordsworth, Emerson, Thoreau, and Wittgenstein all share the perception that we are in a state of boredom. The hunger for fantastic excitement and hence what is at least an intellectual escape from such boredom might seem a reasonable motivation for our attraction to metaphysics. The anti-metaphysical reduction to logic and semantics is not necessarily better off. At least for Cavell these are both fundamentally skeptic responses that cannot satisfy our true needs—Cavell can even state that such skeptical attractions are driven by a will to emptiness (*IQO*, 7). From this state, romanticism must, by means of philosophy and literature, attract us toward the ordinary again, breathe new life into it, which for Emerson and Thoreau means examining and consulting one's experience by means of something phenomenologists would call a reduction, that is, a consultation of your experience by means of "a momentarily *stopping*, turning yourself away from whatever your preoccupation and turning your experience away from its expected, habitual track, to find itself, its own track: coming to attention" (PH, 12).[15] To sum up, the first two strands of the ordinary offer parallel recoveries from our state of loss or skepticism: either, according to the first strand, being led back to the everyday by following the injunction of what we should say when, or by consulting one's experience and re-establishing one's interest in and intimacy with the ordinary, which romantics call our home.

Addressing the third strand of the ordinary, we must ask: What exactly is our home? Where is the ordinary to which we return? In response to the charge of conservatism, inherent to the returning home, Cavell insists on the returning in the sense of turning—both as turning away from a scene of illusions and as turning toward something new, so that the ordinary to which we return is paradoxically a place we have never been (PDT, 9–10). This third strand consists of what Cavell labels moral or Emersonian perfectionism, and it adds a temporal dimension to the ordinary, that is, a future directedness: it centers on selfhood and its split condition between its fallen present state and its striving for its next self through constant change. Even if the foundation for Cavell's so-called Emersonian or moral perfectionism was laid as early as his 1972 book on Thoreau's Walden, it first reaches fruition in the 1980s, particularly with the Carus Lectures he delivered in 1988, which were published as Conditions Handsome and Unhandsome. In Conditions, perfectionism is no longer only Emersonian, but regarded as a dimension of moral life recorded in a vast list of cultural achievements, spanning from Plato to Heidegger and Wittgenstein. The striking presence of writers with a strong religious orientation in Cavell's canon is unsurprising; St. Matthew, St. Augustine, Dante, Milton, Pascal, Kierkegaard, and Dostoevsky have all found their way into Cavell's list (CHU, 5). In broadening the concept of perfectionism in this manner, Cavell makes it clear that there is not merely one way toward perfection, as little as perfectionism is committed to one fixed state of perfection—it rather points to the incessant movement onward. Perfectionism is a particular care and responsibility for the self— a caring for the self by way of transforming the self, or more precisely, a striving for becoming true to oneself (CW, 11). Hence, perfectionist works are knitted together not by a school of thought, a philosophical discipline, or a genre, but by their aspiration to change the writer as well as the reader. Perfectionism is philosophical, moral, spiritual, aesthetic, and political quests—indeed, it is all of these at once.[16]

I said that Cavell's perfectionism strives to turn us toward a place we have never been—perhaps it should rather be said that the ordinary is precisely not a place at all, but instead something like a continuous task, something essentially to be achieved. This does not contradict the thought of a home, but puts the emphasis on the notion of a home as something that can essentially be changed or something we must be prepared to leave. Thus understood, perfectionism works retroactively, as it were, into the first strand of the ordinary and makes Wittgenstein's appeal to the ordinary into an appeal of change from inside, a new birth— a sensibility of change that Cavell says that Wittgenstein shares with Luther, Rousseau, and Thoreau. Consequently, we must distinguish between the actual everyday in which we find ourselves and the eventual everyday, which is essentially ahead of us. Reflecting on Wittgenstein's practice, Cavell writes:

> His philosophy of the (eventual) everyday is the proposal of a practice that takes on, takes upon itself, precisely (I do not say exclusively) that scene of illusion and of loss; approaches it, or let me say reproaches it, intimately enough to turn it, or deliver it; as if the actual is the womb, contains the terms, of the eventual. The direction out from illusion is not up, at any rate not up to one fixed morning star; but down, at any rate along each chain of a day's denial. (*NYUA*, 46)

Within the perfectionist strand, we are met with a handful of metaphors of the everyday that do not necessarily fit happily together: as a journey onward (from the actual to the eventual), as birth (the actual as the womb of the eventual), and philosophy as descent (the downward direction out of illusions). Perhaps they are all crystallized in Cavell's favorite Emersonian figure of transfiguration (*NYUA*, 47): it denotes a change (and thus a journey) that is affected not from the outside but from the inside of the ordinary (as birth), and its change is not a change of place or of occupations, but a change where the same is perceived differently.

Chapter Outline

Despite the unsystematic nature of Cavell's engagement with religion, I try to show how his engagement is internally linked to the central occupations of his oeuvre, turning on such themes as the ordinary, skepticism, and acknowledgment. My central aim is to see how such notions should be brought to bear on the discussion within theology and continental philosophy, and more specifically how they, within this orientation, convey a particular vision of the human, which I call an anthropology of finitude. Such anthropology of finitude depicts humanity as constantly oscillating between skepticism and acknowledgment, or, put in more Pascalian terms, between angels and beasts. In Cavell's perspective, this is expressed in our satisfaction as well as dissatisfaction with criteria, which amounts to our finding us, uncannily, both at home and not at home within the ordinary.[17]

Chapters 1 and 2 discuss the overarching question of how to relate Cavell's commitment to the ordinary to the presence of religion in his thinking. Because Cavell's ambivalence toward religion is perhaps the most obvious stumbling block for this book, I address it straightaway, in the first chapter. I argue that his ambivalence—say, his unwillingness to decide between Kierkegaard's and Nietzsche's perspectives—reflects the positioning of his own thought within what he understands as a modernist cultural state. In chapter 2 I proceed from the possibilities that this position leaves open and explore Cavell's thoughts on what I call the ordinary sublime. In striking what is simultaneously a religious, aesthetic, and ethical chord, the ordinary sublime opens up the ordinary to a register that is highly relevant to this book.

With the conditions for a fruitful conversation with religion established in the first two chapters, chapters 3 and 4 proceed to a theological terrain. Chapter 3 concerns Cavell's concept of acknowledgment, which I argue is internally related to the kind of self-disclosure and self-knowledge that Augustine calls confessions. Moreover, it also conveys important connections with Luther's conception of the ordinary and the acknowledgement of God in faith. Chapter 4 grapples with skepticism and how it offers important clues to renewed consideration on sin, understood as the unceasingly recurring human wish to deny our humanity. It is arguably not our finite condition as such that constitutes sinfulness, but our relation to that condition, which appears to be pervaded by an unceasing and willed repudiation of it. As the secular articulation of sin, Cavell's skepticism mirrors and sheds further light on the dynamic that animates sin.

That original sin has been thought of as both responsibility and fate is a point of departure for the next two chapters, which in different ways portray two further dimensions related to sin. In chapter 5 I discuss the ethics of language and its tragic dimension, taking off from Cavell's dissatisfaction with Derrida's reading of Austin, which fails to perceive how words are at once our responsibility and yet destined to work beyond our best (or worst) intentions. Such predicaments might (but need not) lock us into tragic relations to others and the world. In his response to Levinas, Cavell has noted the striking similarity between their respective accounts of how experience of the other might give rise to violence, a theme I treat in chapter 6. This provides the opportunity for expanding on how skepticism with regard to the other might lead to violence, and also for reflecting on the violent dimensions both implied and potentially overcome in religion.

However sinister such depiction of human finitude and sin might seem, it is not without counterweights—neither within Cavell's philosophy nor in theology. The final chapter, then, turns to forgiveness, especially as it figures in Cavell's readings of Shakespeare and the Hollywood film genre that he has labeled comedies of remarriage. The topic of forgiveness, especially the acceptance of forgiveness, leads to an assessment of passivity—a central concept in Protestant theology that Cavell seems at once to both endorse and resist. In rounding off the book, I treat Cavell's understanding of how humanity, as portrayed in chapters 4 through 6, stands in need of some kind of redemption—but what kind of redemption? In answering this question, I suggest where I think the line must ultimately be drawn between Cavell's philosophy and Christian theology.

ONE

Modernism and Religion

Right from his entrance on the philosophical scene in the late 1960s, Stanley Cavell has insisted that philosophy is confronted with the same cultural problems, burdens, and commitments—collectively known as modernism—that confront art. From some moment during the nineteenth century, artistic conventions for representation and composition no longer seemed to be adequate bearers of contemporary expression; along with the corrosion of the given framework of conventions, the stable relation between artist and audience also became more fragile, at times broken. As Cavell sees it, this situation is mirrored in philosophy: after Kierkegaard, Nietzsche, and Wittgenstein, there is no simple answer as to how one should establish and continue to write philosophy; its past conveys no reliable answer for how to proceed, its future relevance cannot be known, and its attraction of an audience has become a goal rather than a given. Hence, both art and philosophy must find new modes of continuing their respective tasks. The absence of traditional authorities in art and philosophy might be rooted in the corrosion of a shared recognition of God and a cosmic order. From this perspective, modernism can be regarded as a reaction to secularization: the metaphysical isolation of modern subjectivity, its loss in the conviction of another reality, and its various attempts to connect with the finite reality. But it is also viable to regard religion as entering a modernist situation, that is, not as outdated and hence impossible, but as possible although problematic.

While Cavell at times expresses reluctance toward religion in general and aspects of Christianity in particular, this disinclination is but one side of his stance toward religion, the other being affirmative. Consequently, any reading of Cavell's relation to religion that does not take both sides into account will invariably be one-sided. In this chapter I shed light on the motivation behind Cavell's ambivalent stance toward religion by suggesting that the modernist situation, as Cavell conceives it, not only has bearing on art and philosophy, but also sheds considerable light on the conditions of religion.

Between Christianity and Nietzsche

In order to contest the reading of Cavell as presenting a one-sided account of Christianity, I address the passages on which that reading fundamentally relies. It is incontestably true that Cavell does attack Christianity, particularly some of its conceptions of sin, its understanding of the human body, and its fundamental passivity coupled with the requirement for external intervention. In doing so, Cavell draws heavily on Nietzsche's criticism of Christianity, for example when writing the following:

> Can a human being be free of human nature? (The doctrine of Original Sin can be taken as a reminder that, with one or rather with two exceptions humankind cannot be thus free. Yet Saint Paul asks us to put off our (old) nature. What is repellent in Christianity is the *way* it seems to imagine both our necessary bondage to human nature and our possible freedom from it. . . .) (*CR*, 416)

The repellent "way" presumably refers to the Pauline understanding of humanity as bound to sin, and to the depiction of redemption from sin through external grace, made possible through Christ. Though readings of the relevant passage are often restricted to these lines, it is crucial to my reading to cite the passage further:[1]

> In this, Nietzsche seems to me right, even less crazy than Christianity. But he persists in believing both that humankind must get free of human nature *and* that the human being cannot be free of human nature. Hence the logic of his advice to escape this dilemma of our humanity by overcoming our human nature. I hope he was wrong in this persistence . . . that we will . . . overcome ourselves nihilistically, solve the dilemma of our humanity by becoming monsters. (*CR*, 416)

Let me draw attention to two points: first, Cavell's suggested parallelism of the Christian outlook and Nietzsche's alternative, and second, the fact that Cavell hopes Nietzsche is wrong, that to opt for the superhuman (*Übermensch*) implies the quest for the inhumane by becoming monsters. Hence, Cavell does not confront us with two options, one obviously wrong and one obviously right. Even if the perspectives eclipse each other—the Nietzschean critique of Christian sin and redemption, versus the Christian objection to Nietzsche's monstrosity—Cavell is not taking a stance here. He can speak of his conception of philosophy "as the achievement of the unpolemical, refusal to take sides in metaphysical positions" (*PoP*, 22). Accordingly, Cavell's aim in the present case is not to decide, but to put the options on display. Taken to the extreme—as here—*both* options have their own attractions in light of the other option, and both might repel us.

Another decisive passage reads:

> For of course there are those for whom the denial of the human *is* the human. (Cf. "Aesthetic Problems of Modern Philosophy," 96).

Call this the Christian view. It would be why Nietzsche undertook to identify the task of overcoming the human with the task of overcoming the denial of the human. . . . (*CR*, 493)

There is a tendency to read the reference to Christianity as a repudiation of it, and to downplay the presence of Nietzsche, at the cost of elucidating the parallelism that arguably is essential to Cavell's account.[2] If such parallelism between the Nietzschean and Christian perspectives occurs in Cavell's thinking, one must assume that if he rejects the Christian view, he also rejects Nietzsche's. But if one must overcome the human in order to overcome the denial of the human, one moves away from what seems to be Cavell's abiding picture of the human as placed between: between avoidance and acknowledgment, and between the drive to transcend and to inhabit one's condition. Moreover, it is not obvious that Cavell believes that both the Nietzschean and the Christian outlooks are misguided. Rather, it seems more likely that what is at stake here is their *truth*—perhaps similar to how it is essential to Cavell's understanding of skepticism that it also articulates some truth, however distorted it comes out (*CR*, 241).

No serious reception of Cavell would claim that he is invariably hostile toward Nietzsche; other texts reveal that Nietzsche is one of the impetuses behind Cavell's elaboration of his moral perfectionism (*CHU*, 48–53; *PDT*, 116–119). If there is a systematic parallelism of Nietzsche's view and that of Christianity, this would suggest that Cavell holds a similar high regard for Christianity. The quotation above refers to Cavell's own "Aesthetic Problems of Modern Philosophy," where, without mentioning Christianity explicitly, Cavell states that philosophy concerns insights that one "cannot, being human, fail to know. Except nothing is more human than to deny them" (*MWM*, 96). I take the lesson not to be that such denials should be purged from what we regard as human; rather, Cavell suggests that our standing temptation to deny what is human must be included in our conception of our humanity, as an acknowledgment of something that begins to resemble inescapable sinfulness. The upshot of the quotation above is that both the denial of the human (that is, the Christian view of original sin) and the wish to transcend humanity (here phrased as Nietzsche's overcoming of that denial) are integral parts of Cavell's view of humanity.

Cavell's sweeping generalizations about Christianity are not meant to take its historical and systematic complexity into account, but to draw attention to inevitable dimensions of our own cultural heritage, akin, perhaps, to Nietzsche's genealogy. For Cavell, philosophy is designed to confront our culture with our present criteria for meaning (*CR*, 125). The portrait of culture that emerges from these passages is one that accentuates the split between culture's religious and distinctively non- or anti-religious dimensions. The significance of this cultural ambivalence for Cavell's ordinary language philosophy is suggested in what seems to be the most significant passage from *The Claim of Reason* in this respect. Unsurprisingly, we again encounter the juxtaposition of Christianity and Nietzsche:

> You might battle against the Christian's self-understanding from within Christianity, as Kierkegaard declares, or from beyond Christianity, as Nietzsche declares. On both cases you are embattled because you find the *words* of the Christian to be the right words. It is the way he means them that is empty or enfeebling. (*CR*, 352)

As the context makes clear, these "words of the Christian" concern passivity and activity; more specifically, Cavell here refers to Nietzsche's suspicion that Christianity disguises actions as sheer passivity. Again, one must ask, whose self-understanding is right? Cavell replies that "the answer is, Both" (*CR*, 352), and leaves it to the reader to figure out how and to what extent both can be right, but also, in another sense, wrong.

Far from providing a one-sided attack on Christianity, the remarks on religion in *The Claim of Reason* should be read as interwoven with a more complex cultural and philosophical web. Cavell seems to be attempting to depict the human struggle over its own human condition, as it unfolds within the modernist situation. This situation is characterized by modernism's ambivalence toward religion, but also by the unwillingness of philosophy—or at least the unwillingness of Cavell's philosophy—to settle for either side. The modernist culture, according to Cavell's portrait, is certainly rooted in a secular age in which Christianity does not belong to the unquestionable cultural framework, but neither is it in an age in which Nietzsche's prophecy of the death of God has proven right, at least not in its most straightforward sense.

Meaning Too Much

When Cavell writes above that "the *words* of the Christian [seem] to be the right words. It is the way he means them that is empty and enfeebling" (*CR*, 352), he alludes to a distinction between *saying* words and *meaning* them, which is the central theme of Cavell's title essay in *Must We Mean What We Say?* In this essay, Cavell argues that there is no pure semantic meaning at our disposal that in turn can be applied to an external, pragmatic context. According to ordinary language philosophy, there is no such pure or private meaning; what words *must* mean is exacted by the conventions and implications of what we are saying under particular circumstances (*MWM*, 9–12). Ordinary language philosophy wants to draw attention to how we must use words in order to mean anything at all. Words are never self-sufficient unities of meaning, but are only meaningful in a wider context. To learn words is also to enter the world in which words have their distinct application. Ultimately, language can only be understood against the background of the entire form of life, as Wittgenstein has pointed out (*PI*, § 19). Words are consequently exposed to the shifting historical configurations of that form of life; their meaning can contract and expand, become obsolete, and gain a new life. One can discover treasures among apparently obsolete words, but words can also appear to say things or even to reveal further depths when their meaning—their interest, value, and role in our form of life—has in fact been lost (*MWM*, 43). Naturally, this also applies to religious words. More precisely, such insights have a dual consequence for religion, in that religious words can mean both too much and too little. In meaning too much, words have implications and consequences for the speaker or writer that outrun his or her intentions; in meaning too little, words seem to convey information or express depth when they in fact do neither (*CR*, 351).

Mulhall says that Cavell employs "Christian words in essentially unchristian ways," which raises the question of whether Cavell can do this consistently.[3] Mulhall asks, appropriately, whether such words can be employed without being committed to the framework in which the words have evolved and find their proper meaning—in Cavell's case, the framework of post-Reformation Christianity. More precisely, what Mulhall has in mind is Charles Taylor's narrative of the Reformation's contribution to modern moral identity, summed up by what Taylor calls "the affirmation of ordinary life."[4] The Reformation resulted in a new evaluation of daily work, of family life, and of ordinary commitments. Mulhall claims that the appreciation of the near, the common, and the ordinary, whether conceived in English romanticism, American transcendentalism, or ordinary language philosophy—in short, Cavell's concept of the ordinary—must be regarded as heavily indebted to the inheritance of the Reformation.

But in what sense must this affect Cavell's thinking? Taylor's point is that the notion of the ordinary still has an impact on our contemporary conception of the self, and, accordingly, Mulhall thinks this should make us question the coherence of Cavell's criticism of Christianity.[5] One might, however, reply with Simon Critchley that although Cavell's key concepts historically have religious roots, it does not follow that they are still religious.[6] But this is hardly the way Cavell asks us to think about it; precisely the fact that the inheritance of our religious past is not definitively over, though without exactly answering the present problems either, constitutes the central problem of the modernist state. The troublesome aspect is that religion is still present, haunting even.

More pertinently, Critchley openly recognizes that Beckett—or more accurately Cavell's reading of Beckett—regards our world as "overfull with meaning."[7] In Cavell's reading of Beckett's *Endgame,* it is such a conviction that attunes Cavell's attentive ear to the religious register alluded to in almost every moment of that play. Against the widely accepted assumption that Beckett wants to demonstrate the meaninglessness of our ordinary words, Cavell contends that Beckett seeks rather to highlight their total and even totalitarian success. In other words, Cavell does not read *Endgame* as depicting the void after the death of God, but as displaying our *inability* to rid words of their religious meaning: "Positivism said that statements about God are meaningless; Beckett shows that they mean too damned much" (*MWM*, 120). Accordingly, our language always takes on meanings that lead beyond private control—we are exposed to meaning that, among other things, comes to us from the past: "Words come to us from a distance; they were there before we were; we are born into them. Meaning them is accepting the fact of their condition" (*SW*, 64). Hence, it is not up to Cavell, nor anyone else, to prescribe what Christian words must imply; we can certainly choose among various words, but we cannot choose what they mean. This is not to say that meaning takes care of itself independent of us, but neither is it to say that just any form of life will bring the meaning of certain words into life. If words mean too much for Beckett, that proves that they still are intertwined with our form of life, for better or worse.

In *Endgame*, stories of redemption have become a curse to Hamm and Clov; they cannot believe such stories, but they cannot give up faith in them, either. They are torn between despair and hope, entangled with meaning from which there seems to be no escape—and yet, they cannot stop trying to escape. Taken as a clue to how the play asks to be read, this means that Beckett is testing the degree to which we can purge ordinary language of its burdensome religious meaning. One of the procedures Beckett uses is to take words literally: as in positivism, he insists on accepting words only as denotations, omitting their connotations. For instance, what at first sounds like swearing—"What in God's name could there be on the horizon?"—turns out to be an actual question, asking whether there is something on the horizon that appears in the name of God. Its dark humor stems from these words' inexorable meaningfulness, that they cannot but avoid meaning more than we think they mean, which ultimately entails that we, the language animal, are "condemned to meaning" (*CR*, 351).[8] Such condemnation might indeed become a curse. Cavell takes Beckett's attempt to remove that curse to be infinitely difficult, perhaps impossible (*MWM*, 120). In Cavell's reading, the restless, unappeasable movements between such condemnation to meaning and the struggle for silence are precisely what is at stake in *Endgame*.

According to Cavell, to insist that Beckett takes a state of meaninglessness as his point of departure "is as ironically and dead wrong as to say it of Kierkegaard or Nietzsche or Rilke" (*MWM*, 156). But silence does play a significant role in Beckett's plays, but not as depicting the given state of our cultural situation (assumedly pervaded by absurdity and meaninglessness); silence is rather an achievement, indeed Beckett's central goal. One way, and perhaps the most obvious way, to achieve such silence would be to turn one's back on God, his judgment, and his promises. But I note that Cavell leaves open the same ambiguity we have seen before: silence can be regarded as an attempt just as much to abandon God as to preserve our relation to God, perhaps as freed from some illusions. Silence might indicate the state after destroying false hopes for redemption, but also the state that clears the way for a new (or old but forgotten) conception of redemption.[9] Invoking Rilke's approach to silence, Cavell writes, "Then the angel may appear, then nature, then things, then others, then, if ever, the fullness of time; then, if ever, the achievement of the ordinary, the faith to be plain, or not to be" (MWM, 156).

The implied depiction of a troubled, modernist religion keeps the door open for the resurrection of a plain faith along with the transfiguration of the ordinary. In the last pages of his essay on Beckett, Cavell juxtaposes T. S. Eliot's ambiguous Christianity with Beckett's similarly ambiguous atheism, noting how they at once rival and perfectly match each other. Cavell even contemplates the idea that Beckett could be encompassed within Eliot's universe, declaring that within this universe we could understand why we seem to both lack words and have too many. But to take such contemplation seriously means to open up for a radical re-understanding of Christianity:[10]

> We could re-understand the sense in which redemption is impossible, and possible: impossible only so long as we live solely in history, in time, so long as we think that an event near 2,000 years ago relieves us of responsibility rather than nails us to it—so long, that is, as we live in magic instead of faith. And we can re-interpret suffering yet again: I had occasion to complain that we take suffering as proof of connection with God; but a sounder theology will take *that* suffering to prove exactly that the connection has not been made, but resisted; for, as Luther's confessor had to remind him, God appears only in love.—But can we really believe all this . . . ? (MWM, 162)

This passage brings out the standing ambiguity toward faith, as at once impossible and possible: impossible as what has grown into outmoded schemes, clichés, or magic, yet possible if we turn around our conceptions of responsibilities, sufferings, and the conditions of our connection with God. The question is whether it is too late for such renewal, or whether it is still too early. Discussing the pertinence of Becket and Elliot, who struggle with art and religion from opposite sides, Cavell takes them as leaving us with the question of whom we shall follow, to which Cavell replies, "We hang between" (MWM, 162).

Meaning Too Little

That it is not the Christian words that are wrong but the way they are meant might be due to words meaning too much. But this modernist problematic also has its flip side: Cavell takes both Kierkegaard and Wittgenstein—or, perhaps better, Kierkegaard read through the lens of Wittgenstein—to reproach our sayings for meaning too little (*NYUA*, 39). In the latter case, the trouble does not stem from the fact that we inherit a language invested with meaning beyond our control; rather, the trouble relates to the illusion of having said something particularly profound when in fact we are making utterances out of touch with any intelligible context, that is, in Wittgenstein's lingo, when we are speaking outside language games. When for instance Christians draw on words from the Sermon on the Mount, Cavell writes, people are "supposing themselves to know what they mean. But Kierkegaard finds that they do not know, or will not know, what the words really mean" (*TS*, 228). Why don't they know? Illusions emerge as we either choose to neglect the way the context exacts how words must be meant, or when the context on which certain words have been tied up is changed or lost through the course of cultural development. It is not as if words transgress a fixed set of rules or grammar, but rather that the words and our life with those words have lost interest to us.

As Wittgenstein sees it, religious words must have bearing on our lives: "It strikes me that a religious belief could only be something like a passionate commitment to a system of reference. Hence, although it's *belief*, it's really a way of living, or a way of assessing life."[11] Once this system of reference is lost, the words do not take on full meaning. In applying a similar insight to the context of worship, Cavell writes, "We are given to say that man's chief end is to glorify God and to enjoy him forever. But we do not let the words assess our lives, we do not mean what they could mean" (*SW*, 63). In general, language is not learned by attaching names to objects. Not only are there plenty of words that have no such reference, but the idea strips the meaning of their condition—namely, the way they are put into the context of a world that is interwoven with the ways we deal with and invest values in that world. If a child has not yet learned the world of, say, kitties or pumpkins, such things do not yet exist for him or her, Cavell writes, for we essentially learn words and the world together. That such a view clearly has far-reaching consequences is made clear when Cavell continues:

> or like the way God or love or responsibility or beauty do not exist in our world; we have not mastered, or we have forgotten, or we have distorted, or learned through fragmented models, the forms of life which could make utterances like "God exists" or "God is dead" or "I love you" or "I cannot do otherwise" or "Beauty is but the begin-

ning of terror" bear all the weight they could carry, express all they could take from us. (CR, 172–173)

When Wittgenstein insists on leading the words back home—from their metaphysical to their everyday use (PI, § 116)—he is presupposing that the words are already away, exiled from our lives. The idea of the exile of words captures precisely the problem with Christian words and what Kierkegaard and later Wittgenstein will speak of as the confusion of words. However, if one thinks of ordinary language practice as a detached scrutiny of given strings of words, Cavell thinks one is missing both the point and the existential impact of such practice. Words are always *ours*, something we are responsible and answerable for. The practice of calling, guiding, or shepherding words home from their exile must take into account that they do not offer meaning apart from our lives, which means that not only words but also *our lives* must return: sometimes we have to change our form of life in order to let words express what they mean (NYUA, 34–35). As a consequence of the exile of words, we lose touch with who we are, what makes a difference in our lives, and what our real needs are—we become alienated, or as Kierkegaard puts it in one of Cavell's cherished statements, "Most men live in relation to their own self as if they were constantly out, never at home" (MWM, 172; NYUA, 39).

For Kierkegaard, such exile is primarily a matter of a mismatch between words and what he calls a stage of life. Drawing on the affinity with Wittgenstein's form of life, Cavell argues that something similar might apply to an entire cultural situation:

> The religious is a Kierkegaardian Stage of life; and I suggest it should be thought of as a Wittgensteinian form of life. There seems no reason not to believe that, as a given person may never occupy this stage, so a given age, and all future ages, may as a whole not occupy it—that the form will be lost from men's lives altogether. . . . It is Kierkegaard's view that this has happened to the lives of the present age. (MWM, 172)

It is important how Kierkegaard imagines that words are emptied: there is nothing wrong with the words—what is wrong is the way we have come to live with them in a given age. This might cause forgetfulness, confusion, and emptiness.

Take, for instance, the concept of revelation. Kierkegaard's and Wittgenstein's practices aim to remind us of something we have forgotten: not by adding further information, but by pointing to what something means. Kant calls this an investigation of transcendental logic, Wittgenstein calls it reminders of grammar; in both cases, attention is directed not toward the empirical, but toward our conceptual conditions of possibility (MWM, 169).[12] It is endemic of an

age out of tune with what, for instance, revelation means, that it asks for further empirical evidence, whereas what is needed is a clarification of what a concept means, that is, its place in our lives. In the absence of evidence, one is easily
led to search for something beyond evidence, something even more stable—call
it metaphysical foundation. This obeys a skeptical craving that is meant to capture the human impulse at the root of both skeptical rejection and an anti-skeptical search for metaphysical assurance, joined together in their respective repudiation of the ordinary. What Wittgenstein and Kierkegaard offer in response is
apparently not much, no new discovery or metaphysical solution; instead, they
offer a certain sense of silence:

> in both writers the cure seems no cure. All we are given is the ob-
> vious, and then silence. Kierkegaard has some sport with the man
> who feels the need to make profound discoveries before he can find
> his salvation and know his true responsibilities. Kierkegaard's sug-
> gestion is that the only discovery that man needs is that he needs no
> new discovery. . . . Yet they both claim that obviousness and silence
> provide *answers,* and moreover that nothing else does, that is, not to
> *their* questions. (*TS*, 220)

There is silence and obviousness because there is nothing to explain: arriving at
the right answer is confirmed by the evaporation of the question.[13] If religious
concepts are approached from the right angle and anchored in the right form of
life, then revelation will make plain sense and no explanation is called for. A similar silence is probably the peace that the later Wittgenstein strives for (*PI*, § 133).
To repeat Cavell's elliptical passage, "then, if ever, the achievement of the ordinary, the faith to be plain, or not to be" (*MWM*, 156). If faith should come fully
into being (again), all explanation must come to an end; what can be displayed is
the obvious, and then there is silence.

Having brought words back home, will we then reach complete meaning? Will religious words display their full meaning, be totally "present"? If
so, post-structuralists and neo-pragmatists will have an easy prey, and, in fact,
Cavell's and Wittgenstein's "home" has been taken as just another figure of metaphysics of presence or a new *ontos on,* to use Richard Rorty's term.[14] But if this
were so, why would Wittgenstein's investigations continue for another 560 paragraphs after his call for peace in paragraph 133? Surely there is no stable funda-
ment beneath the ordinary; all it relies on is our continued effort and willingness to share interests in our life with words. Since there is no guarantee of this
mutual sharing, speech and intelligibility are exposed to threats and risks. It is
essential to Cavell's reading of Wittgenstein that the appeal to the ordinary cannot refute skepticism; his appeal must remain weak, a weakness that results in

Wittgenstein's unfolding of the argument of the ordinary being essentially un-winnable for either side (*CHU*, 69). But the weakness of the appeal to the ordinary is also its strength, for it makes language emphatically ours, both to acknowl-edge and to disown. There are homecomings and peace, but they are transitory moments—no stable stance or perennial philosophical position is provided. The moment inherited words that have meant too little regain meaning, the mean-ing can again turn into a burden, meaning too much. There is no intellectually defensible relief from such an unstable modernist religious stance. Religion has become not impossible, but inherently problematic.

The Modernist Situation

I have implied that the ambiguity and particularly troubled state of religion, such as Cavell portrays it, can best be understood within the framework of what Cavell calls the modernist situation—most notably in the sense that situation was accounted for in his writing from the late 1960s and into the 1970s. Without measuring the distance and closeness of art, philosophy, and religion with any precision, I restrict myself to drawing attention to how, following Cavell, all three fields are exposed and responsive to the same cultural challenge. As for philosophy and art, Cavell writes that they are faced with

> a difficulty modern philosophy shares with modern arts (and, for that matter, with modern theology; and, for all I know, with modern physics), a difficulty broached, or reflected, in the nineteenth centu-ry's radical breaking of tradition within the several arts; a moment epitomized in Marx's remark that " . . . criticism of religion is in the main complete . . . " and that " . . . the task of history, once the world beyond the truth has disappeared, is to establish the truth of this world . . . " (*MWM*, xxii)

The current relation between art and philosophy is entangled with the religious situation, as the reference to modern theology entails. In this account of mod-ernism, we yet again encounter Cavell's double gesture: on the one hand, the modernist situation is epitomized by the completion of the criticism of religion, but, on the other, this situation does not preclude theology but rather defines its cultural predicament. For the reference to Marx in this introductory note to *Must We Mean What We Say?* is, moreover, a foreshadowing of something Cavell says in his essay on Kierkegaard later in that volume. Indeed, the same quotation from Marx's *Critique of Hegel's Philosophy of Right* is referred to, only to conclude that Kierkegaard can be said to "carry its completion to the North"—this time criticizing Christianity, not to overcome it but in order to preserve faith from its corruption (*MWM*, 174).

The essential difficulty of philosophy and art is first laid bare as Cavell proceeds:

> This is the beginning of what I have called the modern, character-
> izing it as a moment in which history and its conventions can no
> longer be taken for granted; the time in which music and painting
> and poetry (like nations) have to define themselves against their
> past; the beginning of the moment in which each of the arts be-
> comes its own subject, as if its immediate artistic task is to estab-
> lish its own existence. The new difficulty which comes to light in
> the modernist situation is that of maintaining one's belief in one's
> own enterprise, for the past and the present become problematic to-
> gether. (*MWM*, xxii)

The problematic relation between past and present in art, philosophy, and religion can be felt from the inside, as the question of "how to go on?," as Wittgenstein might put it—that is, the question of whether, from the present perspective,
each discipline's future can be conceived in continuity with the past. At a certain
historical juncture, past conventions are felt to be incapable of redeeming the
necessities of the present, thus calling for a break with tradition. However, such
a break must be understood dialectically: the emphasis is not on the break with
the past as such, but rather on changes—in style, look, expressions, and self-understanding—that are necessary precisely to *retain* the commitment to the past
(*WV*, 72).[15] The alternative, Cavell contends, is to yield to the present at the cost
of the past—a route undertaken by what Cavell calls "modernizers," or "the cult
of the new," central to what he conceives as aesthetic postmodernism.[16] But for
Cavell it is crucial to preserve the commitment to the tradition, even when it involves struggles and breaks; for the burden of modernism is precisely to accept
one's exposure to problems and struggles, or more precisely, to struggle with
the problem of inheriting the past in new ways. It is this burden that yokes philosophy, art, and religion together.

In an overarching perspective, the last hundred and fifty years or so are characterized by a disintegration of a common, homogeneous public domain. As long
as there is no universally agreed upon criteria for distinguishing genuine from
fake art, each work of art must explore its criteria: its own artistic medium cannot be taken for granted but is put to the test in each new work issued (*WV*, 103).
Its legitimacy as art cannot be anticipated before it is brought into existence,
since there are no stable conventions that it can rely on. Without any settled
framework in art, the possibility of fraudulence has become unavoidable. For Kierkegaard, something similar is the case for the religious author: the problem is
to establish the author's authority, that is, his or her right to instruct readers and

to discern genuine from fake authority. However, there is no guarantee of authority except for the authority that the work itself establishes through its ability to convince (*MWM*, 176). There is some guidance in discerning a true author: his or her moral relation to the audience, ability to uncover false reconciliation, and readiness to confront the audience with its real needs.[17] But whether or not such things are carried out by the author is not given in advance, but can only be assessed from the equally morally demanding perspective of the receiver. Genuine reception requires a willingness to expose oneself to the work together with the demand of total honesty in response. Cavell suggests that this vulnerable relation is expressed in an analogous way in art, philosophy, and religion: in art, this raises the above-mentioned question of fraudulence and genuineness; in philosophy, the situation is characterized by the experience of its fluctuation between irrelevance and sudden relevance; in religion, this is mirrored in the oscillation between the experience of God's absence and momentary closeness (*MWM*, 214).

Modernism denotes not only the moment when the past becomes a problem for the present and when the relation between writer/artist/preacher and audience has become precarious, but also—as a consequence—the moment when art, philosophy, and religion become their own subject. The problems integral to the modernist situation exact the reflexive interrogation of the conditions of possibilities for each discipline.[18] This reflexivity must be undertaken by each discipline's constant questioning of itself and of its right to continued existence. Cavell finds this mirrored in what he takes as the best expression of philosophical modernism, namely Wittgenstein's *Philosophical Investigations*, with its unending interrogation of what philosophy is, what writing philosophy comes to, and how it must proceed. But such a demand also holds true for art and theology—perhaps due to their inner affinity in the sense that the reflexivity of art can be taken as a late fruit of the religious past: "The idea of self-reference recognizes that the artist's self-consciousness has come between his conviction and his work, between himself and the conventions (automatism) he relied upon, forcing him to justify his works even as he performs them. This is the Protestant malady, and legacy" (*VW*, 123). If modernist art must struggle with the reflexive self-reference, so must modernist theology—call it the Protestant malady or legacy. And indeed, the quest for renewed self-conception was brought to the fore in a radical way by, say, dialectical theology in the 1920s, where Bultmann's question, encapsulated in his essay "What Does It Mean to Speak of God?," can be regarded as emblematic of the movement's constant self-interrogation. The interrogation is directed partly toward its own past (Protestant orthodoxy as well as liberal theology) and partly toward theology's conditions and constitutive limitations. Springing from a sense that theology had lost its proper object, dialectical theology moved toward a new understanding of its language, its task, and the meaning of revelation and grace. Such turning upon itself has later taken other directions, but it has never ceased. To shrink from the responsibility that goes with such self-reflexivity is to shrink from the cultural responsibility that goes with each discipline's right to exist.

Despite incontestable modernist traits emerging from Protestant soil, Mark D. Jordan is convinced that theology still has to receive the lesson that modernism has taught philosophy, or at least Cavell's and Wittgenstein's philosophy: "Christian theology has still not suffered modernity as a general crisis of *form*."[19] To undergo such crisis would require more intense exchange with arts and the aesthetic implication of its own concerns, an interchange that Cavell suggests is already made open, as from the other side: "the activity of modern art, both in production and reception, is to be understood in categories which are, or were, religious" (*MWM*, 175). But is not theology's subjection to a divine authority that cannot be further questioned essentially an anti-modernist premise that theology cannot rid itself of? Cavell seems at times to think exactly this. In philosophy, say, Emerson's philosophy, one has to commit every word to criticism, which is, as Cavell understands it, "not a commitment which religion may make, sometimes to its credit, sometimes not" (*CHU*, 137). But Peter Dula argues convincingly against the depiction of theology that Cavell here presupposes. As Dula argues, if the word of the cross is at theology's center, it should indeed reveal to us the futility of any closure of theology. Borrowing the former Archbishop Rowan Williams's words, he stresses theology's "commitment to subject every word of itself to criticism, endlessly, with nothing held safe."[20]

The Future of Modernist Religion

It is true that Cavell's modernist conception was most explicitly put forward in the late 1960s, during the last phase of what can be labeled high modernism. It is also true that the dominating depiction of the cultural climate, along with the intellectual responses to it, has changed since high modernism, changes that are often summed up in what vaguely has been labeled postmodernism. It is, for instance, interesting to note that Jean-François Lyotard regards precisely *Philosophical Investigations* as depicting the postmodern condition, in which the master narratives have collapsed, leaving us with nothing except islands of heterogeneous language games.[21] Others have pointed out how postmodernism has provided a new soil for religion, beyond metaphysical schemes that identify God with the highest principle or the absolute ground, that is, beyond onto-theology.[22] In sum, one might say that the postmodern condition brings along the de-differentiation of constitutive superstructures and the weakening of strong binary oppositions, thus leading to a renegotiation of the distinctions between religion and non-religion.

Except for some engagement with Derrida, to which I return in chapter 5, Cavell has offered no sustained account of postmodernism. But from the little he does say, it is clear he thinks that the subversion of distinctions or radical de-differentiation leads away from, rather than into, what he takes to be the subsisting teaching of Wittgenstein. If the postmodern perspective, as Cavell takes it, is one in which we can no longer distinguish between what is ordinary and what is out of the ordinary, between what counts as humane and what counts as inhumane, then Wittgenstein's endless conversations with and treatment of the skeptic become pointless. Insisting on a modernist reception of *Philosophical Investigations,* Cavell explains: "However that concept developed for me over those decades, it was always a function of a sense of radical distinction, even of mortal enmity, between reason and sophistry, between conversation and chatter, between the serious and the idle, between the achievement of art, in however unheard-of form, and its withdrawal" *(PDT,* 140–141). The whole project, essential to Wittgenstein's and Cavell's practices, presupposes that it is possible and indeed crucial to distinguish between speaking inside and outside language games, between words' exile and their home; it is a stance from which skepticism is not only annoying but a veritable threat to our humanity. Accordingly, to trivialize skepticism and the distinctions it feeds upon is not to struggle with problems, but to remove them.

Is it still viable in this new millennium to insist on distinctions and seriousness? Or has the postmodern condition made this position outmoded, perhaps insensitive to the real state of religion and its current challenges? In short, is Cavell's modernist account still relevant? An indirect way of answering these questions is through a brief detour into Charles Taylor's *A Secular Age* and its portrayal of our contemporary religious situation. If Taylor's work is representative of the present situation, possible agreements with Cavell's outlook might provide us with hints of Cavell's abiding relevance. Although Taylor depicts our secular age as no less challenging to Christian belief than does Cavell, it might be said that they approach this challenge from opposite points of departures: Taylor from a Catholic position, Cavell from his openly secular position. In Taylor's narrative, secularization is supposed to capture the change from a state in which it was practically impossible not to believe in God, to a situation where such belief is only one among many possibilities.[23] The Reformation not only led to a new affirmation of the ordinary, but some of its impulses have also conditioned the emergence of what Taylor calls an immanent framework, for believers and non-believers alike. Similarly, Cavell points to Luther as one of the pioneering figures of modernity, in heralding a new sense of privacy that paved the way for modern secularity *(CR,* 470). But Luther also prepared the ground for a new sense of community in believing and valuing—for religion as well as for modern art *(MWM,* 229).

Taylor openly recognizes that the immanent framework has grown into a kind of silent premise for questions concerning religious faith, and with it, an unwarranted bias toward non-transcendent perspective on human flourishing, the so-called "exclusive humanism."[24] However, in his detailed rehearsal of various conflicts between Christian and anti-Christian positions (either humanistic or Nietzschean), Taylor is at pains to avoid polarization and to demonstrate that neither position is conclusive. Normatively, the question of religious transcendence should remain open, which, descriptively, leaves us in a cultural situation of instability, often expressed as ambivalence. Taylor has no patience for those who think that secularization has precluded the possibility of God, whether because of the progress of science or exclusive stress on human autonomy; although faith has become deeply problematic, it is still a live option. Most of us do not take extreme positions, but endure the cross pressure of belonging to an immanent, self-enclosed order, yet sensing a strong pull toward something more, something other. In borrowing William James's words, Taylor depicts us as standing in an open space, feeling "the wind pulling you, now to belief, now to unbelief."[25] This highly ambiguous position of the double pull is, I will claim, reflected in Cavell's unease with our Christian words that at once mean too much and too little, leaving us hanging between. Indeed, in my reading this captures the position of religious modernism: it does admit the troubled stance in the cross pressure, but it resists subversion or de-differentiation of distinctions between belief and non-belief. From this perspective, Cavell's claim that reference to God or religion "is no longer natural to the human spiritual repertory" (DK, 198) can be read not as a refutation of religion as such, but as an assertion that it is now neither natural nor impossible, and hence that it is problematic. The utterance can be taken as articulating the spiritual habitat in secular modernity, but it can also be taken as a critique of that habitat—if not in defense of faith, so in defense of a life in which faith would be possible. For the returning of words that Wittgenstein speaks of is twofold: it asks us to put words back into their everyday traffic, but if the words are right, the words reproach our lives—they invite changes so that our lives can become the context in which words might take on meaning again. The upshot is that we must return to the religious words in order to mean them.

But does not Cavell's ambiguous posture preclude such a change of life? The ambiguity seems to undermine the commitment to something beyond human finitude that must be granted authority over our lives. Seen from a religious point of view, this is hardly edifying. And yet, it has its advantages, if seen from a decidedly philosophical point of view; for, arguably, philosophy should take neither theism nor atheism as its points of departure. To demand that philosophy must choose between theism and atheism is already to deaden its attention to all the surprising ways in which religion might occur in life, forcing it into what Maurice Merleau-Ponty has conceived as a "fixed (non-philosophical) position."[26] When facing religion, philosophy must allow itself to stay perplexed and remain an eternal beginner:

> Cynics about philosophy, and perhaps about humanity, will find that questions without answers are empty; dogmatists will claim to have arrived at answers; philosophers after my heart will rather wish to convey the thought that while there may be no satisfying answers to such questions in certain forms, there are, so to speak, directions to answers, ways to think, that are worth the time of your life to discover.[27]

Cavell's presentation of the ambiguous modernist situation provides a basis for such a way to think. Moreover, if one takes seriously Cavell's own aspiration as a perfectionist author, then his writing is supposed to throw us back at ourselves, to bring out the voice in the reader's own life. The absence of religious commitments on his part does therefore not preclude other decisions on the reader's part. For similar reasons, Kierkegaard chose to confront his reader with a wide variety of possible relations to religion presented through his masquerade of pseudonyms, in order to point out that such relations, far from being given, are in fact options that call for a decision. Kierkegaard thereby wanted to elicit the true kind of commitment from the reader that can give sense back to religious words—or, as Cavell interprets it, to encourage progress from chatter to speech.[28]

TWO

The Ordinary Sublime

I have argued that Cavell's ambiguous relation to religion should be understood against a wider cultural backdrop of modernism. If religion and thus theology have become problematic yet not impossible, then we must expect such possibility to show up within what Cavell terms the ordinary. However, the ordinary does not provide the location for experiences of incontestable divine revelations, nor does it unfailingly offer clear criteria by which we can assess such experiences. Nevertheless, the ordinary must be so inhabited as to provide glimpses, events, or perspectives from which religious orientation can gain a foothold in our form of life—or else such orientation seems to participate in the escape from the ordinary. Indeed, the ordinary is religiously open, however ambiguous such initial openness can seem. In order to encircle such a minimal condition for religion, I explore what I call "the ordinary sublime," in which aesthetical, ethical, and religious registers resonate all at once. To be more specific, my interest is in a certain dynamics of the sublime, between its powerfulness and its weakness, which I find reflected in Cavell as well as in Cora Diamond's fruitful and thought-provoking elaborations of related themes. Neither of them treats the sublime at length or unfolds its implications in the way I do here, but they provide sufficient clues for a further elaboration of that concept.

The ordinary sublime sounds like a contradiction in terms—and some of its inner tension should indeed be preserved. The tension in question is not so much between something completely other, breaking into an inside that is otherwise closed in on itself, which is a model that has been attractive to some postmodern and deconstructive treatments of the sublime.[1] Rather, the ordinary sublime must be regarded as a function of the ordinary itself. Inherent to the ordinary sublime, however, is indeed a sense of extraordinariness. If Cavell occasionally expresses unease with the notion of ordinary language philosophy, it is because the label is sometimes taken to contrast, and thus exclude, the extraordinary. What "ordinary language" is meant to contrast, however, is not the extraordinary in the ordinary, but, in Cavell's words, "a fixated *philosophical* language which precisely would pre-empt the extraordinary from disturbing customary experience."[2] Even if it can be argued that such a transposition of the sublime within the ordinary is not necessarily incommensurable with postmodern or deconstructive conceptions, the approach from the ordinary still entails a significant shift of emphasis. An approach from the ordinary is not so much concerned about the otherness, which metaphysics has tended to repress, but the repression of the *familiarity* inherent to the conception of the ordinary. Such repression must somehow first be lifted in order to take the extraordinariness of the ordinary into account.

Transposing the Sublime

In order to indicate some initial points of orientation, let me briefly refer to three relevant features that I take to be central to Kant's influential analysis of the sublime. First, the sublime is, according to Kant, initiated by an experience that transcends the limits of finite understanding. The feeling of the sublime concerns something that our sensible faculties—our senses and our imagination—are unable to represent. Second, the sublime harbors an unappeasable ambivalence between repulsion and attraction, between horror and fascination. Kant explains this ambivalence in terms of the abyss that opens up once we experience the failure of our representations, combined with the satisfaction in realizing that the ideas of reason nevertheless surpass the limits of our sensible faculties. And third, there is something to be gained from the exposure to the sublime, namely an otherwise unrevealed dimension of our humanity. For Kant, this means that we awaken respect for ourselves as bearers of autonomous reason.[3] Throughout the chapter, I return to these characteristics in order to measure the distinct way in which they are transformed according to the philosophical approach from the ordinary.

Wittgenstein occasionally speaks of our tendency to conceive of logic as something sublime, and more generally of our tendency to sublime our language (*PI*, §§ 38, 89, 94). Wittgenstein's invocation of the sublime clearly has negative connotations, which is also reflected in Cavell's writing. The wish for the sublime thus understood is indicative of our rejection of ordinary language, and an urge for something purer, something beyond the instability of everyday speech and acts (*CHU*, 98–99). But there is also a more positive invocation of the sublime in Cavell's writing, an invocation that lies at the center of this chapter. At one juncture, Cavell draws the connection between the sublime in Wittgenstein and Kant:

> Wittgenstein's appearance at this intersection of romanticism and skepticism and Kant is, so it seems to me, encoded in his concept of *subliming*. . . . But whereas in Kant the psychic strain is between intellect and sensibility, in Wittgenstein the straining is of language against itself, against the commonality of criteria which are its conditions, turning it as it were against its origins.—Thus a derivative romantic aesthetic problematic concerning the sublime moves to the

center of the problematic of knowledge, or say of wording the world; quite as if aesthetics itself claims a new position in the economy of philosophy. (*NYUA*, 57–58)[4]

Cavell notices the ambivalence in both Kant's and Wittgenstein's accounts. But there is an important transposition of the sublime in the latter's sense, since the strain or ambivalence is not between intellect and sensibility, but enacted within language. The sublime is therefore at the center of Cavell's occupation, amidst the struggles implied in our wording of the world. This turn to ordinary language suggests something like a transposition from Kant's invocation of the infinite (according to the mathematical sublime) and the mighty (according to the dynamic sublime), to the register of the low, the near, the common. Such transposition invites us to redirect our attention to a humbler concept of the sublime as something far more vulnerable, that is, something that can essentially be missed, even suppressed.

The appeal to what we ordinarily do with words, in Austin and in Wittgenstein, is meant to counter philosophy's craving for metaphysics—unshakable foundations, the purity of logic, or systematic totality. Within such a robust metaphysical framework, everything disturbing is pre-empted or else regarded as wholly other to us. Still, if Wittgenstein is taken as leading us back to rules or conventions of different language games that allow us to draw a clear line between plain sense and metaphysical nonsense, then no progress has been made.[5] According to such a reading, it is hard to imagine that the sublime could come to pass within the ordinary thus construed, since such ordinariness will never really be shaken, either from outside or inside. Both Cavell and Diamond challenge such an interpretation of Wittgenstein, for what they stress is the astonishing flexibility whereby we can project our words into new contexts, together with the constant risks such projections involve.[6] All we can appeal to is our criteria, that is, the knots of our shared interests and intelligibility. But to accept such vision takes an ability to appreciate the criteria's "triviality as much as their importance, their weakness as much as their strength" (*PP*, 155).

The ordinary so conceived is liable to give rise to a sense of the groundlessness, as if the everyday is "a shaky foundation—a thin net over the abyss" (*CR*, 178). What we have to go on is as simple as it is terrifying, or terrifying because it is simple. We learn and teach words in certain contexts, and then we are expected, and expect others, to be able to project them into further contexts. "Nothing insures that this projection will take place," Cavell writes, and, in what has become an almost classic passage, he continues:

> That on the whole we do is a matter of our sharing routes of interest and feeling, modes of response, senses of humor and of significance

and of fulfillment, of what is outrageous, of what is similar to what else, what a rebuke, what forgiveness, of when an utterance is an assertion, when an appeal, when an explanation—all the whirl of organism Wittgenstein calls "forms of life." Human speech and activity, sanity and community, rest upon nothing more, but nothing less, than this. It is a vision as simple as it is difficult, and as difficult as it is (and because it is) terrifying. (MWM, 52)

If such simple and terrible facts are constitutive of the ordinary, mutual understanding, they do not preclude but rather invite the extraordinary within the ordinary, captured in the figure of the ordinary sublime. The task of philosophy is to make us aware of this ordinary reality: "I sometimes speak of the task as discovering the extraordinary in what we call ordinary and discovering the ordinary in what we call extraordinary; sometimes as detecting significance in the insignificant, sometimes as detecting insignificance in the significant" (PAL, 96).[7]

The Difficulty of Reality

It is helpful here to turn to what Diamond has called "the difficulty of reality" in order to reach a clearer understanding of what this ordinary sublime amounts to. In The Realistic Spirit, Diamond's concept of "realistic spirit" is meant to capture and promote a particular mode of philosophy that turns itself patiently toward what we call reality. According to Diamond, philosophy characteristically lays down requirements for what is rationally conceivable, prior to an actual inquiry into how we actually treat the reality at hand.[8] Conversely, the realistic spirit is supposed to call our attention to what is right before our very eyes.[9] In her later "The Difficulty of Reality and the Difficulty of Philosophy," Diamond presses her realistic spirit further, exploring not only how our conceptual life molds what we take to be reality, but also how that spirit urges us to embrace experiences that go beyond our conceptual repertoire, indeed beyond what we took as reality (PAL, 44).

The difficulty of reality is meant to encircle "experiences in which we take something in reality to be resistant to our thinking it, or possibly to be painful in its inexplicability, difficult in that way, or perhaps awesome and astonishing in its inexplicability" (PAL, 45–46). Such a description makes it reasonable to regard Diamond's difficulty of reality as a twin concept of the ordinary sublime: it captures what Kant thought of as the sublime's transgression of our faculty of understanding. Yet, Diamond's very next sentence outlines the distinctively ordinariness of the sublime, say, its vulnerability: "We take things so. And the things we take so may simply not, to others, present the kind of difficulty, of being hard or impossible or agonizing to get one's mind around" (PAL, 46). In other words, nothing commands us to take the phenomena in view as sublime; they might for others as easily pass as nothing worthy of attention.

Diamond's essay provides a number of telling examples of such encounters with the difficulty of reality, of which I discuss only a few. Ted Hughes's poem "Six Young Men" is a meditation on the liveliness of six young men in a photograph, taken in 1914, all of whom had died in the war six months later. The last stanza is as follows:

> That man's not more alive whom you confront
> And shake by the hand, see hale, hear speak loud,
> Than any of these six celluloid smiles are,
> Nor prehistoric or fabulous beast more dead;
> No thought so vivid as their smoking-blood:
> To regard this photograph might well dement,
> Such contradictory permanent horrors here
> Smile from the single exposure and shoulder out
> One's own body from its instant and heat.[10]

In Diamond's reading, Hughes articulates an encounter that we cannot encompass; it circles around the incontestable presence of life, contradicted by its similarly incontestable absence or death. But this presence of a certain absence is at stake not just in this particular photograph but in any photograph or, for that matter, in film. According to Cavell, it is constitutive of photography and film that the persons depicted are in a sense present to us while we remain absent from them. Hughes's poem makes the grammatical fact salient by the literal death of the six young men in the picture: nothing is more lively and nothing more dead. Seen from one perspective, this is quite trivial; seen from another, it is deeply troubling or mysterious—perhaps a mystery we fail to attend to only too often. Some might feel Cavell is making too much of a mystery of it, a criticism to which he replies, "My feeling is rather that we have forgotten how mysterious these things are" (*WV*, 19). According to Cavell, the sense of the ordinariness as well as extraordinariness is essential to our appreciation of both photography and film in general. Or, as he puts it in an essay on Emerson, "without the mode of perception inspired in Emerson (and Thoreau) by the everyday, the near, the low, the familiar, one is bound to be blind to the poetry of film, to the sublime in it" (*SW*, 150).[11]

The sublime's sense of incomprehensibility or alterity can be inflected in two directions: downward, toward absence, horror, or death; but also upward, toward the good, the magnificent, or divine. If Diamond's first example concerns the downward inflection, she offers other examples that concern the upward inflection: the inexplicability of beauty and goodness.[12] The beauty of a tree, the architecture of its branches crowned with green and the singing birds therein, can strike one as nothing short of a mystery. Diamond finds Czeslaw Milosz's words apt: "It should not exist. There is not only no reason for it, but an argument against. Yet undoubtedly it is . . . " (Milosz quoted in *PAL*, 60). Eliciting the astonishing character of goodness, Diamond draws our attention to Ruth Klüger's memoir, *Still Alive: A Holocaust Girlhood Remembered*, and especially to Klüger's account of how a young woman courageously helped her survive the life-or-death selection process at a concentration camp. The author has never stopped wondering about this incomparable goodness, a wonder that again gives rise to impatience in other people: there are altruistic persons, certainly, but that is hardly news (*PAL*, 62). Diamond also notes that the miracles witnessed in the New Testament have been described as at once empirically certain and conceptually impossible (*PAL*, 63). Diamond's point is not that the beauty of the tree or the unexpected goodness in the extermination camps are divine miracles; her point is rather to highlight the astonishment and awe that spring forth from the difficult reality in all those cases.

Such encounters with the ordinary sublime reveal the point where reality and conceptual thinking come apart; they localize rifts where our habitual language games and train of thought do not fully grasp what is there. To others, it is as if the grip has never been lost, not even been questioned. I regard it as a mark of the ordinariness of the ordinary sublime that it is inherently open to such diverging perspectives. No infinity or might imposes itself on the receivers and commands universal agreement in response—the ordinary sublime comes to pass in a vulnerable gesture that is possible to overlook or reject. If we go back to Hughes's photograph, it is perfectly possible to take it as unremarkable. In a Wittgensteinian manner, Diamond invites us to imagine how the language game of photos is taught. If a child asks why her now deceased grandfather is smiling in the picture if he is dead, we might explain that he was smiling at the time when the picture was taken. Gradually, she will master the language game surrounding photos, and the ring of contradiction will evaporate. But her initial position is in some respects similar to that of the poet—they are both unhinged from the language game:

> The point of view from which she sees a problem is not yet in the game; while that from which the horrible contradiction impresses itself on the poet-speaker is that of someone who can no longer speak within the game. Language is shouldered out from the game, as the body from its instant and heat. (*PAL*, 45)

Diamond here sheds light on the divergence between those who feel themselves addressed by the ordinary sublime and those who are not responsive to it: the latter are comfortably settled within the conventional game, whereas the former cannot recognize themselves within it. Yet, neither the child nor the poet is abandoned to silence or absolute nonsense, rather they find themselves on the outskirts of our language games. There are no ready-made means to adequately express the experience, and thus they are left in a state that Cavell finds aptly captured in St. Paul's expression "now I know in part" (*PAL*, 96; 1 Cor. 13:12).

The position of the girl learning the grammar of photographs is, however, not exactly the same as the position of the poet. The girl is *not yet* a master of the language game, while the poet is as fully a master of it as any competent speaker is, though he can *no longer* speak within it. His "outside" is on the other end: he finds that for all the flexibility of the grammar, the sublime experience exhausts it and commands him to express himself beyond any established conventions. This might or might not succeed in communicating—and that is part of the difficulty of poetry, but also of the difficulty of communicating intimate moments outside poetry. Cavell points out that, for all his helpfulness, Austin did not allow for speech acts expressing such intimate moments, moments where one can no longer rely on conventions or manners of speech. In what Cavell calls "passionate utterances," this is precisely the risk we must run: drawing on our affinity with words as we know them, we must project them in perhaps yet unheard-of ways. In these regions of language, there is no accepted convention that must be met at particular occasions for the act to be performed successfully, as Austin will have it. Rather, I reveal myself in a moment of passion in front of the other and invite a response in kind. If an illocutionary utterance participates in the order of speech, a passionate utterance "is an invitation to improvisation in the disorders of desire" (*PDT*, 185). Confronted by the sublime, our criteria run out; we have no more to go on than our most personal improvisations—we cannot even take for granted the shared recognition of the phenomena at stake. Expressions of the sublime are therefore risky business: they might, like prophecy, instill community and mutual recognition, but they might also lead to isolation.[13]

The Missable and the Dismissable

I mentioned ambivalence as the second characteristic of the Kantian sublime. There is a corresponding ambivalence inherent to the ordinary sublime, though with a different accent. The breakdown of our ordinary comprehension can no longer be redeemed by the ideas of reason, as it is in Kant. The ambivalence is rather caught within the everyday itself. All of Diamond's examples can be taken as either perfectly ordinary or absolutely extraordinary; to some readers they are overwhelming, while others fail to raise an eyebrow (*PAL*, 92). This, I suggest, captures the ambiguity of the sublime transposed to the key of the ordinary. But what can this ambiguity more specifically reveal about its ordinariness?

Wittgenstein's philosophical procedure highlights what is going on when someone for example calls something a table, adding a number, following a rule, pointing in a direction, and so on—he is reminding us of things that no competent speaker can fail to know. The only reason this is worth a reminder is that we somehow come to ignore such things. Wittgenstein might be hinting at such ignorance when he writes, "The aspects of things that are most important for us are hidden because of their simplicity and familiarity. . . . [W]e fail to be struck by what, once seen, is most striking and most powerful" (*PI*, § 129). The enigmatic ambiguity turns up again: something that can make the most powerful impression can also pass without notice. It is indeed strange that we can fail to recognize what is most familiar. Cavell captures this as he speaks of experience missed, or more generally, the ordinary as what is *missable* (*PDT*, 11–12, 25–26). The difficulty of such a philosophy consists in showing the obvious, or more accurately, the unobviousness of what we take as obvious, for the significance of the obvious is something we seem prone to miss.

How do we come to ignore such things? There are arguably two distinct ways in which the ordinary, and along with it the ordinary sublime, tend to be missed; I speak of them as passive ignorance and active rejection, respectively.[14] In his juxtaposition of Wittgenstein and Heidegger, Cavell provides a clue regarding this distinction: "Wittgenstein perceiving our craving to *escape* our commonness, even when we recognize the commonness of the craving; Heidegger perceiving our pull to *remain* absorbed in the common, perhaps in the very way we push to escape it" (*IQO*, 32). Starting with the latter, passive mode, phenomenology has pointed out the difficulty of grasping that which is, in Heidegger's lingo, ontically closest, due to our absorption in everyday practice. Our primordial way of opening what Heidegger calls the worldhood of the world is by making it familiar, taking it into our practical mastery, our readiness-to-hand. We do not primarily regard things as objects of inspection, but we grasp them as equipments and fit them into our routines. But such an opening of the world is double edged, for precisely the same means that open the world up tend to level it out. When the equipments are placed into the orbit of all our diverse occupations, they become transparent and then leveled into the average or fallen everyday life. A similar dynamics is operative in social life, where individuals fall into the anonymous life of *das Man*, the "they."[15] Under such circumstances, the ordinary sublime tends to be missed.

Yet another way in which the ordinary can be missed is through active rejection. What Cavell calls skepticism is meant to capture motives behind an, as it seems, ineradicable impulse to willfully alienate ourselves from our familiar life with words. Even though skepticism also results in ignorance of the ordinary sublime, it departs from the first sense of ignorance in important respects.

It is no longer a matter of something "perceptually missable," as Cavell puts it, but of what is "*intellectually* dismissable" (*PDT,* 12). The skeptical indifference is a matter not of inattention, but of willed repudiation. This move does not mean that the skeptic finds the world unimportant—on the contrary, "He forgoes the world for just the reason that the world is important, that it is the scene and stage of connection with the present: He finds that it vanishes exactly with the effort to *make* it present," famously expressed in Descartes's case where he consults the evidence provided by his sense perceptions (*DK,* 94). To make the world absolutely present, to establish it beyond any possible doubt, is a compensatory strategy chosen to avoid the lurking sense of the groundlessness of the everyday. First when that sense cannot be avoided, the skeptic feels that doubt has won out—the world-consuming doubt turns into nihilistic denial: there is nothing for us worth knowing.

Skepticism actively repudiates our criteria for what can possibly count as the other's mind or the external world: by undercutting our intelligible speech, it moves itself into a position from which the world and others are beyond reach. Applied to the ordinary sublime, this means that the skeptical ignorance of the sublime is caused not by the lack of awareness, but, on the contrary, by an overreaction to the acute awareness of it. Diamond's expression for this reaction is *deflection* (*PAL,* 57)—a willful distraction from what is found agonizing in our exposure to reality, to the world as well as to others in it. Why is it that the ordinary sublime urges the skeptic to deflect his or her attention away from it at such a high cost? Diamond suggests that it is difficult enough for philosophy, after Wittgenstein, to demonstrate that the low and common is of real importance to us, but it gets even more difficult once we have to deal with "the possibility of being tormented by the hiddenness, the separateness, the otherness of the others" (*PAL,* 77).

Besides the disappointment with the ordinary and its inherent separateness, there might be even deeper fears hidden behind the skeptic's deflection. For not only does the sublime mark the moment when reality turns out to be resistant to our thinking and withdraws from our efforts to reach it, but it might also mark a moment when reality defeats us. For Kant, the impression of (empirical) defeat is rapidly turned into enhanced regard for the spontaneity of reason, but in Diamond's version it is precisely the image of reason over reality that on such occasions is radically questioned. The ordinary sublime leaves us powerless, fundamentally passive, at the hands of reality. In the occurrence of the sublime, reality addresses us first, leaving us to await and receive its address. Such passivity implies a serious blow to the Kantian philosophical self-perception. Skepticism typically attempts to transmute the experience of passivity into an intellectual riddle—as if the skeptic's incessant intellectual activity aims at deflecting the attention away from our fundamental exposure to reality. Cavell frequently alludes to Pascal's aphorism "I have discovered that all the unhappiness of men arises from one single fact, that they cannot stay quietly in their own chamber."[16] Timothy Gould has encapsulated the motive of the restless activism that Pascal is hinting at as the "false activity [that] conceals an intolerance for the passive."[17] The intolerance for passivity turns out to be the motive behind the deflections, and false activity is the favored route to direct our attention away from what is at the heart of our condition.

The Embrace of the Ordinary Sublime

The ordinary sublime can be perceptually missed and intellectually dismissed, but it is equally possible to *embrace* the sublime.[18] Indeed, the scattered remarks about the sublime in Cavell's writing attest to the inherent ambiguity that Kant found characteristic of the sublime. On the one hand, Cavell makes the following comparison: "Kant's conjunction of excess and abyss seems to me to match Wittgenstein's sense of the conjunction of the hyperbolic (super-connections, super-concepts, etc.) with the groundlessness as the ideal which philosophy finds at once forbidding or terrible, and attractive" (*NYUA*, 58). According to Cavell, the hyperbolic is a function of the fear of the groundlessness of the ordinary; in other words, it is some kind of skeptical deflection. But, on the other hand, there are also passages where Cavell takes the sublime to invite us to appreciate our ordinary conditions in new ways, for instance when he speaks of the romantic "preaching of the everyday as the locale of the sublime" (*CR*, 463).

Hence, it seems as if the very same phenomenon, placed at the limits of our criteria, can both lead us into exile from the ordinary as well as deeper into it. The phenomenon cuts both ways—it can, to borrow Cavell's words, be "turned equally toward splendor and toward horror" (*CR*, 492). To embrace the sublime does not mean that we are able to master it conceptually, but it requires a capacity for passive reception, acceptance, and acknowledgment. Acknowledgment in this respect means to let something separate from me—the human other, the world, or the sublime—make a claim on me, but it also entails my responsibility to respond (*MWM*, 256–257). What if philosophy can also stand being exposed to the ordinary sublime—what will be gained from such an encounter? I mentioned as the third characteristic that Kant thinks the sublime has, despite its threatening occurrence, a deeply humanizing impact: we gain insight into our dignity as bearers of reason.[19] It is likewise central to Cavell that something like the ordinary sublime can turn us toward the everyday. This turn is essentially bound up with the threat of skepticism inherent in the ambiguity of the sublime, because it is only insofar as we realize that our common intelligibility and the meaningfulness of the world can be lost that we understand what it means to inhabit it.

It is therefore understandable why Cavell never thinks that ordinary language philosophy is in a position to refute skepticism, but also why he finds it important to preserve the skeptical voice: something can only come to light after passing through the skeptical ordeal, thereby discovering that we are capable of denying our conditions as intelligible creatures. The return after the sublime is therefore never to the same everyday—something is gained:

> The return of what we accept as the world will then present itself as a return of the familiar, which is to say, exactly under the concept of what Freud names the uncanny. That the familiar is a product of a sense of the unfamiliar and of the sense of a return means that what returns after skepticism is never (just) the same. (*IQO*, 166)

Upon the return, the familiar is changed by the experience of the threats of skepticism. The return is uncanny, or in German *unheimlich* (un-homely), for while the familiar is not exactly alien, it has not been properly recognized before and thus appears not exactly the same. As Cavell indicates, it is the same seen differently, in the manner of what Freud called the return of the repressed.[20]

In his essay on the Wittgensteinian sublime, James Noggle draws attention to Cavell's treatment of the sublime in Wittgenstein, but also to the sublime's power to return us to the ordinary, through what Noggle considers a form of catharsis.[21] Still, the sublime in Noggle's account has no inherent ambiguity. The sublime *is* the point of utter linguistic alienation, which the earlier Wittgenstein identifies as nonsense and the later identifies as the skeptic's desire to speak outside language games. For the sublime to reach such a point of nonsense is an important achievement, Noggle argues, since only from this position can we discover that the metaphysical dream of an ineffable realm beyond the ordinary is nothing but an illusion. *Tractatus* brings us to the threshold of the mystical: "here," Noggle states, "the ethical or the aesthetic is not simply signaled by the nonsensicality of certain expressions, but rather *consists in* it."[22] The sublime, understood as the nonsensical, leads us in a very specific sense back to a beliefless stance, which Noggle says comes to expression in Sextus Empiricus's skepticism: "Sextus claims that his skepticism purges him not only of his beliefs but of itself, landing him as if by accident in a quasi-mystical state of tranquility—*ataraxia*—in which he believes nothing, not even skepticism."[23]

I have no doubt that Cavell and Diamond also think that what I have called the ordinary sublime marks the point where criteria come to an end, but the inexplicability thereby caused is not obviously nonsensical—although, it is true, it exceeds conventional sense. We can still express ourselves, but only in what Cavell calls passionate utterances, unfounded by common modes of communication. The deadness and aliveness in the photograph of six young men are not exactly metaphysical illusions, they do not purge us of beliefs—they are rather deeply rooted in something difficult in our reality. Although the skeptical move takes its cue from sublime moments, it deflects it. But if it embraces the sublime in the sense of Diamond's difficulty of reality, then the return is a return not to Noggle's tranquillity (that would be an escape) but rather to the ordinary as changed.

The philosophical acknowledgment of the ordinary sublime not only accepts that there are phenomena that outrun our established conceptions and leave us fundamentally passive, but also that the experience of the sublime directs us toward something otherwise missed. Put simply, the sublime might initiate the (possible) transition from the actual to the eventual everyday, or as Cavell might also put it, from the ordinary conceived as leveled down by conformity, to what he calls, citing Kierkegaard, "the sublime in the pedestrian" (*NYUA*, 39; *IQO*, 177). The context of this quotation from *Fear and Trembling* is Kierkegaard's reflections on Abraham, the knight of faith, who is called to the morally terrible, inexplicable, and hence in a sense sublime sacrifice of his son Isaac. In the moment when, by divine intervention, Abraham is given a lamb to sacrifice instead of his son, he receives his son back. The son he now receives is certainly the same son, and yet everything is changed; in particular, Abraham's relation to his son is altered. This observation makes it possible for Kierkegaard to distinguish between two movements: the infinite, which also is called a movement of resignation, and the succeeding finite, which is faith—in which one does not lose the finite, but regains it. Despite the magnificence of this double movement, it will not be apparent from the outside. However, those who can carry out only the first movement are easily discernible:

> The knights of the infinite resignation are easily recognizable— their walk is light and bold. But they who carry the treasure of faith are likely to disappoint, for externally they have a striking resemblance to bourgeois philistinism, which infinite resignation, like faith, deeply disdains. . . . But to be able to come down in such a way that instantaneously one seems to stand and to walk, to change the leap into life into walking, absolutely to express the sublime in the pedestrian—only that knight can do it, and this is the one and only marvel.[24]

The sublime in the pedestrian is another version of the ordinary sublime: although it might imply a truly shaking, life-changing experience, it tends to appear disappointingly ordinary—the leap is transmuted to walking. In his reading of Cavell and Kierkegaard, Robert M. Hall sums up the relevant aspects of Abraham's double movement as follows: "Resignation drives us toward transcendence; drives us from the world; faith drives us, as spirit, back into the world. But we do not come back from Mt. Moriah the same. The movement of resignation, when it is really made, irreversibly transforms our relation to finitude."[25] Where Noggle's sublime leaves us in suspense between the states, Cavell's and Kierkegaard's pulls us back into the world; the sublime wrests the world from our possession so that we may possess it again.

If we are able to let the sublime return us to the ordinary, we do not return to a place untouched by the possibility of the loss, but we must embrace the standing possibility of loss as integral to the ordinary. That our human condition contains the capacity to repudiate that condition means that a real acknowledgment of it can be fully reached only after having passed through the ordeal of the sublime.[26] Diamond retains this standing possibility of the sublime in noting "how much that coming apart of thought and reality belongs to flesh and blood" (*PAL*, 78). The difficulty is thus inherent to us as our flesh and blood; the sublime is part of our home, yet departs from it, uncannily. This means that our home—the ordinary—is not a stable settlement, for, as Cavell notes with reference to Thoreau, "in *Walden* the proof that what you have found you have made your own, your home, is that you are free to leave it" (*IQO*, 175).

Postmodern accounts of the sublime, in Derrida and Lyotard, have focused on how the sublime surpasses our comprehension. What is symptomatic, however, is not only that such accounts have so little to say about the ordinariness of the sublime, say its vulnerability to being missed or rejected, but more importantly that they have very little to say of the sublime's power to *return* us toward the everyday. It is indeed telling that in Derrida's reading of Kierkegaard's *Fear and Trembling*, nothing is made of the fact of the return. It is as if Derrida can see the sublime as figuring in the first movement, indeed its stroke of madness. But he does not attach significance to the double movement that arguably makes up Kierkegaard's prime concern: the infinite resignation must be succeeded by faith enacted in the recurrence of the everyday.[27] But precisely this is, as I conceive it, the moral of the ordinary sublime: since we, after being exposed to it, are offered the opportunity to realize that it is *we* who have refused to see what is before our eyes, the ordinary sublime can, if embraced, instruct us back into another relation with the ordinary. Cavell writes, "'Give us this day our daily bread'; it is not something to take for granted" (*IQO*, 171), which in Kierkegaard's version concerns repetition as "the daily bread that satisfies with blessing."[28] The ordinary returns at once as a gift, something to be received passively, but also as an appeal to our responsibility: the ordinary is not to be taken for granted but is *ours* to inhabit—and ours to leave.

At the beginning of this chapter I claimed that the ordinary sublime could provide at least a minimal experiential resource from which a religious orientation could tap. As Diamond constantly alludes to, the change involved in such a return after the acknowledged occurrence of the ordinary sublime does have moral consequences, even when they at first sight seem to be more of changes in aesthetic sensibility. They are meant to turn the philosophical attention toward the finite conditions of our moral life that otherwise is easily left out or repudiated. But besides the aesthetic and moral impact, the omnipresence of religious vocabulary in Diamond's account is striking: grace, wonder, miracles, limits and transcendence, even prophecy. In another context, Cavell is careful to note that the "spiritual fervor" in Wittgenstein's writing can be taken as religious, moral, or aesthetic. They are not separate disciplines for Wittgenstein, neither in *Tractatus*'s speech of the mystical nor in *Philosophical Investigations*—they are all dimensions internal to his method.[29] Adding to the picture of the ordinary sublime's unsettled location between the trivial and the extraordinary, Cavell writes that Wittgenstein's work can "seem too trivial to mention . . . and then suddenly can seem to require a response of particular urgency, as if speaking to a sense of moral or even religious perplexity" (*PDT,* 200). The upshot seems to be that the ordinary sublime strikes a chord that might be responded to in all these registers. Consequently, religion has also found a point of reference within the ordinary, however vulnerable that point might appear.

At one juncture, Cavell considers whether Nietzsche's claims are meant as epistemological, metaphysical, religious, aesthetic, or moral, and he would without doubt be able to pose the same question to Wittgenstein. He goes on:

> I find I am glad to reply—glad only to reply—that it is precisely all of these, all the time. But that means to me that every word we utter, or withhold, is an act capable of responsiveness within at least these registers. No wonder philosophy lives in fear of the ordinary word. (*PDT,* 131)

THREE

Acknowledging God

Having presented Cavell's openness toward the problem of religion, I now proceed to more theologically charged territory in order to explore some possibilities offered by Cavell's philosophy. In doing so, I focus on one of Cavell's signature concepts, namely acknowledgment. Although acknowledgment has a wide application in Cavell's thinking—including our relation to the world, others, different modernist artistic media, and our own conditions as speaking animals—it was initially developed in response to the skeptical problem of other minds. Since the problem of other minds has remained at the center of Cavell's concerns, and since this problem highlights features relevant to related inflections of that concept, I first outline acknowledgment as it is developed in that context. To be precise, it is within the context of a discussion of Wittgenstein's so-called private language argument that Cavell first proposes this concept. In addition to its centrality to Cavell's thinking on the whole, the reason for focusing on this concept in the present chapter is that it has clear implications for the conception of the self's relation to God.

"To what extent, and to whom, can I, or should I, or dare I, make myself known?" are central questions that often go unnoticed or are taken as impertinent to philosophy, Cavell notes, though they are "[n]ot unnoticed, or impertinent, however, to Montaigne or in a while to Rousseau—nor, dare I say?—to Augustine or to Luther.... Does philosophy—ought it to?—care about these outliers of confession?"[1] I hope to convey in the following pages the fact that Cavell does care about Augustine and Luther, and consequently that in his view philosophy as such ought to care about them. To be more specific, confessions in Augustine's sense provides critical guidance in understanding the first-person application of Cavell's notion of acknowledgment, whereas Luther provides a useful background for understanding acknowledgment in terms of faith, or as Luther thinks of it, as trust in a promise.

Acknowledging the Other

In his influential discussion of the problem of other minds, Wittgenstein centers on the question of whether we know our own and other's pain (PI, § 246). In one of the important early comments on Wittgenstein, Norman Malcolm attempts to expound on the way in which he takes Wittgenstein to refute skepticism with regard to other minds. Such skepticism takes for granted that it makes sense to say, for example, that I know (i.e., that I am in a position to establish with certainty) that I am in pain, but that I never know for sure whether the other suffers pain. According to Malcolm's reading, however, Wittgenstein points out that it is meaningless to say from a first-person perspective that "I know I am in pain." The usual requirements of knowledge are out of the question here (such as that you can be right and wrong and that there are public criteria for deciding its correct application); however, Malcolm argues that the utterance makes perfect sense from a third-person perspective. Since there are publicly available criteria in this case for assessing the correctness of the application, I might very well know that the other is in pain. Malcolm takes Wittgenstein to demonstrate that skepticism with regard to other minds is self-defeating, in the sense that the skeptic's assertions are based on conceptual confusions of the ordinary use of "knowledge."[2]

Essential to Cavell's reading of Wittgenstein is that ordinary language philosophy is in no position to refute skepticism in this way; it cannot claim to know our ordinary language in any other, more specialized sense than the skeptic already does. Rather, it must patiently try to call attention to what words convey, without denying the skeptic's ability to renounce it. Malcolm's description of how we speak of knowledge in a theoretical or epistemological case is not as misleading as his surmise that such speech adequately expresses what ordinarily interests us when we are confronted with our own or another's pain. Apart from those interests, ordinary words will be bereft of their point, impact, and consequences, in short, their meaning. To start with the first-person perspective, Cavell points out, counter to Malcolm, that there are indeed ordinary applications of "I know"—for instance, in saying "I know I am childish," or "I know I am late," which is, of course, not meant as a declaration of theoretical certainty. The context is here one in which I admit, or reveal, or confess something—that is, one in which I *acknowledge* something about myself. Cavell's suggestion is that such acknowledgments are also operative in giving voice to my pain:

> It is obvious enough, but unremarked, that "I know I'm in pain" . . . is an *expression of pain*. It may also be an expression of exasperation. And it has the form ("I know I . . . ") of an *acknowledgement*. . . . As an acknowledgement (admission, confession) it is perfectly intelligible. (*MWM*, 256)

Such use of "I know I . . . " requires a particular occasion, for example, if one for some reason wants to conceal one's pain but then decides to reveal it. The point is not that such acknowledgment is an alternative to knowledge, but rather that it demarcates a profound region of knowledge that Malcolm and other philosophers fail to discern. To understand knowledge here as acknowledgment makes it not only possible to see that knowing one's pain can be applied in the first person, contrary to what Malcolm argues, but also that such utterances are not meant to invite epistemological arguments, whether skeptical or anti-skeptical. For there is nothing hidden behind the self-revelation or admission—the exclamation *is* the expression of pain.

The implications of acknowledgment come more fully to the fore as we move from its first-person employment to that of the third person, in acknowledging another's pain.[3] Knowing another's pain does not mean peering through the other's body or establishing evidence with certainty, but might for instance manifest itself as sympathy:

> But why is sympathy expressed in this way? Because your suffering makes a *claim* upon me. It is not enough that I *know* (am certain) that you suffer—I must do or reveal something (whatever can be done). In a word, I must *acknowledge* it, otherwise I do not know what "(you or his) being in pain" means. (*MWM*, 263)

Acknowledging another's pain is a kind of response to the claim laid upon me, a claim that is issued from another as separate from me. Although acknowledgment is surely meant to generate a shift in the understanding of our approach to the other, it is, again, not meant as a replacement of knowledge. Acknowledgment *is* what knowing the other comes to in our ordinary dealings with others. This mode of knowledge goes beyond the epistemological notion of knowledge: it is not enough to state a belief in and establish the certainty of another's pain, one must *do* something—it shifts the emphasis from theory to practice. But acknowledgment also transcends epistemology in the sense that it not only takes responsiveness, but also requires personal responsibility for what to do in response, which adds a moral dimension to it (*CR*, 428).

The centrality of acknowledgment does not rest on the fact that it always is successfully enacted in ordinary life; both its success and its failure attest to the fact that it is acknowledgment that is at stake (*MWM*, 264). For, of course, there are such things as my pain being left unacknowledged by the others, and, conversely, my failing to acknowledge others. The skeptic, however, misrepresents the meaning of such failures. The skeptic depicts the first-person perspective as one in which the skeptic is sealed in his or her own circle of experiences to which he or she has an exclusive access; and correspondingly, from a third-person perspective, the skeptic finds himself or herself sealed out from the other—and from both emerges a feeling of isolation and powerlessness (*MWM*, 261). Although in the grips of what Wittgenstein would call certain "pictures" of the inner, Cavell still thinks the skeptic captures a profound truth: it *is* possible for the first person to hide what he or she feels from others, even to repress the feeling from him- or herself. As for the third person, it is likewise possible and similarly common to refuse to respond to the other's claim and therefore actively avoid the other. Yet, in neither case is there a theoretical problem to be solved, as though some information or evidence were needed but beyond reach. What is needed, and what acknowledgment used in the third person is meant to capture, is that I must *recognize* the other's expressions as the criterion of pain and how that criterion lays specific claim on me.

Now that I have sketched the differentiation between acknowledgment as used in the first and third persons, it is also necessary to stress that there are internal relations between them. For to acknowledge (recognize) the other requires that I reveal myself in my response to the other; and conversely, to acknowledge (reveal, confess) something of myself is always done in the face of the other. Tragedy—at least in Cavell's interpretation of Shakespeare's *King Lear*—not only is a failure of recognizing or denying others, but is internally bound up with the avoidance of letting oneself be acknowledged: "in actuality there is no acknowledgement, unless we put ourselves in [others'] presence, reveal ourselves to them" (*DK*, 103). Whether one, as King Lear, is too ashamed to let oneself be seen and recognized, or one wishes to be relieved of the burden of moral responsibility that goes along with acknowledging others, the avoidance of acknowledgment means that we theatricalize both ourselves and others: we attempt to stage each other into objects that are observable from the outside, quite in accordance with the skeptical wish (*DK*, 90–91). The skeptic as well as the anti-skeptic can be diagnosed as being drawn toward epistemological knowledge precisely to escape the personal demands implied in acknowledgment, especially that acknowledgment of others implies self-recognition and self-revelation. In Cavell's view, skepticism with regard to other minds is a matter of our unwillingness to fully recognize the other. Acknowledgment is meant to comprise also our unwillingness, even denials. In one of the most precise summaries of what acknowledgment implies, Cavell writes:

> acknowledgement is an act of the self (if it is one of recognition, then it is not like recognizing a place but like recognizing a government); and it is not done apart from an admission of the existence of others (denial of which made the acknowledgement necessary) or apart from an expression of one's aliveness to the denial (the revelation in acknowledgement). (*WV*, 124)

Theological Challenges

Reviewing Judith E. Tonning's thought-provoking response to Cavell now helps us turn to the theological significance of acknowledgment. In "Acknowl-

edging a Hidden God," she rightly locates acknowledgment as the counter-con-
cept to Cavell's notion of skepticism, occasionally called sin. Against Cavell's outlook, Tonning contends that it is only by means of the Christian doctrine of sin
and grace that full acknowledgment of humanity can be gained, but such a doctrine in turn only makes sense given the acknowledgment of God. She wants
to move beyond the limits of Cavell's "relational epistemology" toward an embrace of "an original and real relation to God which is ultimately independent of
the present knowledge and attitudes of the individual."[4] From Tonning's perspective, the only context in which acknowledgment can be realized is thus in "the
continual acknowledgement of our existential dependence on God, expressing
itself as a (supernaturally enabled) acknowledgement of his will."[5] According to
her argument, this ontological dependence more specifically implies the givenness of creation, and since the creation is solely God's act, it cannot be made dependent on human acknowledgment. Rather, acknowledgment of God depends
upon God's prior act of creating and sustaining us.[6]

Tonning asserts that Cavell cannot appreciate the sense of the givenness
of creation, since his notion of acknowledgment seems to overly depend on
human achievements. But at this point, I think Cavell's notion comes closer to
Tonning's theological inflection of it than she is willing to admit. True, Cavell
does not affirm creation in the strong metaphysical sense, but he in fact has built
in an awareness of a fundamental *receptivity* or *responsiveness* in the acknowledgment of the other or of the world: "It is true that we do not know the existence of the world with certainty; our relation to its existence is deeper—one in
which it is accepted, that is to say, received" (*SW,* 133). At this most fundamental level, accepting the world as received involves being open to its givenness
and being willing to respond in return—perhaps in praise and gratitude for existence, as Cavell suggests elsewhere (*PDT,* 68). According to Cavell's rendering
of it, acknowledgment is not a distinctively religious concept but is open to a
variety of responses and qualifications. There is, however, nothing with the receptivity of acknowledgment as such that prevents it from being inflected religiously, as in receiving the creation as a gift from God, or for that matter, in accounting for the wonder that keeps the philosopher's fire burning, just as such
receptivity might be something one wants to avoid, say by means of nihilism or
skepticism.

However, if creation is supposed to establish and secure our relation in an
"ontological grounding," then Tonning has moved her theological inflection of
acknowledgment too far away from the context that gave meaning to Cavell's
concept in the first place.[7] Tonning's "acknowledgement of God" seems to suggest that our finitude and separateness is overcome by a metaphysical relation
to God that is established regardless of our responses. This pushes her con-

ception close to the metaphysical wish to establish a relation between one's claims to knowledge and the object of knowledge "without my intervention, apart from my agreement" (CR, 351–352). Precisely the craving for an unmediated attachment, beyond my personal responsibilities, is what Cavell considers to be one of the hidden desires beyond the skeptical impulse. For Cavell, acknowledgment presupposes separation and thus only has a point insofar as no metaphysical grounding can secure our relationship independent of our reception of and exposure to the other, the world, or, I will add, the infinite other—God.[8] Acknowledgment only makes sense for beings who relate to others across separation.

In order to understand why a metaphysical solution cannot work, we recall that acknowledgment, as well as the sense of skepticism that it replies to, is a decidedly modern notion for Cavell—that is, the background against which they emerge is one in which an integral cosmology and metaphysics have become highly problematic. At times Cavell refers to the Reformation as a decisive turning point, presumably since it marks the point where tradition and ecclesiastical mediation no longer guarantee our relation to God. The upshot of it was the emergence of a new sense of subjectivity located at a certain distance to its world; for epistemology, this meant that the world relation could be doubted and that the knowing subject must try to bridge the gaps by its own means, such as by sense perceptions. Its natural habitation was lost and the subject strangely relocated.

> At some point the unhinging of our consciousness from the world's interposed our subjectivity between us and our presentness to the world. Then our subjectivity became what is present to us, individuality became isolation. The route to conviction in reality was through the acknowledgement of that endless presence of self. (WV, 22)

The acknowledgment of the self becomes unavoidable, or else it must be skeptically denied or overcome. The acknowledgment of the self cannot take place without the appeal to others, which means that the claim to a community that is never guaranteed will be the basis on which I can reach a self. Such is also the situation that modernist art is faced with: it cannot simply take its medium for granted; the artist's subjectivity has become interposed between his or her conviction and the work. The medium must be acknowledged, with its limits but also with its possibilities for further reinventions, in order to establish its audience or community. Such "Protestant malady and legacy" has for better or worse forced us into self-reflectiveness (WV, 123). From this perspective, Tonning's metaphysical insistence appears as an attempt to bypass the loss of an integrated community as a given and of the self-reflective attitude that it exacts. But for Cavell, acknowledgment is meant to respond to that predicament, recognizing that we already experience ourselves at a distance, hence separated, from others, the world and, arguably, God. Acknowledgment entails the self-awareness of the modern sense of separateness but also points to the kind of relations that can still be obtained across separation.

Tonning certainly also examines separation as an inescapable part of the human finitude. For Cavell, acknowledgment does indeed involve separation, but it is critical that such separation tends to become distorted in the skeptical interpretation of it, an interpretation he sometimes calls sin. "By contrast to Cavell's account, however, this theological interpretation of scepticism [as sin] places the 'sceptical' desire to repudiate human limitation in the context of real, existential 'incompleteness' arising from the human vocation to *theosis.*"[9] Leaving aside the vexing question of *theosis*, Tonning thinks that only a "real, existential incompleteness" can make sense of sin and hence skepticism. But here we might wonder whether Tonning is saying that the skeptical interpretation is in fact right: that we are created incomplete, with unjustified restrictions, as if separation between self, others, the world, and God is due to a metaphysical lack.[10] What Cavell wants us to embrace, however, is that separation and finitude are constitutive parts of human knowledge and acknowledgment.

Cavell reads *Othello* as Shakespeare's exploration of the difficulty entailed in acknowledging human separation: "Their [Othello's and Desdemona's] difference from one another—the one everything the other is not—form an emblem of human separation, which can be accepted, and granted, or not. Like the separation from God; everything we are not" (*CR,* 496). Human separation is precisely what Othello cannot grant. But the passage suggests that separation also fundamentally determines our relation to God, and hence such a relation must accordingly be conceived as a matter of acknowledgment. The question is not so much whether some ontological incompleteness excludes us from having a real relation to God; what is at stake is whether the separation is "accepted, granted, or not." Faith is, accordingly, the acknowledgment of God, accepting God as available (we know from revelation what there is for us, finite creatures, to know of God) yet as the other to us, "everything we are not" (which the skeptic turns into an argument for denying whatever is revealed to us).

Since, according to Cavell's reading of modernity, we have lost our natural absorption in a sacred cosmos, our relation to God cannot take care of itself apart from our responsibilities. Acknowledging God therefore entails self-reference, a personal relation, one that precludes faith from turning into impersonal knowledge. Theology and philosophy have been burdened by a recurrent drive to establish God with certainty, thereby perhaps betraying a skeptical wish for overcoming personal commitment and responsibility. Cavell notes:

What we forgot, when we deified reason, was not that reason is incompatible with feeling, but that knowledge requires acknowledgement. (The withdrawal and approach of God can be looked upon as
tracing the history of our attempts to overtake and absorb acknowledgement by knowledge; God would be the name of that impossibility). (*DK*, 117)

In Cavell's depiction, acknowledging God is not so much a question of solely human epistemic achievements, as Tonning seems to fear, but rather a question of
willingness to receive what is granted us on God's initiative ("the withdrawal and
approach *of* God"). This is precisely what is missed as long as acknowledgment
is replaced by knowledge, a replacement that comes to expression in the tradition of proofs for God's existence, central to the tradition from Anselm, Thomas
Aquinas, and Descartes onward.

But exactly what is wrong with the proofs for God's existence? Paradoxically, the proofs do not result in establishing the relation to God beyond doubt,
but in God's withdrawal. "Proofs for God's existence, and criticism of these
proofs," Cavell writes, "are apt to be empty intermittently for people whose
conviction is that they are known by God, or to God, or not" (*CR*, 443). For those
who are convinced that they are known by or to God, the proofs are useless and
empty, since the proofs cannot convey any insight of value; for those who are not
convinced, proofs will be in vain, since the proofs do not move them into a position in which they can acknowledge their relation to God. In a Pascalian manner, Cavell can even write that "only someone who lacked the knowledge to find
God, the way to locate him, would offer such proofs" (*CR*, 241). The upshot is
that acknowledgment of God cannot take place without the implication of myself, in self-revelation, perhaps in a confession.[11] If I am left out in the knowledge
of God, it means that my relation will be an unacknowledged relation to God, or
worse, the death of God. One might, however, take such death of God as already
involved in the Crucifixion. Cavell writes that I might shut my eyes to the other
in question or attempt to shut his eyes to me: "Either way I implicate myself in
his existence. There is the problem of the other.—The crucified human body is
our best picture of the unacknowledged human soul" (*CR*, 340).

Acknowledgment and Confession

I have so far delineated only roughly the acknowledgment of God by high-
lighting relevant implications of that concept. However, I think more substance
can be given to Cavell's own fragmentary contributions in this respect and the
way it invites constellations with the theological tradition. In particular, I am in-
terested in acknowledgment as applied by the first person ("I admit," "I confess")

and how it is bound up with Cavell's indebtedness to Augustine as illuminated in his interpretation of Wittgenstein. It is noteworthy that Cavell's acknowledgment seems internally related to confession. As quoted above, the first-person exclamation "I know I . . . " could be read as an "acknowledgement (admission, confession)." The substantial link between acknowledgment and confession appears in the sentence that follows: "It requires a context in which, for some reason, I wish to conceal my pain—say because to admit it would be shameful, or would look like an excuse" (MWM, 256). Confession is one of the ways—probably the main way—in which acknowledgment as applied by the first person comes to expression. The kind of knowledge that is at stake in confessions requires not further evidence or new facts, but rather a new stance toward oneself. This stance takes a willingness to recognize something that one already knows and yet has hidden from oneself and others, perhaps even repressed. Acknowledgment therefore means not only the "recognition of the other's specific relation to oneself" but also that "this entails the revelation of oneself as having denied or distorted that relation" (CR, 428).

According to Cavell, the kind of knowledge acquired through confessions is at the heart of ordinary language philosophy. To engage in ordinary language philosophy, asking oneself what we should say when, is not a matter of a detached mapping of linguistic rules or conventions already fixed prior to the investigation, but rather something that cannot be undertaken without personal involvement and responsibility. The extent to which I make sense of another's words and deeds and others make sense of mine is not a given fact, but constitutes a vulnerable mutuality that ordinary language explores—both its successes and its failures. Since there is no external point from which such exploration can be undertaken, the ordinary language philosopher can only invite the reader to find out for him- or herself whether or not he or she can recognize what the philosopher says as representative. In other words, it is a matter of testing whether one recognizes oneself as included in the "we" of "what we should say when." To engage in ordinary language philosophy is for Cavell to engage in a disclosure of your position in the world and within the community with others—which means that ordinary language philosophy is a search for self-knowledge (MWM, 66). How difficult such self-knowledge is to attain, how anxious we are to let ourselves and others count, and what intellectual efforts we are willing to make in order to avoid such admission—these are, in Cavell's reading, some of the main teachings of Wittgenstein's Philosophical Investigations.

These are equally the themes of Freud's psychoanalysis and Augustine's Confessions—both of which are vital impetuses for Cavell's way of thinking. It has been argued that what is novel with Augustine's theology, and what remains its standing contribution to the formation of Western selfhood, is that God is not directly to be searched for, neither in nor beyond the world, but that our way to God must go *via* the inner, the soul. Such an inward turn makes self-knowledge integral to the awareness of God, and more generally, it promotes a reflexive stand over against oneself and one's occupations in the world.[12] What Augustine discovers inside is not the sheer love of God, however, but a battlefield of conflicting desires or a "grand struggle in my inner house," as he puts it.[13] A true confession requires full acknowledgment of how things are with oneself, against the wish to remain concealed.

Cavell not only takes ordinary language philosophy in general to be engaging in the quest for self-knowledge, but he also reads Wittgenstein as an heir to Augustine in other decisive respects that bear on acknowledgment. In his reading of *Philosophical Investigations*, Cavell is struck by the fact that Wittgenstein chooses to begin his work with letting someone else speak first, namely with a quotation from Augustine's *Confessions* concerning how Augustine reconstructs his own acquiring of language.[14] To Cavell, this literary gesture raises an essential question internal to Wittgenstein's thinking: the question of how philosophy begins. It is as if Wittgenstein is implying that we start not by asserting anything, but by being accosted: someone else speaks first. Such philosophical unassertiveness or silence means that the first virtue of philosophy "is that of responsiveness, [being] awake when all others have fallen asleep" (*PP*, 129).[15] For philosophy in general, as for Cavell's signature concept of acknowledgment in particular, an emphasis is laid upon the initial receptivity and responsiveness.

This might suggest that philosophy must be open to whatever comes its way, but it also suggests that the responsiveness must be vigilant to a call that might seem, at least at first, most unremarkable. However, the remarkable fact about Wittgenstein's chosen passage from Augustine's *Confessions* is that, for most readers (Cavell includes himself), this passage does *not* seem particularly remarkable—it is indeed missable in the sense outlined in the previous chapter. Yet, the unremarkable can have remarkable consequences. Take, for instance, the culmination of Augustine's work: his conversion, as he narrates it, is initiated from something as ordinary as children's play in the neighborhood: "Pick up and read, pick up and read!"[16] To Cavell, Wittgenstein's philosophy on the whole is trying to awaken an attentiveness to the importance of the unremarkable, the common, the ordinary. Cavell takes Wittgenstein to be laying bare throughout his work the astonishingly small degree to which the obvious tends to be obvious, and how this is connected with our various ways of self-alienation. According to Cavell, the remaining 692 paragraphs of *Philosophical Investigations* can be read as spelling out the implications of the quotation from Augustine's account of his acquiring language from his parents. The quotation addresses the question of what it takes to be initiated into language, the conditions and limits of teaching, the confrontation with fundamental criteria of our culture—in short, it addresses the problem of inheriting a language. "Where did you learn—what is the home of—a concept?" are questions that not only surface whenever the figure of the child appears, but they also haunt Wittgenstein's work as a whole (*CHU*, 98).

Wittgenstein takes over Augustine's uncompromising quest for self-knowledge or self-acknowledgment, which moves from the loss of oneself toward regaining the self. From a more systematic perspective, the beginning of philosophy has its starting point in what Cavell has called "the philosophical moment," where nothing and everything is wrong. Wittgenstein has captured this crucial moment in the expression "I don't know my way about" (*PI*, § 123). The German original reads "Ich kenne mich nicht aus," suggesting more strongly than the English translation the loss of orientation internal to the self, or as Cavell reads it, "a loss of self-knowledge, of being, so to speak, at a loss" (*NYUA*, 36). Such an interpretation suggests in turn that philosophy concerns the quest of self-knowledge, which again evokes an Augustinian equivalent, such as "I have become a problem to myself," or within a clear context of confessing before God, "You were there before me, but I had departed from myself. I could not even find myself, much less you."[17] Cavell's comment on Wittgenstein's aphorism might also be read as a comment on Augustine:

> I understand this as a theorization of the search for the beginning of philosophy . . . It conceives philosophy's beginning for me as one of recognizing that I have lost my way, and in that way I am stopped. . . . The progress between beginning and ending is, accordingly, what Wittgenstein means by grammatical investigation, which, since we begin lost, may be thought of as a progress in finding ourselves. (*PP*, 156–157)[18]

Lost and found, exiled and at home, restless hearts yearning for peace—these are, if we trust Cavell, the central axes of both Wittgenstein's *Philosophical Investigations* and Augustine's *Confessions*.

Thus Wittgenstein's occupation with loss and reorientation has consequences for the interpretation of the development of his highly original philosophical style. Cavell thinks that the problems that Wittgenstein's peculiar style responds to are

> the lack of existing terms of criticism, and the method of self-knowledge. In its defense of truth against sophistry, philosophy has employed the same literary genres as theology in its defense of the faith: against intellectual competition, Dogmatics; against Dogmatics, the Confession; in both, the Dialogue. Inaccessible to the dogmatics of philosophical criticism, Wittgenstein chose confession and recast his

dialogue. It contains what serious confessions must: the full acknowledgment of temptation ("I want to say . . . "; "I feel like saying . . . ";
"Here the urge is strong . . . ") and a willingness to correct them and
give them up ("In the everyday use . . . "; "I impose a requirement
which does not meet my real need"). (The voice of temptation and
the voice of correctness are the antagonists in Wittgenstein's dia-
logues.) (*MWM*, 70–71)[19]

In the two footnotes to this passage, Cavell refers to Augustine, Adolf Harnack,
and Karl Barth, which should remove any doubt about whether or not he feels an
affinity between Wittgenstein's style and a certain theological territory. Furthermore, as I pointed out in chapter 1, Cavell insists on reading *Philosophical Investigations* as a modernist work. According to this interpretation, the text's crucial
aim is to establish its own style and voice, not because the tradition is completely
lost, but because the tradition and its authority have become one of philosophy's
own problems. In such an intellectual and cultural milieu, it has been necessary
to regain a philosophy that involves, rather than excludes, the human voice. In
order to do that, Wittgenstein approaches the genre of confession. Confessional
writings are not meant as proofs: no empirical facts, certainty of metaphysical
foundation, or establishing of dogma could do the work. In writing confessions,
I make myself representative of other persons and hence claim a special sense of
authority as speaking for others. I invite them to see what I see and to change according to what they see. In the same way, Augustine invites his readers to trust
him, beyond proofs:

> I also, Lord, so make my confession to you that I may be heard by
> people to whom I cannot prove that my confession is true. But those
> whose wise ears are opened by love believe me. . . . Stir up the heart
> when people read and hear the confessions of my past wickedness,
> which you have forgiven and covered up to grant me happiness in
> yourself, transforming my soul by faith and your sacrament.[20]

Augustine knows that there is no compelling evidence that will convince anyone;
he can ultimately only be received by those "opened by love," those ready to acknowledge him (the third-person inflection) in order to acknowledge themselves
more fully (the first-person inflection).

The criteria for truth of a confession, Wittgenstein writes, reside not in a
correct description, but in the consequences that can be drawn from them and
"whose truth is guaranteed by the special criteria for *truthfulness*" (*PI*, 222).[21] Confessions assert authority over their readers not by their empirical accuracy, but by
their exemplary expressions of something at once intimate and common. Probably with Wittgenstein's passage on confessions in mind (Cavell is here discus-

sing abstract art), Cavell distinguishes between true empirical statements and statements that claim truthfulness and acceptance: "My acceptance is the way I respond to them, and not everyone is capable of the response, or willing for it. I put this by saying that a true statement is something we know or do not know; a truthful statement is something we must acknowledge or fail or refuse to acknowledge" (VW, 157). If philosophy proceeding from the ordinary is to be regarded in terms of confessions, then its voice is destined to alternate between arrogance and humility—arrogance insofar as the philosopher claims to speak representatively of the human condition; humility insofar as such voicing of private moments must subject itself to the laws of the ordinary in order to make them universally recognizable (PoP, 8).

Not only must a confession be accepted, but it is meant to have consequences—we, the addressees, must *respond* to it. Augustine's uncovering of his "past wickedness" and the transformation of his soul invites the reader to inquire into his or her own past, present, and future states. In other words, the reader must be willing to let him- or herself be read, which, in Cavell's lingo, means to let the text reveal previously rejected aspects of the reader's soul (TS, 51–53). Such demands capture not only the situation of a reader of confessions, but also the situation of the confessor before God: it is only after his acknowledgment of the biblical God that Augustine is capable of fully acknowledging himself—exposed to and being read by God. Cavell holds that if the writings of ordinary language philosophy are taken only as opinions that can be believed or not, they are useless. For as both Augustine and Freud demand, a proper quest for self-knowledge must be accompanied by inner change (MWM, 72). It is a change that goes via a kind of recollection of a past that has become fixed and frozen, be it a past life with words controlled by captivating pictures (Wittgenstein) or by repressed fantasies (Freud). Only by such recollection can we hope to break the bonds of our past. Whereas the conversion for Augustine is narrated as one decisive event, ordinary language demands of us the continual conversion, every day, working through the voice of temptation and the voice of correction. Or, as Mulhall has it, "We might think of this as indicating the incompleteness of Augustine's conversion—a conclusion entirely in keeping with his conception of conversion as always essentially incomplete, endlessly in need of repetition and renewal (as his account in book X of the self's essential unknowability to itself . . . would lead us to expect)."[22]

Acknowledgment and Promise

Although confessions imply another to whom one is confessing, such acknowledgment is still located within the first-person perspective. However, acknowledgment also has applications for the third persons, and Cavell has also suggested its theological relevance, indicating that the way one acknowledges the finite other is somehow relevant to the understanding of the acknowledgment of the infinite other. In countering William James's occasional tendency to regard religious testimonies as unverifiable hypotheses, Cavell points out that "the existence of divinity, whatever further intellectual problems, is no more a *hypothesis* than the existence of my neighbor is, though I might deny, or hedge, either" (*CW*, 17). Since the alternative to construing hypotheses with regard to my neighbor is acknowledging the other, so the passage leads us to expect that acknowledgment also pertains to my relation to divinity.[23]

However, such equating of my relation to the other and to God covers over crucial distinctions involved between acknowledging God and acknowledging the other, between what has been regarded as faith and knowledge. Elsewhere, Cavell turns to Luther for clarification:

> When Luther said we cannot know God but must have faith, it is clear enough that the inability he speaks of is a logical one: There is not some comprehensible activity we cannot perform, and equally not some incomprehensible activity we cannot perform. Our relation to God is that of parties to a testament (or refusers of it); and Luther's logical point is that you do not accept a promise by knowing something about the promisor. (*DK*, 95)

Given the context, this passage is meant to clarify the logic of acknowledgment and its relation to what epistemology calls knowledge, and the passage suggests that Cavell finds Luther's understanding of faith as an instance of acknowledgment. Cavell might have several reasons for turning to Luther at this juncture. I have already noted how the Reformation plays a prominent part in Cavell's account of why the modern condition necessitates acknowledgment. Furthermore, as Sarah Beckwith has pointed out, the notion of acknowledgment specifically referred to the sacrament of penance until the age of the Reformation, when it underwent a deep transformation. From having been distributed through ecclesiological authorities, confessions and forgiveness were loosened from those authorities, which made them the business of both no one and everyone. In readings heavily indebted to Cavell, Beckwith points out how acknowledgment became a central human problem in the Reformation's aftermath; in particular, Shakespeare displays acknowledgment's fragility and power in establishing social bonds in his plays.[24] This new perception has much to do with the altered concept of faith, not least due to Luther.

The problem with the epistemological approach to God is that it gives us the impression that there is something out there—a metaphysical fact or *Ding an sich* (the thing in itself)—which we should know but cannot reach. Our failing knowledge of God is understood skeptically as being due to our intellectual shortcomings or human restrictions. In Cavell's account, Luther wants to attract us to another, more useful picture, one in which we are called not to gain knowledge but to acknowledge God by trusting his promise. In *The Babylonian Captivity of the Church*, Luther addresses how metaphysical speculation concerning the Eucharist not only lacks any clear biblical foundation (and hence, in Luther's view, is mere speculation rather than faith), but also blocks faith's access to the sacraments. This might well be read as a logical or grammatical reminder: faith is not a matter of intellectual achievement, certainty, or belief in metaphysical facts. There is reciprocity between promise and faith: without God's promise, the belief is bereft of its direction and content; but without faith the promise is not effective.[25] Faith is then to put trust in the promise and acknowledge the promisor.

Oswald Bayer has argued that the rediscovery of *promissio* is Luther's central Reformation achievement, which reaches fruition in *The Babylonian Captivity*. Drawing on Austin, Bayer thinks of God's promise in terms of performative speech acts: to promise does not refer to matters of fact, but is emphatically to do something—it constitutes what it says.[26] Cavell agrees that ordinary language can shed light on the implications of the speech act of promise, but the characteristics of promise can also shed light back on ordinary language as a whole:

> Conceive the level of this idea [the idea of promise] to be that man is the animal who can give his word, where that is a function of *having* words, that is, having language. . . . "This is simply what I do" [*Philosophical Investigations*, § 217] is the sign of a kind of promise, say of initiation into a culture, and (its) language, and (its) promises, its unattained but attainable states. (*CHU*, 115)[27]

The relevant implications are that both the promise of speech and the promise of faith are anchored in performative acts and that they point toward a yet unattained future. But Cavell argues that this gesture also applies to the kind of utterances we entertain as we initiate people into our culture. "This is simply what I do" or "Here we say . . . " is fundamental both in teaching children how to speak and for the education of grown-ups, that is, for ordinary language philosophy. Although such utterances sound like statements, they should be regarded as promises. This means that Cavell's philosophy, along with Luther's theology, takes on a significant orientation toward the future.

As his epigraph for *The Senses of Walden*, Cavell chose a passage from *The Babylonian Captivity:*

> For all our life should be baptism, and the fulfilling of the sign, or sacrament, of baptism; we have been set free from all else and wholly given over to baptism alone, that is, to death and resurrection. This

glorious liberty of ours, and this understanding of baptism have
been carried captive in our day.[28]

A double temporal dimension is involved in Luther's understanding of baptism:
one points backward, to the inheritance of a promise of redemption once given,
the other points forward, by means of the liberation from captivity, toward something like an eschatological fulfillment of the promise.[29] The present, then, is
kept in suspense between the giving of the promise and its fulfillment, and can
be regarded as a state of bewilderment, in the grips of the temptation of false rec-
onciliations and false hopes.

Now these temporal dimensions might seem out of tune with what Cavell
and Luther are after, namely the repeated recurrence of the everyday, for Luther experienced as the repeated death and resurrection, for Cavell as the loss
and regaining of the self and its words. However, such recurrences are already
inscribed in baptism, which, according to Luther, should be considered as a process of growth. Although Luther thinks that we keep falling from our baptism
and keep getting lost in sin, the promise will last throughout life—and beyond.
Therefore, the everyday is—in keeping with Cavell's depiction—both the place
of our self-exile and the place to which we are called back in confessions. Luther
puts it thus: "Therefore, when we rise from our sins and repent, we are merely
returning to the power and the faith of baptism from which we fell, and finding our way back to the promise then made to us, which we deserted when we
sinned."[30] Our ordinary life requires a *returning*, which simultaneously is a *turn
to* a promise of an eschatological future. Or put the other way around, it requires
a change by means of a return or remembering: "Memory," Cavell writes, "is
the access to that knowledge that constitutes the call for a change expressed as
a (re)turn" (*CHU*, xxx). The temporal chiasm of remembering and of promise is
central to the practice of philosophy, as Cavell sees it, and its working toward
what he calls redemption (in a non-theological sense). There is no antinomy between inheritance and future change; the one presupposes the other, as Ricoeur
pointed out with reference to the eschatology of freedom entailed in the memory
of Exodus and the Resurrection.[31]

In his epigraph to *Senses of Walden*, Cavell's invocation of the promise of
baptism might shed further light on what it means to acknowledge the fact of language. Interpreting Thoreau's understanding of speech and writing, Cavell distinguishes between one's mother and father tongues: the term "mother tongue"
establishes the fact that the language is not my possession, but something shared
and established before me, and hence inherited; the "father tongue" is some kind
of second inheritance, or as Cavell puts it, a rebirth. Here the emphasis is on the
individual overtaking of language and the responsibility for projecting it toward
the future (*IQO*, 133). The first birth is carried out by the mother; the second birth

is the business of the Father. In Cavell's reading of *Walden,* the religious symbols and ideas are invoked as allusions to the inheritance and unfulfilled promise of America. Still, the allusion also reveals Cavell's understanding of birth and of baptism: "Baptism of water is only a promise of another which is to come, of the spirit, by the word of words" (*SW,* 17).

Another way that brings out the future dimension of the epigraph follows immediately. For an alternative understanding of Thoreau's father tongue is to see it as prophecy, that is, the language of the Father, the word of God, as it is put in the mouth of the prophet. From this point in *Senses of Walden,* quotations from Ezekiel and Jeremiah (and to some extent the Gospels and Paul) recur throughout the book. What is relevant here is not so much prophecies of the promise of land (alluding to Thoreau's America) as its inspiration "by water" (alluding to Walden Pond) and that "it is written in captivity," and under the promise of change (*SW,* 18). Cavell can also regard Wittgenstein's writing as some kind of prophecy—say, disagreeable confrontation with the captivity of our way of lives as they stand (*NYUA,* 75). The only way to provoke change is from within, as if valid change can only come to pass when both dimensions of the promise are acknowledged: both our acceptance of our mother tongue and our overtaking of the father tongue. It has been argued that a utopian or even eschatological horizon pervades Cavell's thinking, not least as it reaches fruition in his moral perfectionism and its aspiration to transform the self.[32] But such a view must be held together with how such a horizon is embedded in an inheritance of the promise to which we constantly must return. "On Luther's account, in which the Mass is a promise," Cavell writes, "your acceptance of *this* promise is transformative of yourself."[33]

Acknowledging a promise—faith—requires that we are willing to confess and willing to let the voice of correction reorient the voice of temptation. This change is not one returning to "the given" but an endless task. What remains Lutheran in Cavell is certainly not the way Luther speaks (with Paul) of spirit and flesh, but how he depicts the struggle enacted in daily conversion along with the daily renewal. In Luther's words:

> According to the spiritual nature, which men refer to as the soul, he is called a spiritual, inner, or new man. According to the bodily nature, which men refer to as flesh, he is called a carnal, outward, or old man, of whom the Apostle writes in II Cor. 4, "Though our outer nature is wasting away, our inner nature is being renewed every day."[34]

Caring for Theology

Cavell has indeed something to say on acknowledging God, and by excavating this theological inflection of acknowledgment, further aspects of the concept of acknowledgment are brought to light. Its relation to both confession and promise underscores how acknowledgment revises a one-sided epistemological understanding of knowledge. Cavell's point in referring to Luther is to draw attention to Luther's differentiation between faith and knowledge, but also to the promise of change. And likewise, it is clear that the invocation of confessions is motivated by the particular kind of knowledge that is at stake for a philosophy that proceeds from ordinary language—a knowledge based on self-knowledge. Such an approach to acknowledgment adds to the interpretation of faith the deepening of the personal commitment to the divine other: the claim from the other calls me out and addresses my responsiveness and responsibility across the separation.

One of the arguments I have made is that acknowledging the other is inextricably connected to acknowledging myself. This means that to acknowledge (recognize) the infinite other requires that I reveal myself in responding to that other, but also, conversely, that acknowledging (revealing, confessing) hitherto hidden aspects of myself takes place in face of the (finite or infinite) other. This is mirrored in Cavell's reading of Descartes's argument for God's existence, which he takes to be saying that "it would not be possible for my nature to be what it is, possessing the idea of God, unless God really existed" (*CR*, 481), and we could add, if God does exist, so do I. While it affirms the internal relation between God and the self, the passage has been taken as Cavell's rejection of the idea of God as a guarantor for human existence, since such an appeal begins to resemble a skeptical idea of the human.[35] But as chapter 1 attempted to demonstrate, Cavell is far from unequivocal on these questions—which opens up the possibility for an affirmative answer to Cavell's question of whether philosophy does or ought to care about such "outliers of confession" as Augustine and Luther.[36]

A related objection can be made against the religious relevance of Cavell's proposed link between Wittgenstein and Augustine. Cavell indeed explicitly says that the obvious difference between Augustine and Wittgenstein is the former's appeal to God and the latter's lack of such an appeal. So Wittgenstein quotes Augustine after "the death of God" in order to "bring the question it contains into the ensuing (modern) realm of silence, of sourcelessness." The interesting thing is how Cavell continues: "There is nothing whereof one cannot speak; therefore one must attain silence" (*PP*, 177). The clear allusion to and play with *Tractatus* has its irony: the silence shall, for Wittgenstein, arguably not preclude but *preserve* the religious.[37] Cavell's double gesture seems at first sight to close the door for religion, only in the next moment to reopen it.

But what about Luther—is he not the clear target of an attack, for instance in Cavell's genealogy of modern skepticism, starting with Protestantism? Cavell writes,

From then on, one manages one's relation to God alone, in particular one bears the brunt alone of being known to God. . . . As long as God exists, I am not alone. And couldn't the other suffer the fate of God? It strikes me that it was out of the terror of this possibility that Luther promoted the individual human voice in the religious life. (*CR*, 470)

According to this genealogy, the modern sense of the inner privacy and secrecy that provokes skepticism has grown out of the Reformation—but so has the new sense of possible individual selves and, for Cavell, the decisive task of raising one's voice. And further, such individuality has called forth a new sense of community in religion, art, and philosophy. This new sense of community comes radically to the fore in modernism—and philosophical modernism, I argued in chapter 1, is indeed what Cavell's works aspire to. After Luther, Cavell says, relations and community become more personal—the community means "not the overcoming of our isolation, but the sharing of that isolation" (*MWM*, 229). This is probably a scant foundation on which to build an ecclesiology, but at least it suggests the importance of acknowledgment, in aesthetic, philosophical, as well as religious terms.

FOUR

Skepticism, Finitude, and Sin

Acknowledgment is an interpretation of knowledge, Cavell insists, or perhaps an interpretation of what lies at the heart of any knowledge, entailing a certain sense of receptivity or responsiveness, a willingness to confess and reveal oneself in a practical and responsible reply to the other, the world, or as I have suggested, to God. But such acknowledgment presupposes a separation from that which one responds to, or more generally, it presupposes finitude. Central to Wittgenstein's philosophy, and thus also to Cavell's own philosophy, is therefore the acknowledgment of human limitation, an acknowledgment that, however, seems hard to achieve. A significant passage reads:

> For Wittgenstein, philosophy comes to grief not in denying what we all know to be true, but in its effort to escape those human forms of life which alone provide the coherence of our expression. He wishes an acknowledgement of human limitation which does not leave us chafed by our skin, by a sense of powerlessness to penetrate beyond the human conditions of knowledge. (*MWM*, 61)

Why do we feel chafed by our own skin, and why does this lead to efforts to escape our forms of life? Theology calls this sin, but if "Philosophy cannot say sin" (*IQO*, 26), it calls it skepticism—both sin and skepticism capture the human destructive craving to transcend its humanity.

Although it has been unavoidable to call attention to skepticism in the preceding chapters, this chapter reads skepticism in light of its systematic parallelism or overlapping with sin. It is important to bear in mind what Cavell's occupation with skepticism seeks to accomplish. As Fergus Kerr rightly observes, Cavell is after the inherent truth of skepticism:

> He is not trying to refute scepticism. Nor is he simply diagnosing scepticism. Nor is he half-heartedly out to abandon scepticism. Rather, Cavell is engaging with scepticism, trying to uncover what sense of our condition—what experience of our condition—is voiced in versions of scepticism.[1]

In this endeavor, skepticism must come into an expression of its own, it must be listened to, as to a worthy other. The exigency of listening to this otherness be-

comes even more urgent as skepticism is not meant to capture more or less obsolete philosophical positions, but to name an impulse that wells up in ourselves.
Here I again attempt to extend Cavell's conversations with theology, a conversation that Cavell at times explicitly invites, sometimes only indirectly evokes, and
sometimes probably does not intend at all. Cavell offers occasional readings, or
sketches of readings, of the myth of the Fall in Genesis, but the overarching and
intimate parallelism of sin and skepticism appears most fruitful in this respect:
"skepticism," we learn, "is a place, perhaps the central secular place, in which
the human wish to deny the condition of human existence is expressed" (*IQO*,
5). The religious place, one must assume, is that of sin.

Theology, Doubt, and Skepticism

Let me begin the conversation from the theological side this time, in order
to provide a background for the problem of doubt and skepticism and their relation to sin. In Protestant theology, the stress put on the soteriological importance
of faith—justification by faith alone—turns doubt and skepticism into a serious
theological concern. In Luther's reading of the Genesis story, the Fall is first and
foremost about fall from faith—the turn from the trust in and obedience to God's
words, and the turn toward the self-sufficient posture of human beings, curved
inward on oneself (*incurvatus in se*). When the serpent intimates, "Has God really
said . . . ?," the first seed of doubt is planted, and, consequently, the first and decisive step of the Fall is inaugurated. According to Luther, the doubt is critical and
fateful because it effectively undermines the unconditional trust in God's word.[2]

Among those who have taken doubt seriously in more recent times is Paul
Tillich. For him, there is no faith without an element of doubt, due to fundamental structures of the human condition: although we relate to the infinite—our
"ultimate concern"—we remain finite. Seen in isolation, the infinite should guarantee its own presence. However, as far as the infinite is only received within finitude, our limited and fallible grasp of it cannot be overcome, and hence the "element of uncertainty cannot be removed, it must be accepted."[3] Doubt will not
undo faith since it is a function of our finite relation to the ultimate concern; serious doubt rather confirms faith, Tillich asserts.[4] One can find some of Cavell's
central concerns echoed in Tillich's way of accepting and embracing doubt: both
the importance of finitude and the vulnerability of our criteria. However, one
might also suspect that Tillich's acceptance of doubt smacks of resignation.

At least that is how Karl Barth reads it. Like Tillich, he does not want to con-
flate the useful methodological or Socratic doubt with the faith-related doubt,
since the former is a beneficial companion to any serious theology, whereas the
latter is emphatically not. Still, Barth does not want to deny the presence of faith-
related doubt in Tillich's sense, but to him, it seems more like a destiny of our

present state, "between times," than a constitutional dialectic of faith as such. The ambivalence and wriggling between "yes" and "no" are symptomatic of our cultural condition for believing and thinking, a cultural condition that has become alienated from its origins and hence vulnerable to distortions.[5] Thus, in contrast to Tillich and in keeping with Luther, there is no comfortable reconciliation of faith and doubt—doubt truly threatens faith from within. Doubt is thoroughly ruinous; it is not part of God's good creation, but belongs to the demonic and negating forces. And yet, there is justification for such sinners:

> There is certainly a justification for the doubter. But there is no justification for doubt itself (and I wish someone would whisper that in Paul Tillich's ear). No one, therefore, should account themselves particularly truthful, deep, fine and elegant because of his doubt. No one should flirt with his unbelief and his doubt. The theologian should only be sincerely *ashamed* of it.[6]

Barth makes an important point: skepticism attacks the very center of faith, the very relation between human beings and God, and therefore one should not yield to it. When Tillich says that serious doubt is confirmation of faith, he seems to undermine the full impact of doubt. However, it must be said in Tillich's defense that he distinguishes between doubt, which is internal to faith, and skepticism. Skepticism does not primarily concern judgments, but is much more pervasive— it is an attitude toward all beliefs, from sense experience to religious creeds. It rejects the possibility of knowledge and hardens into a locked position, which in the end must face despair or cynicism.[7] Skepticism is an enemy of faith, indeed of all our vital relations: to ourselves, others, the world, and to God.

Doubt obviously has a place in Cavell's concept of skepticism, but it is not its source, nor its ultimate outcome; skepticism, we learn, concerns not so much knowledge's failure as the disappointment over its success (*CR*, 476). Cavell's concept of skepticism moves beyond methodological doubt and ambivalence— it closely resembles Barth's shameful doubt and Tillich's despairing or cynical skepticism. In Cavell's opinion, skepticism concerns our conditions as humans, and it concerns it insofar as it attempts to overcome our conditions and opts for the inhumane. As he repeatedly points out, there is nothing more human than to deny the human. Such denial is at once natural and utterly unnatural; natural because it seems to flow from our life with words, as if the first fateful step has always already been taken (*IQO*, 59); unnatural because it is at odds with our own humanity. There are indeed points of convergence that encourage further elaboration of Cavell's understanding of skepticism as sin, such as Tillich's underlining of its naturalness, but also Barth's emphasis of the seriousness of the skeptical threat: to Luther it is indeed at the root of original sin. However, to understand

Cavell's intimated parallelism of skepticism and sin, one must understand the particular way in which we relate to our finite conditions.

A Difficult Finitude

One of the most condensed passages in which the problems of finitude come to the fore reads thus:

> If it is inevitable that the human conceive itself in opposition to God; and as debarred from a knowledge of the world as it is in itself; and as chained away, incomprehensibly, maddeningly, from the possibility of a happy world, a peaceable kingdom; then it is inevitable that the human conceive itself as limited. But what is it to conceive this? Let us say it is to take ourselves as finite. (*PH*, 73)

Cavell is here, of course, alluding to Kant's philosophy. However, as we see below, finitude is also essential to Cavell's understanding of Wittgenstein's philosophy as well as of romanticism, or to be more specific, of romanticism's unending struggle with Kant's concept of the thing in itself (*das Ding an sich*).

Kant's chief premise in his depiction of human knowledge is arguably finitude. In contrast to God's infinite knowledge, human knowledge is both conditioned and limited: a thing's appearance is subject to the a priori conditions of possibility of our understanding. The first thing to notice is the inherent ambiguity in Kant's conception: these a priori conditions of possibility are at once our limits to and our positive means of knowing. Attesting to this ambiguity, Cavell remarks that Kant "transforms our very finitude, our limitedness, into power that creates the necessary conditions for the possibility of human knowledge of the world" (*CW*, 125). What from one side looks like confinement can from another side look like the positive conditions of knowledge as such. This view of finitude is, as it turns out, not as stable as one might wish it to be—an instability that Kant profoundly elaborates. He opens his first *Critique* with this: "Human reason has this peculiar fate that in one species of its knowledge it is burdened by questions which, as prescribed by the very nature of reason itself, it is not able to ignore, but which, as transcending all its powers, it is also not able to answer."[8] Even if Kant believes that it is possible to philosophically refute transgressive inquiries into what we cannot possibly know, such inquiries will still invariably recur, insofar as the drive to transcend the constitutive limits of human understanding is like a sickness of which one cannot fully be cured—much in the same way as we cannot rid ourselves of the relentless inclination to believe in optical illusions.[9]

Here one might sense in Kant's thinking a dim echo of something like the doctrine of original sin, as Cavell seems to suggest: "What Kant also recognizes is the human propensity to think of its powers as penetrating beyond the limits of human knowledge, not with faith but with a higher knowledge, rivalling, as I have put the matter, God's knowledge" (*CW*, 128). However irrepressible this drive to self-transcendence is, its aim still remains an illusion—a dialectic illusion, as Kant terms it—that, following Cavell's elaboration of it, might come to expression in philosophy, poetry, drama, and many other areas of life. "So Kant's Critical Philosophy," Cavell states, "may itself be taken as philosophy's interpretation of the Fall" (*IQO*, 50).

Whether appearing in the guise of what Kant calls dogmatism (refusing to listen to critical thought) or skepticism (refusing knowledge as such), the human desire to transcend its own limitations and take the thing itself into possession is common to both propensities. For this reason, Cavell regards the affirmative (dogmatic) and the dismissive (skeptical) modes as inverted reflections of the same phenomenon, two versions representing skepticism's Janus faces (*CR*, 46). Although the thing in itself is posited only as a limiting concept—something that cannot be intuited, but only thought—it is nevertheless destined to give rise to deep-seated misunderstandings and unappeasable desires.[10] In short, it evokes something beyond human limits to which we crave access. Insofar as appearance is the very thing that manifests itself to us, there is nothing for us to perceive outside our conditioned and finite knowledge. "For Wittgenstein," in Cavell's Kantian interpretation, "it would be an illusion not only that we do know things-in-themselves, but equally an illusion that we do not" (*MWM*, 65). Rather, reference to the thing itself should be taken as a negative reminder that it is precisely by virtue of our conditions as finite that we are able to recognize something like a meaningful world of things in the first place.

The fateful step that the skeptic commits is the misinterpretation of limitations as intellectual confinement or metaphysical restriction, as if those limitations illegitimately debar us from what we should know. This corresponds to the irrepressible human longing to achieve God's perspective—the craving for immediate totality—that is, according to Cavell, precisely what is so hard to defeat: "that [the image of God's knowledge] will be as easy to rid us of as it is to rid us of the prideful craving to be God—I mean to *rid* us of it, not to replace it with a despair at our finitude" (*CR*, 236–237). In Cavell's depiction, then, we are destined to oscillate between the desire to rival God, possessing absolute knowledge, on the one hand, and to plunge into the despair of having no knowledge at all, on the other. It is against this abiding oscillation that Wittgenstein wants to attract us to an acknowledgment of limitation, as providing philosophical peace, at least for a while. For in this perspective, "limitations of knowledge are no longer barriers to a more perfect apprehension, but conditions of knowledge *überhaupt*, of anything we should call 'knowledge'" (*MWM*, 61–62).

Kant's picture of human finitude and of the conditions of the possibility of our knowing thus sheds light on the particular restlessness that Cavell believes animates romanticism (*CW,* 128).[11] On the one hand, romanticism finds giving up the thing in itself to be too high a price to pay; but on the other, it accepts and elaborates Kant's pertinent portrayal of our inner ambivalence:

> It [romanticism] appreciates the ambivalence in Kant's central of idea of limitation, that we simultaneously crave its comfort and crave escape from its comfort, that we want unappeasably to be lawfully wedded to the world and at the same time illicitly intimate with it, as if the one stance produced the wish for the other . . . That Wittgenstein and Heidegger can be understood to share this romantic perception of human doubleness, I dare say helps account for my finding its problematic unavoidable—Wittgenstein perceiving our craving to *escape* our commonness of the craving; Heidegger perceiving our pull to *remain* absorbed in the common, perhaps in the very way we push to escape it. (*IQO,* 32)

The trajectory from Kant, via romanticism, to Heidegger and Wittgenstein displays Cavell's way of linking together as well as juxtaposing a number of texts. This is as essential to his way of reading as is its outcome: the depiction of human existence as caught between states. It reveals how deeply the post-Kantian ambivalence runs in Cavell's thinking—an ambivalence that, as I shall claim, has everything to do with sin.

There are, of course, various inflections of Kantian ideas in the texts that occupy Cavell, but all of them focus on conditions of the possibility of knowledge and of human finitude. Emerson, for instance, also perceives our conditions as inhabited by antagonism, as if we were potentially alien to ourselves. How can that be? The answer lies in what Emerson calls the "mysteries of human condition" (though not, as Cavell points out, exactly *the* human condition, one that is fixed and static) (*IQO,* 37). Cavell takes Emerson's use of the term "condition" as an allusion to Kant. According to Emerson, however, the conceptual conditions cannot be restricted to twelve neatly separate categories, but must be read off in every word we utter. Kant's transcendental logic is a matter of understanding the a priori conditions of knowledge, and to Cavell's ear this is reflected in the way Wittgenstein directs our attention, not to the phenomena, but to the grammatical possibilities of the phenomena (*MWM,* 65; *PI,* § 90). This Wittgensteinian displacement makes it possible to regard the human condition, along with its internal struggle, as interwoven with ordinary language. Emerson can likewise be seen as articulating our linguistic condition in terms of the Fall, where traces of our fallenness can be sought in our inner struggle in and with language: as at once foreign to us and our own, as our fate as well as our responsibility (*CT*, 40).[12] Language is our condition for wording the world, but since language rests on our mutual agreement in words and judgments, it simultaneously refers us to others. Language as fate is

> not exactly prediction, but diction, [it] is what puts us in bonds, that with each word we utter we emit stipulation, agreements we do not know and do not want to know we have entered, agreements we were always in, that were in effect before our participation in them. Our relation to our language—to the fact that we are subject to expression, victims of meaning—is accordingly a key to our sense of our distance from our lives, of our sense of the alien, of ourselves as alien to ourselves, thus alienated. (*IQO*, 40)

One might hear central aspects of original sin resonating in words such as "fate" (catching the anti-Pelagian teaching of the West since Augustine), "bonds" (as in, for instance, Luther's teaching about the bondage of the will), and "alienation" (which is Tillich's preferred rephrasing of "sin"). Cavell suggests that our fate is captured by our being conditioned by and exposed to a language that is antecedent to us, not fully under our control, even working behind our backs, but still the only medium in which we can find and realize our voices. No wonder, then, that, as Cavell often puts it, being condemned to meaning or being victims of meaning is felt as a fate that the skeptic wants to flee; for no one wants to shoulder the responsibility of meaning when there is no a priori guarantee that my language will reach out, and nothing prevents it from betraying more than I wish to reveal (*CR*, 351).

From a skeptical point of view, our being conditioned by ordinary language is doomed to result in disappointment. The knots of our mutual language, our criteria, are able to determine the conceptual identity of things and of the world. But since the skeptic wants something more—the very thing itself—this is not good enough; the skeptic demands that the criteria must also guarantee *existence*, first and foremost of the external world but also other minds (*CR*, 45). However, this is precisely what our criteria cannot do, nor are they meant to do. The world and others remain other to me; they stay beyond my command, and I remain separate from them, even as I am separated from God (*CR*, 496). They are other, but not utterly foreign, autonomous but not inaccessible. Nevertheless, the craving for unconditional knowledge will never be satisfied, and since this craving seems unappeasable, it will not come to an end, at least not more than momentarily within philosophy. Having stated that skepticism is the secular version of sin, Cavell then argues that "so long as the denial is essential to what we think of as the human, skepticism cannot, or must not, be denied. This makes skepticism an argument internal to the individual, or separate, human creature, as it were an argument of the self with itself (over its finitude)" (IQO, 5).

Cavell's understanding of our finitude articulates a strange and dark dynamic of our self-relation in the human denial of humanity. Our constitution harbors an enigmatic ambiguity—as if human existence is destined to be at odds with itself: what opens up our perspective of the world are the very same structures that seems to close us off from the world; what makes human speech meaningful are the very criteria that invite meaninglessness; what makes human actions toward one another possible is the same condition that might destroy our relations. Somehow, we come to feel chafed by our own skin. In short, human beings are, to borrow Stephen Mulhall's phrase, "always already turned against themselves . . . by virtue of their very condition as human."[13]

The Myth of the Fall

Cavell's brief but suggestive readings of the myth of the Fall is the raw material for a more theological interpretation. Cavell seems to support such an undertaking when he notes that Kant's interpretation of human existence "is not incompatible with interpretations of [Coleridge's "The Rime of the Ancient Mariner"] as of the Fall; indeed it provides an interpretation of that interpretation" (IQO, 50). If we regard the myth of Eden as produced from a sense of having always already fallen and of projecting backward the imagined life prior to that fall, then that myth should not be taken as a depiction of a state radically foreign to our ordinary lives from which it is projected.[14] When Cavell states that "the world is Eden enough, all the Eden there can be," it is meant not as a dismissal of the myth but as an attempt to turn us toward a reading where the myth is not perceived as an alien state "immune to skepticism" (IQO, 52, 49).[15] In other words, Cavell is confirming that the mythological depiction does not exempt Adam and Eve from finitude and fallibility, they must rather be taken as mythological personification of central aspects of our human condition. On the other hand, neither can the myth of the so-called prelapsarian phase be identical to our ordinary existence, since it is precisely meant to depict a state that we have fallen *from*, one that is now only available via a counterfactual myth. The myth's double relation to life as we know it might in itself be regarded as reflecting the enigma that we are unable to live in accordance with our condition, which is another way of saying that skepticism inevitably haunts our lives.

To insist on finitude as pertaining to Eden might be theologically controversial, but it is not unfounded. For the same idea has been expressed more traditionally by affirming the mortality of Adam and Eve, prior to the Fall. Apparently, but only apparently, this interpretation conflicts with Paul's view that death is the wages of sin (Rom. 6:23). However, insisting on Adam's and Eve's finitude follows the myth's inner logic in taking into account that the tree carrying the fruit of eternal life is also forbidden (Gen. 3:22).[16] If human beings were already immortal, the prohibition does not make sense. The more categorical reason for affirming prelapsarian finitude is the need to distinguish between finitude and sin, without in any way denying their interconnection. While sin is something for which one must somehow be held responsible, the same does not hold for one's separateness and mortality. Indeed, identifying finitude with sin would come close to Manichaeism with its clear distinction between sinful matter and spiritual redemption, a distinction Augustine resolutely rejects and replaces with another: created (and hence good) nature and the fallen will.[17] It is probably more in accordance with the myth to think of humanity's prelapsarian state as one of *harmony* with its own conditions and finitude, as depicting what has been called a state of integrity (*status integritatis*). Something like this seems to be captured in the biblical observation that, although Adam and Eve were naked, they were not ashamed (Gen. 2:25).

Where does the inclination to leave this state of integrity and harmony stem from? The move away from this state is narrated as a temptation originating from the serpent, whose questioning casts doubt on the order of things. I have already mentioned Cavell's "voice of temptation," which suggests by implication that the ordinary is finite in a negative sense, something that must be overcome by what Cavell calls serpentine infinity (*IQO*, 51). Guided by this idea of negative finitude, we get the impression of the ordinary as "limited, as implying a world elsewhere, as beyond a line, against which it is itself something less in depth or intimacy of existence" (*IQO*, 149).

The next event in Genesis is the eating of the forbidden fruit, and the question is how this act shall be interpreted. In his reading of Samuel Taylor Coleridge's "The Rime of the Ancient Mariner," which itself contains a particular reading of the myth of the Fall, Cavell faces the objection that the poem cannot really be an interpretation of the Fall because the mariner is not exactly disobedient, which is assumedly central to the more traditional account of the Fall. However, the poem opens up another possible line of interpretation that Cavell outlines, where the moral of the story is not disobedience to God's prohibitions, but rather the other way around: the sense of prohibition arises from having gone too far (*IQO*, 58). The mariner's ship more or less casually crosses a line, whereupon he drifts toward the pole, where everything is frozen, empty, and dead. The experience of this emptiness in retrospect turns the experience into one of a limiting line, that is, a prohibition.

Cavell expands the reading almost dialectically as he suggests that, granted that the line or prohibition is given, the line or prohibition can in itself give rise to further desires. Or, as Cavell puts it, "The beginning of skepticism is the insin-uation of absence, of a line, or limitation, hence the creation of want, or desire" (*IQO,* 51). This conception depends on the strange dynamics of desire and the Law, known at least since the time of Paul (Rom. 7:5, 7:7). Although the Law is holy and good, it becomes an occasion for sin, since it gives rise to sinful desires. But in order for the Law to be seen as awaking desire by virtue of its power to draw a line against the forbidden, a slumbering, disoriented desire must already exist.[18] Jacques Lacan, perhaps alluded to by Cavell in the quotation above, has famously linked desire to absence. He refers to Paul's precise description of the dialectical relation between desire for the absent and the Law, a desire that flares up only in relation to the limitations marked by the Law and that ultimately leads to the desire for death—not unlike skepticism's will to emptiness.[19] Thus, an un-appeasable restlessness is set in motion, "the restlessness," as Cavell thinks of it, "of a finite creature burdened by the desire of the infinite" (*PDT,* 207). Hence, the eating of the fruit awakens the desire for the infinite, which might be de-picted as the desire for the thing in itself or for speaking outside language games; either way, the desire expresses the wish for an exemption from the human condition.

If one wants to translate the Cavellian outline into a more theological lan-guage, one might call this unrestricted desire "concupiscence." Concupiscence was an Augustinian and scholastic term for lower, sensual desire; its meaning and scope were widened through the Reformation, where it came to involve the entire human being and his or her orientation. The essential trait of concupis-cence is that it knows of no satisfaction but is driven by the desire to draw the whole of reality into its orbit.[20] Paul Ricoeur expounds the concept thus:

At the same time as the meaning of ethical limit becomes hazy, the meaning of finiteness is obscured. A "desire" has sprung up, the de-sire for infinity; but that infinity is not the infinity of reason and hap-piness . . . ; it is the infinity of desire itself; it is the desire of desire, taking possession of knowing, of willing, of doing, and of being.[21]

The desire wants to take everything into its possession, achieve control of oneself and the environment. According to such an interpretation, concupiscence comes close to hubris, the decisive human flaw according to Greek tragedies, in which an attempt is made to wipe out the constitutive distinction between the finite and the infinite, the mortals and the immortals—or, adapted to Judeo-Christian perception, between creatures and Creator. Such hubris amounts to the repres-sion of finitude.[22] The theme is very much present in the canonical literature of modernity as well, emblematically dramatized in the legendary Faust's illimita-ble desire for total knowledge (*CR,* 455), or, for that matter, in Nietzsche's concept of the will to power. Cavell refers to such an aspiration "as the human desire to have God's knowledge; hence, doubtless, to be God" (*IQO*, 148).

Having awakened the unrestricted desire, the outcome of the Fall is first realized upon turning back the gaze, from the infinite to human finitude. But why turn back the gaze in the first place? Because the desired totality cannot be achieved; the gaze is forced back. Sooner or later Adam and Eve were destined to discover that there are things they could not take into possession, and consequently, the separate human beings were thrown back on themselves. In the light of the blissful idea and its corresponding desire, Adam and Eve felt utterly disappointed, not primarily over what they have done, but over who they were. In light of the desired infinite, their own finitude is drastically degraded. For Cavell, disappointment is the expression of the human dissatisfaction with our language, our self, and our ability to know—which he indeed takes to be the conclusive lesson of *The Claim of Reason* (*IQO*, 5). For Adam and Eve, nothing has changed, yet everything has changed. Put more precisely, it is not that their condition has changed, but their *relation to* their own condition has changed, from harmony to alienation. The first sign of this change is telling: as they previously had felt at home in their nakedness, that is, in their human condition, so now their first reaction is a feeling of shame or fright over their being naked—they bound fig leaves and made themselves aprons (Gen. 3:7).[23] What before appeared as guiding rules for life and mutual flourishing now appears as limitations. Limits are interpreted as restrictions, conditions as constraints.[24]

The fact of our finitude now appears as constrained, and the skeptic reacts to this by repudiating our condition entirely—as if the first transgression finally leads to the revolt against our very humanity. If we cannot have everything, so the skeptical logic goes, we will have nothing at all. The skeptical impulse also sheds light on perhaps finitude's most characteristic mark, namely death; for although humans are made from dust and must return to dust (Gen. 3:19), what is noteworthy is that the whole attitude to death antecedent to the Fall is now converted from a natural end of human life to the wages of sin, as Paul writes.[25] Although sin is intrinsically connected to finitude and death, finitude and death are not in themselves sin. As Cavell succinctly observes, "Not finitude, but the denial of finitude is the mark of tragedy. This denial of finitude has also been taken as the mark of sin" (*CR*, 455).

This turning back on itself, along with the human reactions that this provokes, constitutes sin as distinct from finitude. This turning back follows the inner skeptical logic: in the light of the sublime idea and unrestricted desire, the reaction is one of disappointment over who we in fact are. This leads to the next step, where the skeptic feels that there must be a way to reach what lies beyond our condition, beyond our communal agreement in criteria (*IQO*, 60). The skeptic attempts to carry this out by depriving words of their reference and indebtedness to others, instead wanting to secure their meaning privately. The skeptic discovers that there is nothing that prevents him or her from denying his or her relation to others. But the price is high: it deprives the skeptic of his or her voice, his or her individuality as well as communality, and leaves the world dead in the skeptic's hands.

Separation and Participation

In Cavell's writing, there are traces of another account of the Fall, an account that captures a somewhat different aspect by focusing more particularly on our relation to the other. This account suggests that the skeptical focuses on doubt and that the lack of knowledge hides a still deeper fear. There is something the skeptic is desperate to flee because it is all too *certain:* that we exist as separate, for no conceivable reason (*CR,* 369). This discovery comes as a further assault, which again leads to further overreactions, as if "the reaction to the discovery of my separateness is to perpetuate it, radicalize it, interpreting finitude as a punishment" (*IQO,* 60). In his readings of *Othello,* Cavell regards the doubt about Desdemona's fidelity as a cover story of a much more horrible fact that Othello knows too well. And likewise, Hamlet's doubt about the ghost is also read as an intellectualization of something Hamlet already knows but avoids facing. In both cases, they try to avoid their fear of separation. For Hamlet this means that he cannot accept his mother Gertrude as a separate sexual being (*DK,* 189); for Othello, the unforgivable fact is that Desdemona exists separate from him. She is not in his possession, and yet she is somehow related to him. The relatedness implies further that Othello himself is partial, imperfect, and also dependent, for according to the dialectic of acknowledgment, only by her knowing him can he be assured of his own existence. He realizes that he is essentially dependent on something beyond himself, which he nevertheless is separated from. To doubt her fidelity or the existence of her mind only conceals the issue at stake:

> Nothing could be more certain to Othello than that Desdemona exists; is flesh and blood; is separate from him; other. This is precisely the possibility that tortures him. The content of his torture *is* the premonition of the existence of another, hence of his own, his own as dependent, as partial. According to me further, his professions of skepticism over her faithfulness is a cover story for a deeper conviction; a terrible doubt covering a yet more terrible certainty, an unstatable certainty. (*CR,* 493)

Skepticism toward the other arises most profoundly, not out of a lack of knowledge, but rather from being too certain about something we would like to ignore. The certainty of the other's separate existence is not, however, foreign to the original state prior to the Fall. Nevertheless, something in the manner in which the existence of the other tends to be represented becomes intolerable— such as the feeling that I am excluded, that he or she is beyond my reach or control, combined with a lurking awareness of my dependence upon that other and hence an awareness of my own partiality.

I have pointed out the link between finitude and separation, but Cavell here adds the second half of our finitude, namely our dependence and hence participation. For what one is alienated from is something one truly depends upon, or else separation would not be threatening; and conversely, what one depends on is something one also desires separation from, perhaps in favor of an uncontaminated autonomous perfection. If the union between me and the other is not seamless and complete, the skeptic opts for splendid isolation. At least for the narcissistic skeptic, such as Othello, his exceptionality and perfection cannot tolerate anything less. Such a skeptic is driven by a yearning "at once unappeasable and unsatisfiable, as for an impossible exclusiveness or completeness" (CR, 452). Hence, Othello turns Desdemona into stone (alabaster); only in that way can he master her epistemologically and make her existence open to ocular proof (CR, 496). In this manner, he can know her and simultaneously avoid acknowledging her. However self-imposed, the skeptic will not only become out of reach of the other, but also undercut the condition that makes his access to the world and others in it possible. When such an outcome is paradoxical, it is because the separation that the skeptic winds up with is a radicalized version of the separation that caused his consuming disappointment in the first place.

Cavell does not fail to detect the topic of separation and participation in the story of Genesis, especially as it comes to the fore in the creation of man and woman. God recognizes that Adam is alone, despite the company of his other nonhuman fellow creatures. Cavell notes that the creation of the woman is prepared for by the naming of the animals, perhaps to suggest that a common language is constitutive of mutual acknowledgment, desire, and intelligibility (CT, 28, 37). Of course, this is in keeping with the centrality of language and its criteria for ordinary language philosophy in general. But by the same stroke, the human relation is thereby deeply implicated in something that tends to be unstable. For language at once makes the relation to the other possible and simultaneously invites its refusal—in short, it underscores the fragility of the intertwinement of separation and participation.

Genesis is also the authorization for marriage: Adam and Eve are supposed to be one flesh. Relevant in this respect is that, according to Cavell, some particular insight dawns on Eve, namely that her former blindness had veiled the fact that the two of them remain separate (CT, 21). Once she has eaten the fruit, her desire for knowledge is not satisfied; on the contrary, Eve finds herself essentially unknown, both to Adam and subsequently to herself. But the senses of separation and deficiency fuel the unappeasable desire for more knowledge, at the cost of acknowledging each other. In Cavell's account, marriage is an emblem of acknowledgment (or the failure thereof), a continual quest for the acceptance of separation as part of the union. For, Cavell writes, "what is wanting—if marriage is to be reconceived, or let's say human attraction—is for the other to see our separate existence, to acknowledge its separateness, a reasonable condition for a ceremony of union" (CT, 22).

For Cavell, marriage is not only an emblem of human relations, but also an allegory of our relation to our ordinary conditions, conditions that are always already in the grip of skeptical denial and that need reconfirmation and renewed acknowledgment every day. And the same arguably holds true of our relation to God in faith: faith acknowledges God in a way that makes the fact of separation salient, as in God's hiddenness, but faith also names the relation to God, in terms of dependence. Our relations to the other, to the world, and consequently to God are thus twofold. This twofold character of separation and participation gives rise to the skeptical wavering between the desire for absolute union beyond separation and the desire for absolute privacy in order to escape participation, partiality, and dependence.

Inhabiting the Inhumane

Cavell suggests that the perversity of our skepticism runs deep, but he also brings to theology a related teaching: wherever the skeptic impulse is awakened—in tragedies, film, philosophy, or in daily concerns—it is never solely something foreign to each of us, but always also part of us. In a central passage quoted earlier in this chapter but worth repeating here, Cavell writes that "skepticism is a place, the central secular place, in which the human wish to deny the condition human existence is expressed." And importantly, Cavell adds that "as long as the denial is essential to what we think of as the human, skepticism cannot, or must not, be denied" (IQO, 5). With reference to Milton's *Paradise Lost,* Cavell writes that "[Lucifer] is in us, in our awaiting transformation . . . but we expel him, more or less, instead of transforming ourselves" (SW, 115). Whatever the upshot is in that context, it at least suggests that the discovery of Lucifer in us leaves us with two options: either he is expelled or else we must confess that presence and transform ourselves accordingly. Perhaps the former names another face of the skeptic temptation, for our potential inhumanity is all too easily avoided precisely by externalizing it—be it in terms of Lucifer, the stranger, or monsters. Freud teaches that we are not masters of our own house, that we harbor unconscious drives and repressed desires that at any time might return in the figure of something uncanny. If this is so, we have reason to suspect that we harbor an inclination to continue denying this inner otherness only to project it outward. Richard Kearney captures this succinctly when he writes that "the monster remains a personification of our repressed Other. It functions as that negative mirror image of ourselves which we project onto a fantasy world."[26]

Also according to Cavell, we tend to perceive the monstrous as external to our humanity; the monster is viewed as the outsider. It gives rise not so much to the fear of danger as to horror, because the threatening fact about the monster is that it cannot be completely cut off from our own identity. The idea of monstrosity is nourished by the horrifying precariousness of human identity as such, in the sense that there is nothing—no stable barrier or wedge—that debars us from becoming other. On the one hand, the monstrous signifies the inhuman, but on the other, "only what is human can be inhuman . . . If something is monstrous, and we do not believe that there are monsters, then only the human is a candidate for the monstrous" (CR, 418). This means that to the extent that we want to keep talking about the monstrous, it must be regarded as a distinctively human possibility.

Cavell points out that this sense of horror—in contrast to fear—is central to religion; we could also say, in a Christian inflection, that it is central to a particular way of thinking about sin: sin denotes our inclination toward the inhumane. To be sure, this inclination should be resisted, and yet Cavell insists that it cannot and should not be denied. For our ability to deny our humanity must not become yet another denial, projected onto others, but should be integrated into what we think of as human. Or again: "Nothing is more human than the wish to deny one's humanity, or to assert it at the expense of others" (CR, 109). But, then, how is the inhumanity in our humanity to be worked upon? And how do we stop asserting it at the expense of others, say by demonizing or scapegoating the other? A first step might be to confess, a confession that requires both self-revelation before the finite or infinite other, despite the inclination to remain hidden. True confession, Cavell has said, involves a willingness to change (MWM, 71); this means that an acknowledgment of the otherness in oneself is a preparation for the acknowledgment of the otherness of others. Or put slightly differently, Cavell says that one can "see others only to the extent that one can take oneself as another" (CR, 459).[27] The abiding skeptic in us—our original sin, if you will—must be worked on constantly, something that Protestant theology has called sanctification. But if such constant working on oneself presupposes a turning away from the self-destructive relation to what is entailed in our finitude, the question is whether the power for such turning lies in our hands.

FIVE

The Tragic Dimension of the Ordinary

Following the Augustinian tradition, original sin is something that we are responsible for and hence guilty of, yet in another sense it is a destiny that befalls us. At stake is hence a fine balance between necessity and freedom, between personal guilt and delivery to destructive structures. Accordingly, acknowledging sin takes a personal sense of the I, confessing or revealing itself as the originator of deeds and speech, while acknowledging that this I is indebted—for better and for worse—to the inheritance of and continuous participation in a form of life that bestows coherence to those deeds and utterances. Against this background, the present chapter elaborates a similar structure that might be considered a tragic dimension inscribed in the ordinary, and that will focus not on inheritance but on the subsequent consequences of our deeds and acts. I contend that this tragic dimension can be seen as a further articulation of the implications of original sin: there are indeed limits to our mastery of our own destiny, and hence the Pelagian perception—in which we are in principle fully in control of ourselves—does not seem to accurately capture our moral position in the world. Admittedly, the relation between the tragic and the Christian outlook is a topic of considerable controversy, turning on, among other things, the emphasis on responsibility and destiny along with the question of whether Christian hope and reconciliation have a place within a tragic worldview.[1] But at least it seems to me that if we want to reflect on how responsibility and uncontrollable destiny are interconnected, we would do well to engage in further conversations with Cavell's writing on the tragic potentialities of our ordinary words and deeds.

Cavell's central yet often overlooked premise for the tragic dimension bears on our relation to meaning. One of Cavell's most frequently recurring statements is that we are "condemned to meaning," a statement that harbors both an indicative and an imperative. It is indicative of the unavoidable significance of every human gesture. That we can also be "victims of meaning," where that inexorable meaningfulness becomes a curse, is central to our exposure to tragedy, or, as Cavell parenthetically remarks, to original sin: "The human condemnation to intention and consequence is the sequel, if not the meaning, of original sin" (*VW*, 188). There is, however, also an imperative implied in the indicative: not only are we condemned to meaning, but, to repeat this central teaching, we *must* mean what we say.[2] The point is not only that what we say has practical implications, but also that we do not always understand adequately what we say—and in the face of both, we are responsible for trying to make ourselves intelligible. Since we cannot control in advance the full implications of what we say, what we mean is not so much a given as a task.

Cavell's most extensive treatment of tragedy is found in his reading of Shakespeare's dramas, in which he finds the skeptical problem of other minds and the existence of the external world enacted in human lives. The wake of modernity brings with it a new sense of freedom, separation, and finitude that calls for a change in the perception of subjectivity and responsibility in a potentially groundless world (*DK*, 3). This perception distinguishes Shakespeare's sense of tragedy from the Greek tradition in which the cosmic order and fate are the stable framework for drama. Put in Cavellian terms, the tragedy enacts both the need for acknowledgment of others and of the world, and our avoidance of such acknowledgment. Such central themes are however also related to Cavell's understanding of our lives with words. For Cavell, as Anthony J. Cascardi interprets it, the power of Shakespeare's work "rests on his ability to envision characters who live out the fate of their words relentlessly, without compromise or escape, or who suffer disastrously from their failure to do so."[3]

I will not pursue Cascardi's account of Cavell's Shakespeare further, but rather investigate how living the fate of our words bears on our relation to ordinary language as such. More specifically, I shine light on how ordinary speech and actions are liable to become unbearable, following Cavell's comments on and extension of Austin's theory of speech acts. These comments and extensions are provoked by Derrida's deconstructive reading of Austin. In "Counter-Philosophy and the Pawn of Voice," Cavell praises Derrida for identifying central and often unrecognized dimensions of Austin's thought, while his reading, more critically, gives rise to further reflections on Cavell's own inheritance of Austin's philosophy.[4]

Exclusions: Excuses, Pretending, and Tragedy

In Derrida's view, Austin still clings to phonocentrism, where the voice is depicted as present to the conscious I, which, by means of the stable and homogeneous realm of signs, can convey meaning to others. Such insistence on the primacy of a consciousness hearing itself speak is, more generally, an instance of the metaphysical tradition pervaded by a relentless demand for presence.[5] In accordance with such a metaphysics of presence, Austin's speaker is located at the center of a set of conventions by which he performs his speech acts. In Derrida's reading, Austin not only appeals to a total context, but also to "consciousness, the conscious presence of the intention of the speaking subject in the totality of his speech act" (*LI*, 14). Austin thus joins in the marginalization of writing according to which writing is regarded as a secondary supplement in absence of the present voice. Derrida, however, famously argues that it is the other way around: he argues that writing—in the wide sense of possibility of signification—is decisively bound up with iterability or repeatability, which is the condition for any conventional utterance or written sign. For any sign must be able to be repeated in the absence of a particular sender or voice—not only sender, but also in the absence of a particular receiver. It is the principal possibility of absence of any voice or intentions present to itself that makes all production of meaning possible, which in Derrida's lingo is tantamount to admitting the primacy of writing.

A central point is the two exclusions that Derrida accuses Austin of, namely Austin's purported exclusions of failures and citations from his theory presented in *How to Do Things with Words*. From Derrida's sense of iterability, it follows that writing can be grafted onto an infinite number of new contexts, which unavoidably means that meaning will be altered according to each of those shifting situations and horizons (*LI*, 7). Thus, failures (where meaning turns out differently than intended) and citation (in the absence of the original author) are not threats to meaning, but are rather exemplary manifestations of writing. Austin does admit that failures are a misfortune that can affect all utterances in the cases where the context is inapt. Still, the first exclusion Derrida detects is Austin's lack of any *general theory* of such failures, that is, a theory that is able to show that they are a constitutive part of any sign and thus writing (*LI*, 16). The second exclusion concerns iterability more directly, insofar as Derrida thinks Austin would need to take into account how every utterance in fact quotes a previously written text. Derrida's notion of text is meant to comprise conventions and their application in varying contexts, which is at the heart of Austin's concern. But the problem is that Austin brushes off quotations, whether in poems or plays, as parasitic and non-serious use of ordinary language; hence they are excluded from his theory of meaning (*LI*, 16).

Cavell does not think these two "exclusions" are really matters of repudiation; rather, they are excluded "for the moment," as Austin writes, since Austin presumes his readers know that he has dealt with both at length elsewhere (*PoP*, 86, 91). Regarding the first exclusion, Austin writes, "I mean that actions in general (not all) are liable, for example, to be done under duress, or by accident, or owing to this or that variety of mistake, say, or otherwise unintentionally" (*HDTW*, 21). Adding that such considerations are part of what we normally would call "extenuating circumstances," Cavell seems right in taking this as an allusion to Austin's own "A Plea for Excuses," which attempts to reveal the kind of speech act that an excuse is and, indirectly, what it reveals about us and our actions in general. The second "exclusion," regarding a theory of citation (*HDTW*, 22), is discussed in another essay with the telling title "Pretending."[6]

Here Austin deals with the distinctions between serious and non-serious, between pretending, shamming, rehearsing, and so on, which bear on the distinction between saying and quoting. Thus, it is ironically Derrida who turns out to be excluding, by refusing to take aspects of Austin's work into account.

Cavell is implying that Derrida, whose philosophy depends on attentive reading, has not really read Austin well enough. One further exclusion on Derrida's part points in this direction, namely his blindness to the tragic element inscribed in Austin's project. In a concrete and subtle way, Cavell turns Derrida's weapon back on Derrida himself. Cavell draws our attention to one particular quotation, inscribed, as it were, at the margin of Austin's own text, namely Austin's citation of Euripides's *Hippolytus*: "My tongue swore to, but my heart did not." Austin is here after false accounts of intentionality, as something private, spiritual, or profound in a metaphysical sense:

> But we are apt to have a feeling that their being serious consists in their being uttered as (merely) the outward and visible sign, for convenience or other record or for information, of an inward and spiritual act: from which it is but a short step to go on to believe or to assume without realizing that for many purposes the outward utterance is a description, *true or false*, of the occurrence in the inward performance. The classic expression of this idea is to be found in the *Hippolytus* (1. 612), where Hippolytus says . . . "my tongue swore to, but my heart (or mind or other backstage artiste) did not." (*HDTW*, 9–10)

According to Cavell, Derrida's failure to notice this quotation is symptomatic of a general unwillingness on Derrida's behalf to detect Austin's distinctive voice, more specifically the peculiar profundity implied in Austin's voice. The ignorance of the quotation is perhaps due to the common perception of Austin as averse to profundity as such (i.e., not only the false profundity of philosophy that he openly scorns), and hence the tendency to regard him as superficial. However, the tragic depth *is* explicitly inscribed in Austin's texts, and, as Cavell puts it, "soon the diagnosis of the sense of his superficiality darkens" (*PoP*, 88).

What is the relation between this invocation of the tragic and the two temporary "exclusions"? Regarding the first exclusion, Austin thinks that excuses (and justifications) in general presuppose that someone has done something untoward and is trying to get out of it. In excuses, "we admit that it was bad but don't accept full, or even any, responsibility."[7] Austin hints at this in his lectures on speech acts, referring to "extenuating circumstances." Cavell finds a strange relation between Austin's and Freud's "slips": for Freud, slips are matters of overdetermination that always reveal more about yourself than you want to be—and yet have to be—answerable for, whereas for Austin, slips betray the tendency, due to our embodied being, to produce effects and consequences that we cannot fully be responsible for (*CW*, 333). To consider human actions to be in need of excuses presupposes that actions are not under our full control and that they can be done unintentionally, unwillingly, involuntarily, and so forth—in short, excuses presuppose the fallibility implied in human finitude. Hence, Austin's writing of excuses concerns the "unending vulnerability of human action" (*PoP*, 87).

Inadvertent actions seem to be the price for being capable of acting in the face of human finitude, for having a body, and for our exposure to the world. From this perspective, Cavell finds it surprising that Derrida accuses Austin of considering failures to be external to our actions:

> Who, such as Austin, would so dwell on excuses who did not surmise that the human necessity for action, and of action for motion, is apt to become unbearable—its consequences, concomitants, upshots, effects, results, and so forth (another favorite chain of Austin's) unsurveyable, the body a parchment of its displacements. (*PoP*, 87)

Without excuses, our actions will become unbearable. But Cavell also thinks that Austin's interest in excuses implies another region, *beyond* the excusable. Austin's interest in excuses must be understood, as the presence of Euripides's Hippolytus suggests, against the background of its flip side: the possible tragedy that human failures can involve.

Turning to the other "exclusion," that of quotations and non-serious utterances, Austin referred us to "Pretending," or at least, that is Cavell's opinion. Although Cavell invites the surmise that "Pretending" should do the same for utterances that "A Plea for Excuses" did for actions (i.e., attest to speech's vulnerability to insincerity), he readily admits that it fails to do so. On this point, Cavell's response to Austin moves closer to Derrida's concerns. Cavell points out that Austin is unwilling to go into the region between sincerity and insincerity and the problem of skepticism that it implies. To Cavell's disappointment, Austin never takes seriously skepticism about the existence of other minds or the external world, but he regards such skepticism as a matter of philosophy's false profundity. Cavell's departure from Austin on this point turns on their different conceptions of criteria. The kind of criteria that occupy Austin is the criteria of identity of specific objects, those that make it possible to discern, say, the identity of a goldfinch as distinct from other birds. To the extent that Wittgenstein appeals to criteria, they do not concern such distinctions that require some expertise, but they concern the generic objects that any speaker is supposed to be able to identify: if you do not know the criteria for chairs, pain, hands, or sorrow, you simply have not learned the language and the world that goes with it. What

Wittgenstein further adds to that picture, and what Cavell takes as essential to it, is an understanding that all criteria come to an end: criteria give us access to a differentiated world, but they are impotent for determining existence in general. Consequently, there are differences that criteria cannot make (*CR*, 45–46). This comes to the fore in the skeptic's occupation with distinctions between dreams and reality, between real and feigned pain, of which failures put our knowledge of the outer world and the other mind in jeopardy. The same also holds true for the distinction between sincerity and insincerity.

Cavell thinks that such a view entails that "human utterances are essentially vulnerable to insincerity and that the realization that we may never know whether others are sincere . . . is apt to become unbearable" (*PoP*, 92–93). The possibility of tragedy follows from the essential exposure of utterances to skepticism. Austin's disregard for skepticism as shallow philosophy constitutes his general reason for avoiding any such conclusions, but Cavell senses that, more particularly, there is something similar showing up in *Hippolytus* that Austin would like to pass in silence. The mendacious nurse has told Hippolytus's father, Theseus, the lie that Hippolytus has had incestuous relations with Theseus's wife (Hippolytus's stepmother). The tragic fact is that Theseus is not able to tell whether or not the nurse tells the truth, hence Theseus's ungrantable wish:

> If there were some / token now, some mark to make the division / clear between friend and friend, the true and the false! / All men should have two voices, one the just voice, / and one as chance would have it. In this way / the treacherous scheming voice would be confuted / by the just, and we should never be deceived. (quoted in *PoP*, 101)

The problem is that there is no token that once and for all distinguishes real from fake, sincere from insincere, which to Cavell's mind is another way of admitting that there is no way of blocking skepticism and its potentially tragic outcome— in this case, Theseus driving his innocent son to what turns out to be his death.

Excuses and the Bond of Words

Austin's interest in excuses presupposes a view of human action as fallible. Our embodiment brings with it a tendency to produce unintentional effects, effects that contrast with Austin's urge for the justice of language. Excuses are therefore meant to delimit our responsibilities, even as our actions are over-determined and over-indebted to others and to meaning in general. I take it as an interpretation of such a perception when Cavell speaks of the need for what he terms "elaboratives," that is, explanations, justifications, or excuses: "elaboratives make it tolerable to act not knowing in advance what we may do, what consequences we may be faced with, e.g., that we have been . . . unperceptive, betraying, rejecting all unknown to ourselves, and without even seeing how" (CR, 325). We are, as intelligible creatures, condemned to meanings that stick to us as expressive agents, and yet, since we issue expressions beyond our control, we need to make such a burden tolerable by means of elaboratives.

But when it comes to tragedy, Cavell surprisingly states that the burden of utterances and deeds can no longer be lifted by excuses; Hippolytus's "my tongue swore to, but my heart did not" is probably meant as an excuse—but of no avail. Even granted human fallibility, our utterances and deeds cannot be cut loose from our responsibility:

> Excuses mark out the region of tragedy, the beyond of the excusable, the justifiable, the explainable (the civil?). . . . This [is a] route to the sense of the unbearableness of human action—of its overdetermination and its over-indebtedness, as of the unreachableness of justice . . . It is the most sensitive point of Austin's inscription of tragedy—say, of the tragic hedge of ordinary life—in his invocation of Euripides's *Hippolytus* in the opening lecture of *How to Do Things with Words*. (PoP, 87–88)

Why are tragic speech acts "beyond" the excusable? Cavell has at least a negative answer to that question. Hippolytus's silent heart is meant to be an excuse that prevents him from the responsibilities and burdens that accompany the promise. According to Austin, such thinking captures a common spiritualization of promise, perhaps of meaning and intentions in general—Wittgenstein calls it private language. Austin brings out the moral dimension of Hippolytus's paradigmatic utterance very clearly:

> It is gratifying to observe in this very example how excess of profundity, or rather solemnity, at once paves the way for immodality. For one who says "promising is not merely a matter of uttering words! It is an inward and spiritual act" is apt to appear as a solid moralist standing out against a generation of superficial theorizers: we see him as he sees himself, surveying the invisible depths of ethical space, with all the distinction of a specialist *sui generis*. Yet he provides Hippolytus with a let-out, the bigamist with an excuse for his "I do" and the welsher with defence for his "I bet." Accuracy and morality alike are on the side of the plain saying that *our word is our bond*. (HDTW, 10)

That our word is our bond resonates with the tragic evoked by Austin, but it clearly also resonates with dimensions of the Christian tradition that attract Cavell. For the binding force of words is also echoed in Cavell's choice of the ep-

igraph for the third section of *The Claim of Reason:* "For by thy words thou shalt
be justified, and by thy words thou shalt be condemned" (Matt 12:27; *CR,* 245;
cf. *LK,* 299). The significant overlaps between the tragic and Christianity are discussed later in this chapter; it suffices here to note the connection in Austin's passage between a particular "spiritual" vision of meaning and the absence of responsibility for meaning.

In Cavell's ears, such spiritualization sounds like a traditional skeptical
move: to appeal to metaphysical images in order to evade the obligations of the
ordinary, that is, an attempt to say something without meaning it (*PoP,* 101; *PP,*
62, 76). Indeed, such spiritualizing might be regarded as bound up with a religious outlook, for, as Cavell notices, an outward visible sign for an inward spiritual act is more or less a dictionary definition of a sacrament. Such a religious vision of meaning (he also includes political ideology that becomes doctrinal) is
clearly at odds with Austin's theory. Cavell pauses to ask himself if Austin's orientation to the ordinary means the championing of the secular and the liberal,
and finds a reasonable answer: "Only to the extent that religion and politics are
essentially detractors of the ordinary; which perhaps means, only to the extent
that they are metaphysical" (*PoP,* 103).

Even if religion thus in principle can have a legitimate position from such
a perspective, Austin understands the spiritualization of meaning to be the impact of the denial of words as our bond. Still, Austin clearly regards Hippolytus's
promise as an excuse. What Austin misses, however, is that for Hippolytus the
excuse does not get him out of the situation—not even from the fire and into the
frying pan, as excuses are supposed to do, according to Austin.[8] Rather, Hippolytus remains in the fire, and he is even consumed by it: he is—due to his blindness,
or to a character flaw, or perhaps to some tragic *nemesis*—unable to take back
the word he gave to the nurse, who both betrayed to him his stepmother's illicit
passion and bade him keep it a secret. Thus bound to his word, Hippolytus's relentless sincerity is the anti-type of Don Juan, for whom apparently no word is
binding (*PoP,* 101–102). But even if the promise were broken, there would be no
criteria at Theseus's disposal to establish Hippolytus's sincerity beyond doubt.
Upon his stepmother's suicide and Theseus's accusations, Hippolytus is deprived
of indubitable signs that prove the accusations wrong.

According to Cavell, the tragedy is terrifying because it reveals that even a
quite ordinary, casual remark may be irretrievable. Cavell therefore focuses on
the way utterances—speaking as such—always remain open to tragedy:

> so my tongue swore without my heart—*nevertheless I am bound.* In re-
> jecting Hippolytus's glimpse of a profundity in making a promise—
> in speaking as such—Austin says, as noted: "Morality and accuracy
> alike are on the side of the plain saying that *our word is our bond.*"

But this overlooks the fairly blatant fact that on Hippolytus's view of promising, the saying that our word is our bond proves a fatal *curse*. (PP, 62)

Even if Cavell and Austin agree that metaphysical claims to intentionality, privacy, and secret ceremonies of the heart should not and cannot free us from ordinary obligations in speech and promising, the question remains: why is there no excuse? Of course, promises are meant to be held, and it would undermine the very meaning of promising if we always forfeited them, but sometimes we are indeed excused for forfeiting them. Why not here, why not in tragedy? According to Asja Szafraniec's reading of Cavell, Cavell is trying to steer free of two pitfalls: on the one hand is what Szafraniec regards as the typically Christian, sacramental sincerity, which obviously does not help clarify what we mean by our words; on the other hand is the tragic pitfall of becoming bond to our words. In the tragic version, words "functioning as our bonds (petrified bond, like the bond of the Old Testament) lead to tragedies as in the case of Hippolytus." If religion leads into false metaphysics, tragedy (obviously not foreign to the Old Testament) portrays a situation where we are completely controlled by words that are not our own, words that will run their course, no matter what.[9]

There is some truth in Szafraniec's characterization of both pitfalls, though I find them overstated to the point of becoming misleading. As in the case of religious understanding, Cavell does not, as mentioned above, think such a sacramental model of meaning makes religion as such incompatible with his or Austin's conception of the ordinary, as Szafraniec insinuates. What makes Christian words both right and feeble is therefore clearly not meant to hinge on these considerations (cf. chapter 1). As for the tragic, I find that Cavell wants more from *Hippolytus* than a representation of a rigid and petrified image of meaning—in the passage above, Cavell speaks of Hippolytus's glimpse of a true profundity in making a promise that Austin nevertheless rejects. True, Cavell asks himself why Hippolytus cannot simply break his promise, since there are several legitimate reasons for doing so, and then he continues: "Philosophers have said—my parents said—that if you do not keep your promise . . . people will not take your word again. . . . I felt it meant that I would become unintelligible, that the words I would give in my utterances would become ungraspable, not receivable, not currency" (PoP, 104). Put in this way, the perception gives rise to skeptical despair, and therefore exaggerates the point in the opposite direction. Yet Cavell is eager to bring out the truth of this despair. The moral is not so much that there are no ways in which promises can be broken—for surely there are—but that the conditions for having such an institution as promise, and indeed for having such things as speech as such, cannot be forfeited at will.[10] In this sense, we must as a rule keep our words, since we must mean what we say—or else not even the excuse would retain its logic. More generally at stake here is the promise of language as such: "[I]n *How to Do Things with Words* Austin identifies speaking as *giving one's word*, as if an 'I promise' implicitly lines every act of speech, of intelligibility, as it were a condition of speech as such."[11]

But equally important, I think Cavell's invocation of *Hippolytus* is supposed to turn our attention to what it means that something is intended. For Austin, excuses concern actions that are undoubtedly bad, but for which the person in question cannot be held responsible. They are unintentional in one sense or another.[12] However, tragedy does not concern unintentional words and actions and their consequences—that would made it a farce—so much as *intended* words that are fatefully taken up and repeated in others' lives (*CW*, 29–30). Even intended words convey an uncontrollable destiny, and yet they do not release us from our responsibility for meaning them. It is, I take it, their being intended that makes them "beyond the excusable." The question then becomes how we are to understand intentions.

The Implications of Intentions

At least in Austin's rendering, the sentence from *Hippolytus* depicts intentions as inner, spiritual acts. According to this picture, the meaning of words is ultimately at my disposal, because the inner intention ("my heart") governs what is meant. Even if Derrida rightly identifies this picture as a version of metaphysics of presence, Derrida argues that ordinary language philosophy in effect is offering a subtle version of the very same picture, when he writes that the "conscious intention" on which it is said to depend "would at the very least have to be totally present and immediately transparent to itself and to others, since it is a determinating center of context" (*LI*, 18). But according to ordinary language philosophy, intentions are far from always transparent, and they cannot therefore be the determinating centers that are sovereign over the context—neither in reality nor ideally. There are indeed intentions, but they are not sacramental or mental entities under the privileged authority of individuals; to qualify as intentions, they must be invested in the media of shared language. Even though intentions are as inevitable and decisive to human expressiveness as meaning is, they presuppose that all the vital functions of language are already at work:

> For Austin as for Wittgenstein intention is anything but something inner making up for the absence of something outer; it lines the outer. Intention can guide the variation of signal flags through a sequence of positions, but it cannot—that is, *that* intention cannot—guide the establishing of the flags, and what counts as their positions, and what the positions signify, and so on. In the absence of this institution no such intention of variation is formulable. It may

help to say: a context *is* what allows such a thing as an intention to do so much and to be so little. (*PoP,* 111)

The establishment of conventions is simply presupposed, and in this sense intentions are so little, however important this "little" is for human agency and speech. In Hippolytus's case, there is no excuse for having given his word because there is no way in which his inner denial could alter what the words means publicly. His inner intention, understood metaphysically, is in this sense inessential. I can, of course, decide whether to make a promise or not, but what counts as a promise is not up to me.

The same qualification of intentions applies to actions: their intentions cannot be prior mental acts that somehow cause them. However, Cavell has pointed out that unintentional, excusable actions are common (thinking of our daily bumps and crashes into one another), whereas unintentional words are harder to find (*CW,* 29). This makes the relation between action and speech more complex than Austin foresaw (*PoP,* 104–105).[13] Nevertheless, since only intentional actions are relevant to tragedy, the similarity between speech and actions still holds in this respect. Intentions in speech and actions mark out the different ways we come to express ourselves within the cultural repertoire; they refer to what is implied or meant in all our gestures, condemned to meaning as they are. Intentions do not apply to physical objects or natural events, neither are they regarded as some hidden causality within a private consciousness. Intentions are inevitable because human expressions are meant to be meant (*MWM,* 228). To elicit intentions is a matter of interpretation or explanation. Our interest in intentions is in finding an expression's point in response to the question "why?"—why thus and not otherwise?[14] They lead not back into the conscious, private choice, but more deeply *into* the utterances at stake. Moreover, intentions do not play the same role in different contexts; they obey different grammar. In a rather dense passage, Cavell lists the relevant differences:

In tragedy, consequence altogether outstrips the creature's preview, and nature and society exact their price for a manageable world; in comedy, the price is born by nature and society themselves, smiling upon their creatures. In morality, our interest in intention, given the need to confront someone's conduct, is to localize his responsibility within the shift of events. In art, our interest in intention, given the fact that we are confronted with someone's work, is to locate ourselves in the shift of events. In all cases, the need is for coming to terms, for taking up the import of a human gesture. In all, I may use terms to describe what someone has done which he himself might not use, or may not know. (*MWM,* 236)

Despite the differentiation, intentions are in every case directed toward the importance and the costs of meaningfulness of human gestures—in the case of tragedy, society and nature will exact their price for an intelligible world. It is important to note that even when the intention is elicited according to an interpretation, such interpretation can only be realized in a community of speakers, and is not subject to the agent's control ("I might use terms to describe what someone has done, which he himself might not use, or might not know"). Furthermore, both the question of intentions—the "why" of an utterance or action—and the act of articulating them occur as a rule *post festum* ("to describe what someone *has done*"). Of course, there is a sense in which one can articulate one's intentions or one's preview of what one wants to say or do; however, what one said or did—its point and hence its intention—will reach its full realization only in public space and in due time.

In contrast to Derrida's depiction, intentions are here displaced, from the private to the public, and postponed, from a prior temporal position to a retrospective one. In both cases, intentions become entangled with possible tragedy, due to its exposure to the uncontrollable responses of others and the unpredictable prospect of the future. On the one hand, consequences outstrip the agent's preview, because intentions are carried out beyond the present and beyond one's control; on the other, nature and society nevertheless exact the price for a manageable world. The latter I take to encapsulate the requirements for a meaningful world, which bind the tragic hero to his utterances and acts and keep him responsible for their outcome.

Some perspectives from outside ordinary language philosophy may help shed further light on how speech and actions tend to outstrip our preview. The discussion of moral luck is relevant here, since it concerns how we in fact make moral judgments depending on factors outside of our control. In this way, moral luck has indeed much to do with tragedy, as Bernhard Williams has pointed out.[15] One of his central arguments is that morality cannot be cut loose from external contingencies, as the Kantian ideal of autonomy requires, where moral judgments are exclusively tied to motivation. Actions can only reach their justification, or lack thereof, in light of how things turn out. This means that an action can only be fully assessed in retrospect, and not at the time the decision is made.[16] To use Williams's focal example: when Gauguin broke up from his civil life, leaving his family and his job in order to pursue a life as an artist, his choice would lack justification if he had failed as an artist. We now know that he did succeed, but the point is that there was no way Gauguin could have known this in advance—it was a matter of how things went and how his gifts managed to reach fruition. I have mentioned that tragedy concerns not unintentional slips and consequences, but rather what intentional acts and speech turn out to mean.

In accordance with this, Williams also distinguishes between "extrinsic luck," referring to incidents that are contingently connected with the project concerned (e.g., that Gauguin broke his arm), and "intrinsic luck," which concerns factors that are essentially entailed in the project but not determinable in advance (e.g., Gauguin's artistic failure or success).[17] Only the latter leads us into the tragic, that is, into what is beyond the excusable.

For us to fully realize why speech and deeds can only be assessed retrospectively along with the distinction between extrinsic and intrinsic luck, let us turn to some Hegelian accounts that shed further light on the matter. In a Hegelian perspective, intentions are regarded not as private meanings or mental causes, but as something that demands that we take their full realization into account—the materialization of their consequences. As Robert Pippin has noted, this is in keeping with ordinary language philosophy.[18] The need for a retrospective perspective on actions is exacted by the way intentions are regarded: they are not behind or prior to action, but they first become manifest through the unfolding of the implications of the action. The agent has no privileged access to its meaning prior to action by means of introspection, nor is his or her judgment privileged over against others' judgments of what in fact happened, for the agent first comes to realize the intention of what he or she has done in light of others' responses. In this view, extrinsic luck can turn out to be bad for the action, but can still be excused; however, failures owing to intrinsic luck must be part of the tragic component of action, and hence beyond excuse.[19] Even if it cannot be foreseen, such a tragic component is essential to the meaning, hence the intention, of the act of which I am the author. It is not necessary, however, to assume a metaphysical teleology of intentions to appreciate this, and certainly not the *telos* of absolute and pure presence that Derrida accuses Austin of (*LI*, 14). Allan Speight speaks more modestly of intentions "shaped by a process of revision," as we revise our understanding starting from the preview and continue to revise this until we retrospectively reach a more adequate understanding.[20] Such understanding of meaning in action has the ability to preserve the narrative unity of actions and the agent's identification with the action that is necessary for holding the agent responsible.

Pawning and Redeeming the Voice

Let me return to the discussion with Derrida. The inscription of tragedy into Austin's own performatives is reflected not only in his citing *Hippolytus*, but also in his statement "our word is our bond." Derrida regards Austin as fundamentally subjected to the paradigms of the metaphysics of presence, in which the voice is regarded as a presence and writing as extending the limit of the voice by transferring the message in a homogeneous medium. Responsibility, in this account, would be a function of the voice's immediate presence to the speaker, holding its meaning in check. Against this, Derrida conceives of writing as cut off from such presence and responsibility:

> This essential drift bearing on writing as an iterative structure, cut off from all absolute responsibility, from *consciousness* as the ultimate authority, orphaned and separated at birth from the assistance of its father, is precisely what Plato condemns in the *Phaedrus*. (*LI*, 8)

Derrida's portrayal of writing can be described as one outward-going movement, sometimes called dissemination, or as here, depicted as creating orphans. Cavell finds no reason to deny—neither for his own part, nor for Austin's—that words exist beyond the speaker's control. But there is another twist to it, because Austin will not only agree that I have to abandon my words, but, furthermore, that I am abandoned *to* them (*PoP*, 125). This abandonment to words only awaits their *return* to me (*PoP*, 73). This return is crucial to Cavell's understanding of the voice and our responsibilities for our words.

Cavell is suggesting a double movement, which he calls pawning and redeeming the voice, in contrast to Derrida's single movement—the outward movement of creating orphans. For us to understand the logic of Cavell's double movement, it is instructive to compare Cavell's understanding of speech and self with Speight's view of action and agent:

> Coming to know oneself as an agent, then, would involve a move from the personal and immediate sense that one is "in" the action one intends, to the impersonal and corrigible consideration of what exactly that action was and how it might be "mine," given the motivations or intentions I can retrospectively read off of it.[21]

The inner logic of the double movement, here portrayed as one from personal immediacy to impersonal and corrigible consideration, brings out the implicit senses of one's action and what makes it mine. The question of the voice is for Cavell tied to personal responsibility and at the same time exposed to the public. Cavell's first movement starts with the investment of the voice in the medium of speech—the *pawning* of the voice—a medium that is not foreign, yet not fully mine either, and certainly not under my full control: language is inherited (it precedes me), it refers me to others (it rests on the shared agreement in criteria), and it demands of me the continuous willingness to project words into new contexts (into a yet-unknown future).

The first movement, the pawning of the voice, takes place as the voice is abandoned *to* words of others, leading to the insight that the voice "will always escape me" (*PoP*, 126). The second movement occurs as the words return to me, when I have to *redeem* the voice—pay the price for its pawning, as it were. It must be redeemed, as the words "will forever find its way back to me" (*PoP*, 126) and hence exact the price for its meaningfulness, according to a movement that mirrors the trajectory of the tragedy (cf. *MWM*, 236).[22] The redeemed words are what define me and make me responsible for what my intentions turn out to be, just as Speight pictures the revision of my sense of myself in light of the public response. The words' destiny does not absolve them from me meaning them, or from my response to and responsibility for them as they come back to me. Capturing the double movement, Cavell writes, "I recognize words as mine when I see that I have to forgo them to use them. Pawn them and redeem them to own them. What does that say, otherwise (that is, allegorically), about having a self, that is about putting myself into the world, and receiving it from there?" (*PP*, 103). When I put myself into the world, what I say and do will inevitably be taken up in others' lives and be the object of various interpretations. But it is by being responded to or, in Lacan's sense, mirrored, that I receive a sense of my own self in the first place.[23]

In Cavell's reading, this sense of the self is something like the moral of Austin's invocation of signature. Derrida, however, mocks Austin's invocation of signature as an exemplary expression of a metaphysical picture of writing coupled with the metaphysical privilege given to the pure identical self. For Derrida, signature makes the essential absence of the signer salient, and hence any tethering of the signer to the signature is effectively forestalled (*LI*, 19–20). Cavell, however, does not believe that Austin's invocation of signature and tethering is meant in the way Derrida takes it, since Derrida does not consider that in order to understand its implications, we must take its practical point into account. Attending to how we use signatures, it is clear that it picks you out as the one who has signed, but "not in your . . . absolute purity . . . but in your relative and impure identity, not from any possible human that could exist . . . but from whom . . . you . . . might need distinguishing" (*PoP*, 121). So Cavell's Austin and Derrida agree that signature cannot resolve the irony of finite human identity, and it is not meant to. But they draw different conclusions. For Derrida, the iterative structure of a signature means that writing must be "cut off from all absolute responsibility," whereas Cavell implies that it is the very impurity of the signature that calls on responsibility—not of an absolute self immune to moral luck and the drifts of meaning, but one whose responsible *task* remains to tether our signature—our voice—in responding to what has become of our utterances and deeds (*PoP*, 123).

Now, it seems that Cavell's frequent choice of notions, such as returning and recurrence of words, in effect draws him near to Derrida's sense of repetition and iterability. To make their perceptions even more closely related, Cavell can speak of the unpredictability of recurrence as a fact of language (*DK*, 232). However, Cavell is careful to distance himself from a radical decentering or even replacing of the self, and along with that, the denial of personal responsibility (*DK*, 233). How far this fits Derrida's concerns, or whether they are even meant to, is open to discussion, but in any case it highlights one important difference: Derrida's recurrence or iterability does not imply a return to a responsible self in the way it does for Cavell.[24] According to Cavell, Austin's interest in such things as signature is that of

> *limiting the (inevitable) extension* of the voice, which will always escape me and will forever find its way back to me. As if the price of having once spoken, or remarked, taken something as remarkable (worth noting, yours to note, about which to make an ado), is to have spoken forever, to have taken on responsibility for speaking further, the responsibility of responsiveness, of answerability, to make yourself intelligible. (*PoP*, 126)

The facts that we are exposed to our words, that those words might betray us, that they will be taken up into others' lives and then returned to us, make a claim on us. Cavell does not say that we are nailed to every consequence of our deeds, as if we were fixed forever by having once spoken. He says that having once spoken, our responsibilities are that of responding to the destiny of our words and thus making ourselves intelligible.

Cavell thinks Austin's philosophy aspires for justice of speech, such as in tracing intentions and limiting man's responsibility (*CW*, 356). Not only in Austin's explicit discussion of the limiting of responsibility in excuses, but indirectly in every appeal to what we mean, he implies that there must be some moral limit of the inevitable extension of the voice. The problem with Austin, from Cavell's point of view, is not that he is unaware of the fallibility inscribed in human existence, as his preoccupation with excuses reveals, but that he is too certain about how and when to draw the limits of our moral responsibility. Austin's aspiration for justice of speech certainly arises from its occasional injustice, and it is the injustice of speech that arguably makes excuses important to him. We are nonetheless left with the feeling that Austin has not pursued such inherent injustice far enough, at any rate not into its possible tragic implications. This is one reason why Austin is unable to unpack the full implications of his quotation of Hippolytus. Unlike Austin, Derrida places minimal trust in ordinary language, leading him to one-sidedly emphasize writing's unavoidable injustice. In Derrida's view, this emphasis locates responsibility at the limit of ordinary comprehension— as if decisions are always aporetic, made in the face of the undecidable (*LI*, 116– 117). Cavell's position is located somewhere between. He shares Austin's aspiration for justice of speech and for taking full responsibility for meaning what one says. However, this aspiration for justice is played out against the background of the injustice of speech; meaning is not completely up to me, but it is always an appeal, not to Derrida's movement of *différance*, but to "agreements we do not know and do not want to know we have entered, agreements we were always in, that were in effect before our participation in them" (*IQO*, 40).

Tragedy and Original Sin: Destiny and Responsibility

I noted at the beginning of this chapter that balance between destiny and responsibility is as central to tragedy as it is central to the doctrine of original sin. According to Cavell's understanding of the tragedy inscribed in the ordinary, we are condemned to meaning: although we constantly issue meaningful gestures that are exposed to a meaning that outreaches control, we are nevertheless answerable. When Mulhall writes that original sin is "more than an error but less than a fate," he captures precisely the central task of striking the right balance between destiny and responsibility in accounting for original sin.[25] Against a Pelagian quest for full self-mastery, expressed in the power not to commit sin, Augustine also wants to preserve the personal responsibility yet underline that sin is priori to us, indeed an unavoidable destiny into which all humans are born. Or, as Augustine puts it in *Confessions:* "many people living long before me had constructed the laborious courses which we were compelled to follow by an increase of the toil and sorrow of Adam's children."[26] From both the tragic and Christian outlooks thus described, it seems that we are destined to find ourselves handed over to uncontrollable dimensions of life, along with the call to responsibility for that life, which together appear as a burdensome predicament from which one can understand the skeptical drive to flee or else revolt against it.

However, tragedy and the doctrine of original sin focus their attention on a contrary temporal dimension: the former toward an unpredictable future, the latter toward an inescapable past. Augustine, in his problematic reading of Paul (Rom. 5:12), detects our present destiny as tied to the inheritance of a past. It is clearly no longer possible to defend Augustine's quasi-biological thought about heredity, but the decisive insight can still be recognized, namely that, despite its lack of metaphysical necessity, sin has become inextricably connected to our humanity. On the other hand, this destiny is counterbalanced by Augustine's quasi-juridical invocation of our guilt for whatever evil that stems from our will. Ricoeur gives a convincing interpretation of Augustine's concerns: "We *inaugurate* evil. It is through us that evil comes into the world. But we inaugurate evil only on the basis of an evil already there, of which our birth is the impenetrable symbol."[27] Heredity and birth symbolically suggest an "already there" of our sinfulness that still cannot unburden us from the fact that we confirm the evil that passes through us.

But we are not only born and initiated into an inheritance that we cannot choose, but there is also a future that awaits what we inaugurate in the present, and that is the material of the tragic as brought forward in the preceding pages: the tragic error (*hamartia*), even if only as a casual remark, might in extreme cases become the destiny of a life. Both Pippin and Speight stress that intentions gain their full meaning through their public manifestations—the preview is pawned, and their meaning must be retrospectively redeemed. According to such a view, we are exposed to what seems to be the destiny of our words and deeds. Even if the meaning of our words and deeds goes through a process of revision, it remains true that what is once done cannot be undone; and moreover, our intentions are realized in a social weave of receptions, reactions, and new responses in a way that is in principle unforeseeable. Hannah Arendt sums this up in writing that once acts have entered history, they are both irreversible and unpredictable.[28] And nevertheless, we are held answerable.

This suggests that original sin and the tragic converge on the intertwining of destiny and responsibility, and further, that they can be taken to complement the various temporal dimensions entailed in that intertwining. In this perspective, the tragic articulates an essential dimension of the fallen condition, more precisely, the dimension that ties the present to the future.[29] While he certainly did not want to undermine the differences between original sin and the tragic, the ambiguity of responsibility is at the forefront of Kierkegaard's reflections: the tragic error is intermediate between action and suffering, he argues, which means that it is undertaken by the protagonist and yet not fully within his control. The latter makes sorrow so profound in the Greek tragedies, Kierkegaard contends, since sorrow testifies to a kind of destiny, and yet it cannot be understood without its tension with pain, in which the protagonist recognizes his own hand in the cause of sorrow.[30] In the "aesthetic sorrow" of Greek tragedy, sorrow will be prevalent, but a stain of guilt will always remain in it. According to Kierkegaard, however, this aesthetic ambiguity of being guilty, yet not being guilty, cannot be transferred to the destiny of Christ, not because his fate ultimately turns out for the best, but because the categories of guilt and innocence only have an absolute, not relative and ambiguous, application to Christ. Nor is tragic guilt subjective guilt by which the individual stands and falls; it is rather "heredity guilt, like heredity sin." There is hence a profound sense of a pre- and supra-individual dimension that belongs to the tragic heredity guilt, just as in heredity sin, and Kierkegaard explicitly adheres to the Judeo-Christian tradition in his account as he continues:

> One might promptly think that the people who must have developed
> the profoundly tragic was the Jewish nation. For example, when it is
> said of Jehovah that he is a jealous God, that he visits the iniquities of

the fathers upon the children to the third and fourth generations, or when we hear those terrible curses in the Old Testament, one could easily be tempted to want to seek tragic material here. But Judaism is too ethically matured for that; even though they are terrible, Jehovah's courses are also righteous punishment. It was not this way in Greece; the wrath of the gods has no ethical character, only esthetic ambiguity.[31]

What matters for the present is that the distinctions between tragic heredity guilt and Judeo-Christian heredity sin stem from the distinction between the aesthetic and the ethical. While Kierkegaard insists on the ethical character of God, the mutual entanglement of destiny and responsibility remains characteristic of both the Judeo-Christian and the tragic case, even as they differ significantly in the moral they draw from it.

Kierkegaard points out that if one compares classic and modern tragedies written after the Christianization of Western outlook, the accent shifts from sorrow to pain, from destiny to individual responsibility.[32] A version of this perception is taken up by Cavell. In contrast to the Greek fatalistic dimension of the tragic, a modern sense treats our freedom in a sense that displaces a possible interconnection between responsibility and destiny. Cavell has pointed out how modern understandings of the tragic presuppose a sense of freedom and responsibility of interpretation, of the past, present, and possible future:

> It was not wrong to read the sense of inevitability in terms of a chain of cause and effect; what was wrong, what became insufficient to explain our lives, was to read this chain as if its first link lay in the past, and hence as if the present were the scene of its ineluctable effects, in the face of which we must learn suffering. With Kant (because with Luther) and then Hegel and Nietzsche, not to say Freud, we became responsible for the meaning of the suffering itself, indeed for the very fact that the world is to be comprehended under the rule of causation at all. (DK, 89)

Cavell's point is that the interpretation of the inevitable has changed significantly in modernity. The interpretation of suffering—its origins, what understanding we gain from it, and where it leaves us—is not given, but it is something we must find meaning in and hence something we have become answerable for.

Interpretations are significant for how we understand our moral conduct. Even if Cavell can state that I am totally responsible for all that happens as a consequence of what I have done, what happens can still be described in many ways (CR, 324). The act is not fixed to one description, but the description that is opted for will fix us, or more specifically, it will fix our relation to the action. In this sense, an action can become our destiny and its consequences can become inevitable for us. We are not simply responsible for every consequence of our intentions, but, as Mulhall puts it, for "determining [our] *relation* to them—whether and how to claim them as unforeseeable or simply unforeseen, to accept them as meant or excuse them as unintended."[33] To understand our intentions and their consequences in that way is decisive for arriving at self-knowledge: it reveals something about our relation to our intentions and more broadly to our moral position in the world (*CR*, 312).

In tragedy, as in the Christian sharing of the tragic outlook, acts and speech are often not for the best, and according to the modern vision, this cannot be understood apart from how we are implicated in them. In this perspective, the inevitable is not, as in classical tragedy, due to the character flaw of the hero, *nemesis*, or to divine revenge, but to a self-imposed blindness of my relation to my intentions. The blindness, as portrayed in *King Lear*, is not the inability to see, but the *refusal* to see, and such refusal and lack of self-recognition becomes a destiny as long as it blocks any possibility to change. So even if words and deeds have consequences that outrun our preview, they will track us down, Cavell writes, "because we go on doing the thing which produced these consequences in the first place." After turning us to religious themes in his characteristically ambivalent way, Cavell concludes: "What we need is not rebirth, or salvation, but the courage, or plain prudence, to see and to stop. To abdicate. But what do we need in order to do that? It would be salvation" (*DK*, 81). Cavell leaves open what such salvation consists of. At least, it might suggest that we need to be aided, perhaps from outside ourselves, in order to reach self-knowledge, to see and then to change, or more precisely, to stop avoiding ourselves and others.

To arrive at such self-knowledge, one must start from the outcome of one's utterances and deeds; one must see oneself expressed in that outcome and from there reflect back to the outcome's source, in order to acknowledge oneself as the author of the utterances and deeds. This acknowledgment takes the form of a confession. At least, this is how Ricoeur sees it:

> I declare myself, *after the fact*, as being he who *could* have done otherwise; this "after the fact" is the backlash of taking upon oneself the consequences. . . . This movement from in front of to behind the responsibility is essential. It constitutes the identity of the moral subject through past, present, and future. . . . The future of sanction and the past of action committed are tied together in the present of confession.[34]

The act of confession exemplarily reveals the responsible self's redeeming of pawned words and deeds: it acknowledges what intentions turned out to imply and accepts the responsibility for responding upon their return—in excuses, explanations, regrets, or remorse. Under the circumstances in which we live, where inexcusable evil is undeniably operative, to avoid the sensitivity for guilt is to jeopardize one's identity as human. On this background, one might say that confessions are not an exotic, optional religious practice; rather, they are necessarily bound up with arriving at an understanding of one's position in the world.

Cavell suggests that words seem destined to transgress the excusable and thus progress toward tragedy, in which one must claim responsibility for the consequences, "[a]s if the price of having once spoken, or remarked, taken something as remarkable . . . is to have spoken forever" (*PoP*, 126). While we might be condemned to meaning, we here become victims of it. But in such cases, are we bound by the word to its eventual fatal outcome? Typically, this is the implication of Greek tragedy. But if Christianity agrees with tragedy that the conditions of this life are inescapable, there is nevertheless a sense in which the overarching Christian vision cannot accept the final lack of reconciliation as having the last word. Against tragedy, it insists that there is such a thing as a *felix culpa* and hope against hope; in a narrower scope, in intimate relations, there is the offer of forgiveness. But there is a sense that such forgiveness can first truly be recognized against the backdrop of the tragic. By almost echoing the tragic dimension in the quotation from Cavell, Arendt holds that "without being forgiven, released from the consequences of what we have done, our capacity to act would, as it were, be confined to one single deed from which we could never recover; we would remain the victim of its consequences forever."[35] But before exploring the possibility of forgiveness, let us consider another expression of skepticism or sin, namely violence.

SIX

The Other and Violence

Whereas the previous chapter elaborated what might be thought of as a destiny to which we must be answerable, I now turn to another, more active face of skepticism or sin, namely violence. What is the connection between violence and my relation to the other? How can the motives behind violence be understood, and how is it entangled with religion? Levinas's understanding of how violence is bound up with the face of the other provides a rich phenomenological account, one that I believe can be supplemented with Cavell's subtle understanding of its motivation.

Despite the fact that Levinas and Cavell are embedded in distinct traditions, they have in common at least two themes that deserve mention at the outset. First, there are parallels in Cavell's and Levinas's philosophical focus on the other. Cavell's pivotal notion in this respect is, of course, acknowledgment, which presupposes that the other lays a claim on me, singles me out, and that I am exposed to the other in a way that requires my response (*CR*, 84). For Levinas, my exposure to the call of the other, along with my responsibility in return, not only constitutes a striking parallel to Cavell's acknowledgment, but is perhaps the sole theme of his entire oeuvre, defined against the Western philosophical tendency to reduce the other to the same. Levinas's key concepts, such as alterity, separation, and proximity, can be derived from his account of the concrete face-to-face encounter. Perhaps Cavell's and Levinas's common perception can be encapsulated in the following passage from Cavell: "Speaking together face to face can seem to deny that distance, to deny that facing one another requires acknowledging the presence of the other, revealing our positions, betraying them if need be. But to deny such things is to deny our separateness" (*SW*, 65).[1]

This leads into the second similarity: both locate their philosophical interests at the interface between the ordinary and the extraordinary. As discussed in chapter 2, Cavell speaks of what I called the ordinary sublime in terms of "the extraordinariness in what we find ordinary (for example, beauty) and the ordinariness in what we find extraordinary (for example, violence)" (*CW*, 34). At first glance, Levinas's philosophy seems far removed from the ordinary; his preoccupation with absolute alterity, height, trauma, and epiphany feed the suspicion that Levinas participates in what Cavell calls the flight from the ordinary. But then Levinas repeatedly insists that his philosophy is summarized in discrete and ordinary gestures, such as "After you, sir." If we take this insistence at face value, it means that Levinas also wants to turn our attention to what Critchley has called "the moral grammar of everyday life," employing extraordinary terminology to circle in the impact of most ordinary encounters.[2] Whether this reading captures the overarching orientation of Levinas's philosophy is open to debate—there are indeed tendencies in his prose that clearly push beyond the grammar of ordinary life. But to the extent that Critchley's reading is legitimate, the constellation between his and Cavell's thought might be summarized as follows: whereas Levinas strives for an approach to the ordinary from above, as it were, by overturning the Western metaphysical tradition, Cavell starts from below, disclosing the various impulses to escape the ordinary, and turning them toward a more mature perception of the eventual ordinary.

In the first half of this chapter, I show how Levinas's account of violence and the other is relevant to Cavell and elucidate how Cavell's skepticism can shed further light on the underlying motives of such violence; in the second half I relate violence to religion, both with regard to the potential violence connected with the idea of God and with regard to ways of overcoming violence. However, I first prepare those accounts by discussing Levinas's and Cavell's views on skepticism.

The Truth and Threat of Skepticism

The point of convergence between Levinas and Cavell on skepticism has attracted surprisingly little attention from commentators.[3] Although Cavell mentions Levinas's writing on skepticism, he resists any elaboration on that common occupation (*LK*, 528). In introducing skepticism in his late opus *Otherwise than Being*, Levinas remarks that the epistemological attention to uncertainty and risk entailed in our relation to the other displaces the real impact of uncertainty: if one believes that uncertainty should be mended by certainty, one has already fallen prey to the assumption that our relation to the other is a matter of knowledge and reason. The uncertainty or risk that should be preserved resides rather in our practical engagement with the other as transcending ourselves (*OB*, 167). This recalls Cavell's idea of skepticism's distorted depiction of separateness and finitude—it turns them into matters of epistemological problems, where in fact the other's separateness should give rise to practical, even ethical, responses (*CR*, 81–82). Despite Levinas's uncoupling of uncertainty and risk from certain philosophical preconceptions, he nevertheless stresses that "[p]hilosophy is not separable from skepticism, which follows it like a shadow it drives off by refuting it again at once on its footsteps" (*OB*, 168). However, such refutation will not win out, but only displace the rebirth of skepticism, due to its "invincible and evanescent force" (*OB*, 171). The thought that skepticism cannot and should not be dismissed is of course central to Cavell, as well; they both regard the skeptic as the respectable other who must be carefully understood.

And yet, Cavell and Levinas diverge when it comes to the more specific understanding of philosophy and skepticism. For Cavell, skepticism is internal to philosophy, because the ordinary, in which philosophical thought evolves, is by its very nature vulnerable to repudiation. This vulnerability is not a weakness, but rather is what makes language emphatically ours. But for Levinas, skepticism opposes the Western philosophical tradition in its entirety, a tradition that can only assume what falls within the coherent system of thought, its so-called "synchrony." The corresponding sense of skepticism is thus one that resists being subsumed and that thereby indicates a dimension that escapes synchrony, called "diachrony." Diachrony marks the temporal difference between me and a certain absence in the other, that is, between my time and the time of the other that only leaves a trace of an immemorable past. By way of such temporal asymmetry, the other is forever exterior to me and my consciousness of time. According to Levinas, in order to account for skepticism we must distinguish between two levels: the synchronic, on which philosophy operates, and the diachronic, in which skepticism resides. Skepticism is not so much an inherent part of the instability of the ordinary as a stubborn reminder of what is forever beyond comprehension, presence, and being. Seen from the perspective of traditional philosophy, the skeptic rejection of philosophy must be refuted—it is, according to Levinas, indeed self-refuting. Yet, what makes it inevitably return is that it bears witness—even if only indirectly—to the dimension of diachrony that cannot otherwise be articulated within philosophy: "This return of diachrony refusing the present makes up the inevitable force of skepticism" (*OB*, 169).

Following Cavell, the skeptical truth fails to arrive at philosophical articulation due to the skeptic's own inadequate self-perception, whereas for Levinas, it is philosophy's dependence on synchrony that prevents skepticism from conveying its truth. Consequently, Levinas thinks that even if skepticism could put forward its insights in a way that was acceptable to philosophy, it would have betrayed the medium in which it bears witness—in Levinas's idiom, it would betray the saying by reducing it to the said. However, Levinas then writes that "language is already skepticism" (*OB*, 170), which, strange as it may seem, refers directly to this distinction: everything that is said (articulated as a theme) is ultimately only achievable due to the fundamental possibility of meaning stemming from saying (my response or awakening in the exposure to the other, ultimately reflected in the prophetic response "Here I am"). This saying certainly exceeds the said, and yet it has no other philosophical way of expressing itself than through the said. According to Robert Bernasconi's reading, "Skepticism is not just a denial or rejection of the possibility of knowledge. In its saying it is an affirmation which transcends the realm of the said at the same time as sustaining it."[4] Levinas therefore assesses skepticism's contribution positively, as an evanescent voice that reminds philosophy of its necessary openness to alterity. For Cavell, however, skepticism retains the character of rejection of knowledge, thus his question becomes not so much whether skepticism can be refuted or should be confirmed, but why the skeptic feels compelled to reject the condition of what we all somehow know.

Although both Cavell and Levinas interpret skepticism in a manner that goes against the grain, some significant differences nevertheless start to emerge, differences that have bearing on the understanding of violence. For, as will become increasingly clear, Cavell's unearthing of the motives behind violence is inexplicably linked to his sense of skepticism. Skepticism is potentially violent because it fuels my denials of the other and simultaneously conceals my responsibilities for doing so. Skepticism is internally tied to both philosophy and ordinary life, for there is no special class of language games that are philosophical or skeptical (PP, 143). As Levinas sees it, skepticism has another purpose: it shall remind philosophy of its other by interrupting it. Levinas also sees a connection between skepticism and violence, but in the inverse form of Cavell's view: reason and its political equivalent, the state, are intolerant to what interrupts it, and hence their violence is tantamount to the repression of skepticism (OB, 170). By not regarding skepticism as lodged within philosophy, but instead understanding skepticism as emerging from an outside to which philosophy must remain open, Levinas is prevented from considering skepticism's part in violence. I follow two of Levinas's different accounts of violence to show how skeptical motives can nevertheless be said to be implied in them.

Violence, Knowledge, and Separation

The link between the emergence of the other and the propensity to violence occurs relatively early in Levinas's works, where two related yet distinct accounts of the relation between the face and violence can arguably be discerned. In "Is Ontology Fundamental?," the thesis seems to be that the face's transcending character vis-à-vis knowledge gives rise to a murderous impetus, and this remains a focal approach in several succeeding texts, most notably in Totality and Infinity. However, in "Freedom and Command," Levinas changes the emphasis somewhat, this time concentrating on how violence already presupposes a denial of the face.

At stake in the first account is a conception of knowledge in which knowledge itself entails some sense of violence. In my knowing an object, the object is taken under my dominance—I comprehend it in the way I hunt down an animal, overcoming it as an individual being in its own right.[5] Despite this dominance, Levinas writes, knowledge must essentially not annihilate its objects; it should only negate its autonomy: "A partial negation can be described by the fact that, without disappearing, beings are in my power. The partial negation which is violence denies the independence of beings: they are mine."[6] Knowledge's partial negation is therefore led by the drive to take things into possession and subject their separate existence to my domination. Knowledge, thus conceived, forces the world into an orbit around the self and makes it inherently narcissistic.[7]

When it comes to the human face, Levinas contends that a new dimension is opened, a dimension that comes from beyond the world and invites a relation that is incommensurate with power and domination. To be sure, the face can also be regarded as a phenomenon in the world—its contours, the colors of the eyes, even its character and environment can be regarded as internal to its empirical manifestation. As such, the face is merely another object in the world. But such a perception requires a detached angle from which we have not yet entered into a relation with the other; for the face of the other is not solely, not even primarily, a phenomenon, but what Levinas (and later Derrida) calls a trace. A trace is not a sign in a context or a mark left by some kind of causality, but meaning that traverses any context and horizon. The trace means itself without showing itself; it indicates an irretrievable absence, temporally conceived as an irreversible past that has never been present. The trace is, more specifically, something that manifests itself between presence and absence, between the phenomenon and its beyond: it presents itself in the world by withdrawing from it.[8] While such descriptions might give the impression of something infinitely hidden or distant, Levinas nevertheless insists to the contrary that the face is epiphany par excellence—it speaks.

But what does the face say? According to Levinas, the content of the speech is essentially "You shall not commit murder" (TI, 199). In drawing on the Decalogue, Levinas signals that the face is resistant to murder, and that its speech transposes us to another register—from knowledge to ethics. Though Levinas admits the banal fact that the other, taken as an empirical phenomenon, can be hunted down and killed, the *ethical alterity* of the other only slips away from strangling hands—it transcends the empirical world. The question then becomes: if the other, or more precisely the otherness of the other, cannot be annihilated, what is the point of prohibiting its killing? As it seems, the prohibition must correspond to a specific temptation or wish. Levinas stresses that the face is deeply ambiguous: it simultaneously forbids and incites murder; indeed, the human other is the only thing I can want to kill (TI, 198). Unlike any other object, the face is precisely that which absolutely defies my possession; it cannot be partially negated as objects can, because it is impossible to overcome its independence or separation from me. The other says "No!" to any violent appropriation, and does so in preserving its integrity, its "for itself." But knowledge's wish for dominion is nevertheless not silenced. So if the negation of the face cannot be partial, it must be total—the other must be killed:

> Murder alone lays claim to total negation. . . . To kill is not to dominate but to annihilate; it is to renounce comprehension absolutely. Murder exercises power over what escapes power. . . . I can wish to kill only an existent absolutely independent, which exceeds my powers infinitely, and therefore does not oppose them but paralyzes the very power of power. (*TI*, 198)

So far, Cavell affirms Levinas's account: otherness, separation, and knowledge as possession are essential for understanding the source of the murderous impulse. But in order to come to grips with these factors as they are deployed in Cavell's work, they must be derived from what he considers their source: skepticism. And this seems particularly welcome here, since Levinas's portrayal of knowledge seems to fit into the skeptical picture. The epistemological discussion of skepticism has traditionally centered on what Cavell calls "the best case of knowledge." To know Descartes's piece of wax, Kant's boat, and Moore's hands requires no expertise: the wax, the boat, and the hands are generic objects, which means that any competent speaker must know what they are. The skeptic upshot is that if we do not know such things, we know nothing at all—which is precisely what skepticism claims and what traditional epistemology opposes. If such best cases can be doubted or rejected, skepticism will generalize and thus concern the world's existence as such (*CR*, 131, 145).

But what is the best case of acknowledging the other? As did Levinas before him, also Cavell contends that our relation to the world and its objects is categorically different from relations to human others. One important indication of the difference between skepticism of the external world and skepticism of the other concerns precisely the extent to which such best cases can be established (*CR*, 430). A best case of the other would have to be one that was able to represent humanity as such, and—leaving aside the obvious Christian candidate for the moment—there is no such individual available. From this asymmetry follows another: even if there were such a best case of the other, the failure to acknowledge it would not generalize, for the acknowledgment of the other cannot be carried out once and for all, but must be conducted or denied each time anew, and each time it can be done only on my own behalf (*CR*, 426).[9] Such significant differences attest to the different sense of separation entailed in the relation to the other and the one (purportedly) overcome in knowledge. Argument, evidence, and grounds for doubting capture neither my interest nor my difficulty in acknowledging the other (*PDT*, 149). Skepticism is a way to respond, or better, refuse to respond to the demand the other places on me: "I call skepticism my denial or annihilation of the other. It is epitomized in what happens to the other's body, as when Othello's imagination turns Desdemona into alabaster" (*PDT*, 150). Note that this turning into alabaster is carried out precisely by an act of murder.

For Levinas it is the particular way in which the face remains separate that offends the murderer. Interestingly, Cavell also claims that Othello commits murder as a reaction to the other's separation, Desdemona's alterity. Deliberately adjusted to Levinas's lingo, Cavell writes that the separation concerns a

> recognition that this particular other, this creature among all the creatures of the earth similar to me, is also, or rather therefore, absolutely different, separate from me, I would say, wholly other, endlessly other, the one I single out before whom I am I, eternally singled out. It is the unbearable certainty of this separation to which the torture of skepticism over Desdemona's faithfulness is preferable. (*PDT*, 145–146)

What Othello wants to overcome ultimately belongs to our finitude—our separation from the world and from others. So what the skeptic desires is the impossible state in which all separation is undone, and the "object" is under his dominion. Now, since the skeptic is disposed to depict his relation to the other in terms of what Cavell and Levinas understand as narcissistic knowledge, his understanding of knowledge becomes possessive:

> He seeks a possession that is not in opposition to another's claim or desire but one that establishes an absolute or inalienable bonding to himself, to which no claim or desire *could* be opposed, could conceivably count; as if the jealousy is directed to the sheer existence of the other, its separateness from him. It is against the (fantasied) possibility of overcoming this hyperbolic separateness that the skeptic's (disappointed, intellectualized, impossible, imperative, hyperbolic) demand makes sense. (*DK*, 9)

In Cavell's hands, the link between knowledge and possession, already invoked by Levinas, is given an additional turn—namely that it stems from some form of jealousy. It is incontestable that *Othello* centers on jealousy, but, in Cavell's reading, Othello's jealousy is not originally rooted in his suspicion, implanted by

Iago, that Desdemona is having an affair with Cassio; as noted in chapter 4, he is jealous of her sheer independent existence. Cavell sometimes suggests that skepticism of other minds is more fundamental than skepticism of the external world; he does this in the context of the theme of jealousy, which only derivatively can be applied to skepticism of the external world. In both regard to the external world and the other, jealousy easily leads to the urge for revenge—whether in a world-consuming nihilism or in a revenge on the other's resistance to my possession. Such insights reflect light back onto Levinas's analysis: the powerlessness against the other that feeds the temptation of murder has its motivational root in jealousy and revenge.

Violence, Mania, and Passivity

Although "Freedom and Command" reiterates many of Levinas's observations from "Is Ontology Fundamental?," the former essay seems to be guided by a somewhat different idea. In the previous account it was the face itself that invited, but also forbade, violence, but in "Freedom and Command" violence does not originate in the face—on the contrary, violence comes into being as the face is *avoided:* "violence consists in ignoring this opposition, ignoring the face of a being, avoiding the gaze."[10] My suggestion is that both these accounts defend their legitimacy by capturing different possible motives of violence; more specifically, they can both be interpreted as different stages in Cavell's understanding of the skeptic recital.

One way to conceive the internal logic of these distinct stages is to follow Cavell's reference to Melanie Klein, references made precisely in his reception of Levinas.[11] In doing so, I am not claiming that either Levinas's or Cavell's accounts can be reduced to psychoanalytic explanation. Rather, I highlight figures of thought that help track the inner development of skeptic motives. The first account of violence in the analysis of the face has a psychoanalytical parallel in what Klein calls the paranoid-schizoid position of the infant. The child's yet-fragmented ego defends itself by splitting bad from good objects in order to expel the bad ones and project them outward. This is a pre-Oedipal development, Cavell explains,

> in which the child begins acquiring its recognition of the other (of the other who represents otherness as such, shattering the narcissistic ego) when the other, which sustains life with its nourishment, manifests its separateness, its inevitable, however momentary, withdrawal or withholding of nourishment, causing a murderous rage in the child which threatens to destroy or damage that source of sustenance. (*PDT*, 148)

This reading captures the violent reaction sketched in the previous section: the representative other, emblematized by the mother's breast, causes an enormous disappointment to the narcissistic, possessive ego by manifesting its separateness. The child responds to the inevitable withdrawal of the breast by projecting all malevolence onto the breast. This "bad" breast becomes the target of the child's aggression, as a payback for a certain jealousy directed at the breast's resistance to dominance. Cavell suggests that Klein's aggressiveness and Levinas's murderousness both seem derivative, albeit in distinct ways: "in Klein's case from the other's withdrawal and separateness, in Levinas's case from the other's presentation of the face" (*PDT*, 148).

However, this account does not shed light on Levinas's second account of violence, in which the face is not attacked but evaded. But if we follow Klein further, the paranoid as well as the depressive position tend to alternate with some form of *mania*—a hyperactivity that is designed to combat paranoid threats or excessive feelings of guilt.[12] As the child grows, it comes to comprehend objects as whole objects, and hence the splitting and projecting loses its force. It is as if the child has realized the other's exteriority but is utterly disappointed by it, especially its reluctance to obey its possessive grasp. So the child moves on to another strategy, where it seeks to detach itself from others without renouncing them totally, in order to execute control from this position. According to Klein, this is accomplished by the manic reaction: "It succeeds in this compromise by *denying the importance* of the good objects and also of the dangers of the bad objects and the id. At the same time however, it endeavours ceaselessly to *master and control* all its objects and the evidence of this effort is its hyperactivity."[13]

The manic denial of the other's importance, along with the violent strategy of mastering it, provides a gateway to Levinas's second account of violence. In this account, the violent action requires some form of detachment—it is in fact "an action where one is as though one were alone."[14] "As though one were alone" does not mean that one's acts do not affect others, since an essential aspect of violence is that it is inflicted on someone, but it implies the denial of the importance of the other: the violent agent avoids the gaze and ignores the face. While it is too late to deny the other's existence, the violator now takes advantage of the duality implied in the face. The face is a trace, a manifestation, and yet a manifestation of a certain absence or transcendence. Following Levinas, however, the face's transcendence is not only absence but also an appeal—it speaks. This speech implies that the other is turned toward me, but by being turned toward me, the face also opposes me in the ethical sense of saying "No" to me. In the manic phase, it is precisely this speech of the face that is deflected, and by deflecting it, the ego can win detachment from the demand of the other—indeed from its "You shall not commit murder."

For the violator, the other appears not as a face but as a mask; it is neither received directly as an expression nor encountered directly, but, in Levinas's words, the violator "approach[es] it from an indirect angle."[15] The other is accepted as a phenomenon, but its ethical meaning is avoided. From this indirect angle, the "No" does not present itself as an ethical opposition as it is transposed to the spatial opposition along with other phenomena. The face reduced to a mask can thus be pushed back into the order of possessive knowledge in which the narcissistic ego can conduct its control: others can be dominated as objects of knowledge. But according to this strategy, the resistance of the other appears differently: the "face becomes a hostile or submissive force."[16] This is a typical skeptical re-interpretation, in which the other is deformed in order to make it accord with the ego's fantasies, eventually to prepare it for its counter-attacks. If violence in the most general sense is war, such re-interpretation of the other's resistance as a hostile force certainly underpins the violent logic. The "pacific opposition" of the face is deformed into a hostile force.[17]

For Klein it is important that what is denied paradoxically is what nourishes and thus sustains life. Such denial might also take the form of jealousy and envy, not owing to the withdrawal and separateness of the mother, but this time destructively bent toward the source of life. Reflecting on various expressions of envy, Klein points out that, among the mortal sins, envy is rightly held as the most severe: it directs its destructive force against the very gift of life.[18] But what exactly is the enigmatic motivation for such destructive aggression? One might suspect that such violent impetus is moved by a denial of something intolerable to the skeptic, and, following Cavell, this might have much to do with a certain intolerance of passivity.

Cavell has considered how (potentially manic) activity can be linked to the demand for knowledge and certainty. Drawing on Freud's equation of the active with the masculine and the passive with the feminine, Cavell then diagnoses skepticism as typically male. Not that there is anything problematic with the intertwining of active and passive in the economy of knowing (such intertwining has in fact been employed with different emphasis in the tradition from Kant to Emerson and onward); rather, the problem occurs as the masculine and feminine are conceived of as mutually exclusive rivals:

> The violence in masculine knowing, explicitly associated with jealousy, seems to interpret the ambition of knowledge as that of exclusive possession, call it private property. Othello's problem, following my suggestion that his problem is over success, not failure, is that Desdemona's acceptance, or satisfaction, or reward, of his ambition strikes him as being possessed, as if he is the woman. (*DK*, 10)

Othello's exaggerated fear of being possessed mirrors the exaggeration of his own demand for complete self-possession. Yet the exaggerated and deformed depiction underlying the skeptic's fear harbors some truth—not, this time, the truth of separateness, but the other side of the coin, my dependence on the other. But, of course, relative dependency implies acceptance of passivity, that is, that I accept that human identity and integrity can only be established and maintained by way of the other. Perceiving this as a threat, the skeptic follows the manic strategy in devaluing the other's importance, and in turn he subjects the other to his possessive control.

Passivity certainly resounds in Levinas's writing, and its importance seems to be elaborated further in his later thought, where the condition of ethical subjectivity is at the forefront. It seems reasonable to say that Levinas's main project in *Otherwise than Being* is precisely to dispossess the identity of the self, so that the self is no longer understood as an ego for itself, primarily active, spontaneous, self-reflecting, and fully autonomous. The self is rather understood in terms of *substitution*: even before it becomes self-consciousness, the self is taken hostage by the other. Substitution means not only that the other lays claims on me to which I must respond, but more radically that I am put in the other's position and am held responsible for his or her responsibilities, deeds, and misdeeds (*OB*, 13). That this state of passivity is linked with violence afflicting the I—in terms of trauma, persecution, being taken hostage, and so forth—is something Cavell notes (*PDT*, 145). But whereas Levinas draws the connection between violence and the passivity of the I, he does not elaborate the way in which passivity can fuel the murderous inclination directed toward the other.

Levinas certainly locates such passivity at a level of the genesis of subjectivity that goes beyond Cavell's concerns. It even seems as though Cavell does not so much embrace Levinas's description of passivity as suspect the depiction of reflecting the exaggerated vision at the forefront of the skeptic interpretation. Such exaggerated passivity can be returned in undoing the other: "As if the alternative to passiveness—or receptiveness—is rejection, which I take as a certain kind of confirmation of the intuition I have expressed in saying that skepticism with respect to the other, the failure of a proof of the existence of the other, is not a discovery but an annihilation" (*CW*, 117). In this manic phase of the skeptic recital, the rejection or annihilation of the other comes to pass as an imposed ignorance of the face, the willed rejection or even the wish to annihilate the other.

The Other and the Idea of God

There is an inextricable religious dimension in Levinas's concern for the other. Even his insistence that ethics—not metaphysics—is the first philosophy does not block the religious resonance of such a move. On the contrary, for Levinas, ethics is indispensable to the way in which he thinks the idea of God can emerge, for as he puts it: "Ethics is the spiritual optics" (*TI*, 78). Given the ambiguous relation that Cavell has to religion, this raises the question of the intimacy of their philosophy, or more precisely, how they respectively think of the relation between the finite and the infinite other. It is this relation that is at stake as Cavell draws attention to their mutual interest in Descartes's third meditation, his proof of the existence of God.[19] Cavell observes that he and Levinas draw different conclusions from Descartes's meditation (*PDT*, 145). Cavell also picks up on the way Levinas appeals to the (infinite) other as the breakup of my interiority, to which Cavell responds, "I can imagine being told that this investment is equivalent to the idea of God. While I would not wish to deny that, to accept it promises to require philosophical and religious responsibilities I do not know are mine" (*PDT*, 151).[20] To be more specific, there seem to be two issues at stake in Cavell's hesitation: the direct religious connection between the finite other and the invocation of the infinite other with its dimension of height, or of *Illeity* (Levinas's conception of God); and the way in which this relation seems to imply a sense of violence.

In order to shed light on the first issue, I take their differing interpretations of Descartes's idea of God as my point of departure. Cavell holds that tendencies found in the Reformation and in Descartes implies an altered understanding of the distance and intimacy between humanity and God. "As long as God exists, I am not alone" (*CR*, 470) can, following Cavell, be thought of as a fundamental idea to both Luther and Descartes. However, Cavell suggests that, during the aftermath of the Reformation—broadly conceived as secularization—the human other now takes on God's role in overcoming my isolation. For Cavell, the obvious question becomes what is the result of such an escape from isolation in the relation with the other: "I wish to understand how the other now bears the weight of God, shows me that I am not alone in the universe. This requires understanding the philosophical problem of the other as the trace or scar of the departure of God" (*CR*, 470). It is hard to read this passage without thinking of how Levinas also regards the other as a trace (albeit in his technical sense), and how this trace is invested with religious significance. However, for Cavell, the challenge inherent to modernity has become one of reorienting us, from the infinite to the finite other, whereas for Levinas the challenge has been to displace the sense of the divine other. Levinas does not see any mutual exclusiveness between God and the other; quite the contrary, the former can only come to pass through the latter.

Cavell's question then is "why is the existence of a finite other not sufficient to create the reality of such claims upon me?" (*PDT*, 144). In a different formulation, focusing not on the ethical call but on isolation, Cavell asks, why it is that "Descartes does not try to defeat that possibility of isolation in what would seem (to whom?) the most direct and the surest way, by locating the existence of one other finite being" (CR, 482). Viefhues-Bailey argues that Cavell invokes Descartes's conception of God at this moment in *The Claim of Reason* in order to highlight the typically skeptic fantasy by which the skeptic attempts to evade the real problem: "Theologizing is part of the evasion of the real work of accepting responsibility and being responsive to one another; and it is part of the evasion of the realization of how what counts as human is precariously dependent on the kind of acknowledgement we give or we withhold."[21] Admittedly, such a reading sheds light on Cavell's resistance toward Levinas's detection of the trace of God in the other, and yet there is something overstated in such a reading. Viefhues-Bailey's explicit aim is to overcome skeptical theologizing in order to prepare the way for what he deems a more fruitful religious imagination, beyond Christian theology. But could one not turn these questions toward theology without abandoning it entirely? And has theology not already addressed these questions? At least one of the standing preoccupations within a modernist situation, accounted for in chapter 2, should be that theology interrogates itself—especially with regard to metaphysical depictions of God that prevent real acknowledgment, of the finite as well as the infinite other. Levinas's standing contribution to theology should be located precisely here.

Before I discuss how theological ways both maintain the stress on the finite other and preserve a religious meaning, I turn to Cavell's second issue with Levinas's idea of the infinite. Levinas's indebtedness to Descartes's third meditation surely does not rely on Descartes's success in establishing the existence of God beyond doubt, but is centered on how the idea of the infinite enters us. Both Levinas and Cavell focus on Descartes's claim that I could not possess the idea of God unless it came from God. Levinas reads Descartes's point as invoking the idea of the infinite, in which the *ideatum* surpasses the idea itself; the idea of the infinite entails a thought that thinks more than it thinks (TI, 49). In Levinas's rendering, Descartes's idea of the infinite emphasizes that it must be *put* in me because such an idea cannot be produced by means of finite resources. In a way, Levinas reaches a sense of "God in me," and yet the infinite escapes the realm of consciousness and comprehension. The passivity by which the idea is put in me affects my identity, since it marks a breakup of the thinking ego: "The breakup of actuality of thought in the 'idea of God' is a passivity more passive still than passivity, like the passivity of a trauma through which the idea of God would have been put into us," Levinas writes.[22] The passivity of putting in and breaking up thus has the character of a trauma—a shock from a past that affects me so that I can represent it only retroactively, as a trace.[23]

Cavell is undoubtedly right in detecting some sense of violence at work here:

> Levinas's idea is that my openness to the other—to a region "beyond" my narcissism—requires a violence associated with the infinite having been put into me: he speaks of this intervention or aggression in images of trauma, breakup, monstrosity, devastation. This event creates as it were an outside to my existence, hence an isolated, singular inside. (*PDT,* 145)

Levinas probably found such powerful imagery necessary in order to counter the violence inherent to the reign of the same in Western metaphysics. Included within this tradition is the epistemological project that fosters the modern skeptic as understood by Cavell. A passage from *The Claim of Reason* sheds light on Cavell's reading of Levinas at this juncture, both with respect to the mutual creation of outside and inside, exteriority and interiority, but also with respect to violence. Having Descartes and Protestantism in mind, Cavell writes that the creation of a "singular inside" was accompanied by the idea "that to know or be known by another is to penetrate or be penetrated by another, to occupy or be occupied. . . . Hence its overcoming will take the form of violating that privacy" (*CR,* 470).

From Cavell's perspective, however, such violent images as breakups and penetration might contain a strange attraction—a skeptical attraction. The idea of privacy is, following Cavell's suggestion, interlocked with the idea of God by way of penetration, which has its sexual counterpart in sadomasochism. But closer to Cavell's concern, such sadomasochism trades on the skeptic fantasy of absolute activeness and absolute passiveness in human affairs (most central to Othello), or, in a parallel version, the skeptic alteration between the craving for omnipotence and the feeling of impotence. The attraction in masochism is its suggested promise of unconditioned recognition by another (*CR,* 470). In this sense, I am relieved of my responsibilities for acknowledging the other, since that is taken care of regardless of my response. But I am also relieved of the responsibility of making myself known, since according to the masochistic model the authentication of my existence can be passively received, as Viefhues-Bailey has argued.[24] The invocation of sadomasochism might be turned critically toward Levinas, in asking him whether there is more than a hint of it in his account (taken hostage, traumatized, persecuted). While it is obviously unreasonable to think that Levinas's God would alleviate me of my responsibilities, Levinas's depiction leads to Cavell's question of whether his ethical and theological ideals "can become a monstrous undertaking, placing infinite demands upon finite resources" (*CR,* 470). Cavell is thinking of my ethical responsibilities not only to the other, say in substitution, but also to overinvesting in the idea of the other. Yet for Levinas, the possible monstrosity of the demand put on me is a subscription to the phenomenological urgency of my infinite responsibility for the other—I am elected, responsible for all. But is this something that can be endured without lapsing into skeptic violence, either in the form of paranoid attack or manic denial? To endure it, one might have to be Christ or messiah.

Christ and Violence

Such Christological or messianic themes are indeed present in both Cavell and—in a Jewish inflection—Levinas. If there is a "best case" of acknowledging the humanity of the other, it must for Cavell be regarded as pertaining to each and every other that we encounter every day. But might it not be someone who represents humanity as such in an exemplary way? For Christianity it is crucial that humanity as the true *imago Dei* is represented exemplarily in Christ. In discussing Descartes, Cavell both makes use of and displaces related Christological motives. Descartes's conception of being composed of contrary substances

> is the idea of a double nature, symbolized centrally in the culture we share with him (but perhaps now only in literature) as the figure of Christ. So the thing of incarnation, the mysterious meeting of heaven and earth, occurs in Descartes's thought not only in the inspirer of Christianity but in each individual human being. From here you may conclude that the human problem in recognizing other human beings is the problem of recognizing another to be Christ for oneself. (CR, 483)

It is possible to read Cavell here as distancing himself from Christianity by showing how it has inspired the impasse of Descartes's mind-body dualism. But the passage certainly allows for more fecund readings, as well. In one of his alternative formulations, Cavell mentions the Christological theme in a discussion of the modern problem of acknowledging individual existence: "[W]e are as capable of knowing our individuality, or accepting the individuality of another, as we are of becoming Christ for one another" (VW, 93).

Such ideas are paralleled in Levinas's thought. Reflecting on the meaning of a Man-God, Levinas points out that it concerns the humiliation of the most high. Even though Levinas never allows for the revelation of God in one particular historic person, he still emphasizes divine manifestation in human humility—in the vanquished, the poor, the persecuted. Only in such radical humility can God disturb the order absolutely without participating in it, entailing that

God always manifests himself through my neighbor. More specifically, its man-ifestation is found in the naked face that leaves a trace, a trace that signifies "the proximity of God in the countenance of my fellowman."[25] As we have seen, it is also exactly this transcending dimension or trace that triggers violence: in the first instance because it escapes my appropriation, and alternatively, because it puts me in a posture of passivity that I want to deny. Now, since this trace is the dimension of the revelation of God or *Illeity*, this adds a further insight into vio-lence: the aggression is directed toward God.

But if *Illeity* must be sought in the trace, messianism must be found on the hither side of subjectivity, according to Levinas. Such possible messianism is con-nected to Levinas's discussion of incarnation, which for him means being "in one's skin" as vulnerable to wounds and outrages (*OB*, 108). Incarnation can fur-ther only be understood within the logic of substitution, which is the full impli-cations of subjectivity as "one for the other." If one moreover takes up Cavell's problem of recognizing another to be Christ or messiah, a strange, inverted echo can be found in Levinas. It is not a question of letting "another be Christ for one-self," as Cavell will have it, but that *I* must be messiah for the other. No one can demand sacrifice of the other for oneself—I can only demand such a sacrifice of myself for others:

> I alone can, without cruelty, be designated as victim. The *I* is the one
> who, before all decision, is elected to bear all the responsibility for
> the World. Messianism is the apogee in Being—a reversal of being
> "preserving in his being"—which begins in me.[26]

To the extent that Cavell supplies sketches of a Christology—taken more as a figure than an object of faith—he does so by giving full weight to finitude with-out immediate recourse to the infinite. This is, I suggest, a way of maintaining focus on the finite other, without abolishing the possibility of a religious dimen-sion. In his remarkable discussion of whether *King Lear* is a Christian play, Cavell argues that its possible Christian bearing cannot mean that the play illustrates theology, nor that Cordelia depicts the resurrected Christ and thus shows us re-demption. One might, however, regard the play as Christian in a narrower, but perhaps more fertile way, by centering on Cordelia's suffering rejection along with her uncompromising acceptance of it. Cordelia becomes fully human by ac-cepting her separateness despite her father's inability to acknowledge her, and by her maintaining love despite its unacceptability (*DK*, 73). In this, Cavell's apho-rism seems to apply to her: "The crucified human body is our best picture of the unacknowledged human soul" (*CR*, 430). Cavell also suggests a more daring in-terpretation, which is that we regard Cordelia as throwing our redemption into question, which suggests that all appeals to gods and miracles are distractions or excuses, "because the imagination uses them to wish for final solutions, when what is needed is at hand or nowhere." But significantly, Cavell then immediately asks, "But isn't this what Christ meant?" Cordelia's grace is not unearthly, as she is "the only good character whose attention is wholly on earth, on the person nearest her" (*DK*, 74).[27]

I do not rule out the possibility that Cavell might be suggesting a way to human self-redemption that only parallels Christ. But following the leads in the opposite direction—that is, against Cavell's insistence on the finite other as our best case, along with his reservations against Levinas's infinite other—does not necessarily exclude a Christological reading. Such a Christology, however, has to be reached indirectly, not by invoking signs of divine identity (miracles and final solutions), but by accepting that their renunciation is part of Christ's uncompromised acceptance of finitude. If this is so, revelation does not so much indicate a realm "beyond," as it does refer to the revelation of God's humanity in its descent to the ordinary. Such Christological themes are foreshadowed in the classical teaching of God's *kenosis*, the self-emptying of divine majesty in the lowliest, with Paul's hymn to the Philippians (2:7–8) as its biblical background. The humiliation of incarnation is fulfilled in the death of God, where God identifies himself even with the godforsaken.[28] Merleau-Ponty has captured this insight: "There is a sort of impotence of God without us, and Christ attests that God would not be fully God without becoming fully man. Claudel goes so far as to say that God is not above us but beneath us . . . Transcendence no longer hangs over man: he becomes, strangely, its privileged bearer."[29]

Cavell's reading of *King Lear* opens up a possible way to conceive the relation between violence and God. In chapter 4, I pointed out how sin could be regarded as a revolt against and denial of our own human conditions, and consequently how sin comes to expression in our relations to ourselves, the other, and God. On the cross, all these relations are compressed and crystallized; Jesus's death is the moment when Christ takes the human condition fully into himself (*DK*, 73). It demonstrates that human finitude and separateness can indeed lead to denial and its utter consequence, murder—and at the same time, God posits himself amid this murderousness, as its victim. Christ starts to take on the role of a scapegoat, as does Cordelia, bearing the consequences of our violent rejections of one another.

If we bring the themes of violence, sacrifice, and incarnation together as humiliation, and add the trope of the scapegoat that comes up in Cavell's reading of *King Lear*, we have a cluster of themes that makes the reference to René Girard's non-sacrificial reading of the cross irresistible. Girard's socio-psychological theory of mimetic violence—a theory where society is depicted as harboring potential violence due to the rivalry of the same desired objects—is of course not re-flected in Cavell. Neither is there in Cavell any general theory of the scapegoat mechanism, where this mechanism provides a temporary relief from the potentially violent state of crisis. What makes Girard's conception relevant, however, is the way he thinks of the cross as unmasking the lie at the heart of the scapegoating, namely the false conviction that the cause of the crisis is the innocent victim, not us. At first sight, the passion story seems to fit perfectly into the scapegoat mechanism: Christ is regarded as the cause of the crisis state and therefore sentenced to death. But, according to Girard, the point of the story is to deconstruct emphatically the sacrificial logic: it assumes its structure in order to burst it open from the inside. For when God identifies himself with the innocent victim, the basic belief in the sacrifice's justification becomes impossible, and this also undermines the effectiveness of the scapegoat mechanism—no longer can we believe that real or ritualized scapegoating is a legitimate solution to violence.[30] The responsibility is returned to its rightful place once it becomes clear that *we* are the ones who are participating in and perpetuating the violence. The cross is not seen as God demanding satisfaction and hence a perfect sacrifice; what the Gospels lay bare, in Girard's rendering, is that the cross is the consequence of unjustifiable and entirely human violence. It does not undo the thought of Christ as both God and man, the transcendence in immanence, but displaces it: the transcendence is the resolutely non-violent Kingdom of God transcending the kingdom of violence in which it is enacted.[31]

Much of Cavell's reading of Cordelia as a reflection of Christ depends on seeing her as a scapegoat, and also for Cavell, the moral of recognizing her as such is to reveal our own hands in the scapegoating. In Cavell's view, this is strangely reflected in the way the medium of theater works. As long as we, the spectators of *King Lear,* are not ready to absorb this lesson, Cavell argues, we regard ourselves at a distance from what happens on the stage. Precisely by showing how Cordelia is Lear's scapegoat, the play offers us a reflection of how Lear is *our* scapegoat (*DK,* 75). For our relation to him on stage literalizes our refusal to acknowledge ourselves and others outside theatre: we prefer to stay fixed and hidden, construing distance, and denying our presence in front of the other. Our theatricalization of others is, in Cavell's reading, our way of denying how we make them suffer our distortions and rejections. Unlike Girard's projected violence, Cavell emphasizes our withholding of our presence, acknowledgment, and love. But all the same, Christ remains the exemplary human who bears the full weight of our violence: "Christ receives reflection in every form of human scapegoat, every way in which one man bears the brunt of another's distortion and rejection" (*DK,* 80).

For Girard, the cross means, or should mean, the end of scapegoating and the redirection of our mimetic desires, and similarly, Cavell thinks that in *King Lear* we are offered a disclosure of ourselves, an occasion to stop, to turn around, and hence to change. This must be theater's offer of catharsis. But if it can offer such catharsis, theater must compete with religion (*PDT*, 59) for it is perhaps only forgiveness and grace that can bring about such a change.

SEVEN

Forgiveness and Passivity

In the previous three chapters, I have attempted to outline what I have sometimes called an anthropology of finitude. The basic findings seemed less than cheerful, such that we are finite and mortal and yet revolt against our conditions (chapter 4), that we are vulnerable to tragic consequences because we speak and act in ways that outrun our previews (chapter 5), and that we, confronted with the otherness of the other, harbor violent impulses (chapter 6). If one holds these considerations together, one reaches a reasonable backdrop of what makes forgiveness important to human affairs—that is, why humans stand in need of some kind of change or new start that alters those constellations.

In his essay on Austin and Derrida, discussed in chapter 5, Cavell offers no hope for a quick resolution. Indeed, Austin's understanding of excuses is frequently drawn upon. However, excuses are neither able nor meant to relieve us of our responsibility for what we have said and done, but serve more modestly to delimit our responsibility. Indirectly, however, Cavell takes Austin to point toward a region beyond excuses: "Excuses mark out the region of tragedy, the beyond of the excusable, the justifiable, the explainable (the civic?)." Cavell then asks, "Who among philosophers has a theory of forgiveness, and whether it is givable? It would be a theory of comedy" (*PoP*, 87). Despite the strange dismissive ring to this question, Cavell cannot be taken to mean that we lack philosophical theories of forgiveness, for Cavell would surely have known the number of prominent philosophers who have offered such theories. Admittedly, Cavell himself has never developed a sustained and systematic account of forgiveness as such, even if he touches upon the topic at significant junctures. But Cavell has surely much to say about comedies—first and foremost as they were developed in the Hollywood genre he dubbed "comedies of remarriage." If we also include Cavell's writing on Shakespeare's late romances, we see that Cavell in fact brings up the topic of forgiveness exactly in this context.

In his readings of those works, Cavell's understanding of forgiveness is, unsurprisingly, understood within the framework of skepticism and acknowledgment. This means that the theoretical level at which forgiveness is discussed moves on a level other than the widespread moral-philosophical discussion of forgiveness and its typical traits and moral qualities. Similar to how morality enters Cavell thinking, forgiveness is discussed never in isolation, but always as part of the reflection of our conditions and our relation to those conditions. Charles Griswold has suggested a subgroup of forgiveness that captures the apt level and the central themes in Cavell's discussion. What Griswold labels "metaphysical forgiveness" is designed to counter vengeful desires directed against existence as such, not least as they are captured in Nietzsche's *ressentiment*.[1] In keeping with this, I begin here by tracing forgiveness in Cavell's writing on Shakespearean romances and Hollywood comedies of remarriage, focusing on vengeance and forgiveness. The second half of the chapter attempts to circle in the difficulty in being forgiven. The latter problem of letting oneself be forgiven leads to an abiding and ambiguous theme in Cavell's writing, already encountered more than once, namely human passivity.

Revenge and Forgiveness in *The Winter's Tale*

In the previous chapter, I made extensive use of Klein's understanding of the paranoid-schizoid position and the manic defense against it as it occurs in early psychological development. However, little was said about how, during normal maturation, the paranoid-schizoid position tends to progress into what Klein calls a depressive position. Such a depressive position is one in which the sense of guilt comes into being, and such a sense of guilt, Klein argues, is expressed in the urge to make reparation and achieve reconciliation. Both the paranoid-schizoid and the depressive positions are, in Cavell's reading, reflected in the trajectory of Shakespeare's *The Winter's Tale*:

> *The Winter's Tale*, as what is called a romance, epitomizes this phase [i.e., the paranoid-schizoid phase] in its first half (the first three of its five acts), then moves to the reparative phase in its second half, whose closing acceptance by Leontes of the gift of the live Hermione I have spoken of as Shakespeare's competition with religion. The question of Hermione's resurrection apart, . . . Leontes's acceptance of forgiveness for his unforgiveable actions requires an achievement of something I am prepared to call a passiveness beyond passiveness. (*PDT*, 153)

In these rather brief remarks offered at the end of his response to Levinas, Cavell not only connects Klein and Shakespeare's play in a suggestive way, he also betrays that his reading of that play has everything to do with forgiveness, even resurrection and (competition with) religion. In order to understand the implications of forgiveness at this juncture in Shakespeare's play, it is necessary to see what the forgiveness is supposed to forgive—which reveals yet another face of the recurrent skeptic.

In fact, the quotation can be regarded as the conclusion to an earlier essay of Cavell's, namely his reading of *The Winter's Tale* in "Recounting Gains, Showing Losses." Shakespeare's play opens by introducing us to the mutual friendship between Leontes, king of Sicily, and Polixenes, king of Bohemia, and with the happy marriage between Leontes and Hermione that has brought them two children, including their son Mamillius. Seemingly without motivation, Leontes becomes obsessed with the most drastic jealousy found in Shakespeare's entire body of work (perhaps only matched by Othello). Occasioned by casual and insignificant utterances, Leontes begins to suspect not only that Polixenes and Hermione are having an affair, but also that their affair might have resulted in the conception of Mamillius. Leontes soon seeks criteria that can prove his parenthood: comparing features and marks of his son and himself, but to no avail. Such marks and feature cannot offer compelling evidence for parenthood, for, as we know by now, criteria cannot provide the kind of epistemological certainty that the skeptic craves. Even to search for such a certainty betrays a distortion of Leontes's relation to his son, since in general to take one's children as one's own is not a matter of knowledge, but of acknowledgment, expressed in the various everyday ways in which one affirms the relation to them (*DK*, 203). To the extent that the skeptic refuses acknowledgment and unceasingly craves certainty for himself, his ability to participate in our mutual language proportionally fades. In this play, the refusal proves severe: going increasingly mad, Leontes comes to repudiate the mutual attunement on which our criteria depend, only to arrive at a situation where words are bereft of their significance (*DK*, 206).

This interpretation of the first part of the play, consisting of acts 1 to 4, only diagnoses, as it were, the symptoms of Leontes's madness; Cavell's interpretation goes further into its original source. In accordance with Cavell's understanding of skepticism in general, Leontes's doubt is not originally caused by some epistemic failure to assess his parenthood (which is, however, how he sees it himself), but by a *willed* avoidance: he secretly does not want to be Mamillius's father, but wants to deny their bonds as well as the son's independence. Nevertheless, Leontes's rejection of his own son is derivative of an even more profound rejection, Cavell argues. Not only cannot Leontes bear the existence of his issue, he cannot bear the entire field of issuing and breeding, that is, the circle of life as such. In light of such a perception, Leontes turns into a full-fledged nihilist in Nietzsche's sense by assuming the nothingness of ordinary life. In *On the Genealogy of Morality,* Nietzsche thinks that the *ressentiment* of the (Judeo-Christian) slave revolt is nourished by the same desire as the noble masters, namely the will to power. However, being frustrated by their own impotence, the weak cannot exercise such will directly and therefore seek to win through other paths: through their spiritual revenge on life as such.[2]

What is it about life that insults Leontes and fuels his wish for revenge? Behind Leontes's vengeful nihilism, Cavell detects a wish for absolute plenitude without separation, that is, an existence without the need for counting. Counting here implies recounting or telling what counts, an ability that rests on a common appreciation of the values at the heart of our criteria of common intelligibility; but counting also presupposes the acceptance of the economy of exchange between separate beings, call it the economy of life (*DK*, 208; *CR*, 94). Given the economy of life in which we take part, the wish for absolute plenitude is doomed to be disappointed. More specifically, the disappointing truth is that all are "apart from everything of which we are part, always already dissevered, which above all here means . . . that each is part, only part, that no one is everything, that apart from this part that one has, there is never nothing, but always others" (*DK*, 208). Leontes is craving for absolute plenitude, or else nothing at all. But the inescapable facts such as separation and disserving mean that each one of us is only partial. There is, however, also another side of the coin, as Cavell repeatedly points out: separation and disserving are also conditions for being related. Cavell notes how the relation between the kings of Sicily and Bohemia has previously been expressed in their exchange of gifts. But as Leontes comes to regard it, the troubling thing is that one cannot receive gifts without becoming indebted to the other, and by trying to reciprocate the gift, one only deepens the relation. Fearing indebtedness, Leontes despairs at such mutually deepening bonds and longs for metaphysical evenness where nothing counts, the annihilation of any debt whatsoever:

> Payment in such case would do the reverse of what he wants, it would increase what he wishes to cease; it would imply the concept of indebtedness, hence of otherness. And this sense of the unpayable, the unforgivability of one's owing, as it were for being the one one is, for so to speak the gift of life, produces a wish to revenge oneself upon existence, on the fact, or facts, of life as such. (*DK*, 211)

The metaphysical indebtedness is for Leontes deeply threatening, because it inscribes passivity and dependence in his own identity; it also causes despair since there is no way to get even for the gift of life, except in renouncing participation in it. To Leontes, owing his existence to the generosity of life or creation is an unforgiveable insult to which he reacts with the drastic revenge upon existence as such.

Cavell has called the second part of the play, deployed in the fifth act, both the reparative phase and the path to recovery. It culminates in the scene where Hermione, whom Leontes believes to be dead, is disguised as a statue that miraculously returns to life. It seems clear that Shakespeare here is both playing

with the art of theater, which has the power to bring words to life, and mirroring the resurrection of Christ.[3] Cavell does not directly deny the pertinence of
a Christological reading of the resurrection scene, but he takes the scene primarily as a wedding ceremony, or perhaps better: a ceremony of remarriage.
For Leontes and Hermione have already had a marriage, which, as a result of
Leontes's nihilism, ended in turning them both dead to each other, envisaged
in Hermione's appearance as a statue. Literalizing both Leontes's former cold-
ness to her and his blindness for her humanity, the illusion of Hermione being a
statue is unveiled as she starts moving toward him, in flesh and blood. According to Cavell's insistence on this scene as a wedding ceremony, the recognition
must be mutual: as she moves toward Leontes, he must reply in kind. Hermione
must become alive, and Leontes must acknowledge her, both in the sense of confessing his former blindness to her and allowing for their mutual recognition of
each other. When the marriage is re-enacted, it is a matter of mutual resurrection to one another. They must become both one flesh, according to Genesis,
while remaining separate:

> Then let us emphasize that this ceremony of union takes the form
> of a ceremony of separation, thus declaring that the question of two
> becoming one is just half the problem; the other half is how one be-
> comes two. It is separation that Leontes's participation in parturi-
> tion grants—that Hermione has, that there is, a life beyond his, and
> that she can create a life beyond his and hers, and beyond plenitude
> and nothingness. (*DK*, 220)

In Leontes's case, the recovery from his nihilism not only involves their mutual
creation of each other, but also their capability of having children, and the latter requires further acceptance of separation as the condition for offspring created beyond the two of them. For Leontes to achieve this, he must surrender his
revenge on life by accepting the indebtedness that goes with the exchange implied in the gift of life.

In a sense, interpreting the scene as a marriage ceremony is compatible with
the Christological interpretation of the resurrection scene: leaving aside certain
mystical visions of a marriage with Christ, it is in both cases a matter of turning
death into life, resulting in becoming "new creation" (1. Cor. 5:17). But there is an
even stronger sense that makes such compatibility feasible: in both cases, the resurrection is bound up with the offer of forgiveness.[4] As Cavell takes it, Hermione
does offer Leontes such forgiveness for his rejection of her and his family and perhaps for his entire rage against life; but the question is whether Leontes is prepared to *allow himself* to be forgiven. "Has Leontes accomplished this?" Cavell
asks, and points out what that would require: "It seems to be the form in which

the revenge against life (as Nietzsche almost said), the weddedness to nothing-ness, is foregone, forgotten" (*DK*, 220). I return to the question of allowing oneself to be forgiven, but for the moment it is sufficient to observe that Leontes seems to allow himself to be forgiven. Although Cavell is rather brief when it comes to forgiveness at this decisive juncture, it cannot be doubted that much of the logic of his reading finds its resolution here. Accepting forgiveness is the proper remedy for Leontes's nihilism, for while the source of his malaise is revenge on life, forgiveness means the foregoing of that revenge in accepting its gifts. Leon-tes's wish for nothing has changed; "*The Winter's Tale* shows what it may be to find in oneself the life of the world" (*DK*, 221).

Forgiveness, Remarriage, and the Recurrence of the Diurnal

The marriage scene in Shakespeare's play dramatizes the way forgiveness is the key to a renewed mutual acknowledgment, implying at once separation and dependence. Cavell has identified in the Hollywood comedies of remarriage a similar structure that is constitutive of the genre: The couple reaches a crisis in which the female part is disappointed with the marriage as it stands, leading to some form of divorce. The future of the couple then depends on the man and his ability to take the next step: he must overcome his limited perception of his spouse in a way that allows her to come fully into existence beyond the restrictions of their previous marriage or relation. Having attracted her attention again, the man must offer his confession and request some form of forgiveness (*PH*, 31–32). Or as Espen Hammer aptly puts it,

> He [the male part in those films] confesses his guilt of having denied her, and by implication of having rejected his own dependence on her. If she accepts his confession, that is, if she responds in kind, with appropriate emotion and action, thus showing her unrestricted ac-knowledgement of him, then the couple achieves what Cavell calls a state of forgiveness.[5]

Forgiveness is central to these films because it marks the way out of the mutual circle of revenge—the focus on such circles has led Cavell at times to speak of the genre as "revenge comedies." Forgiveness, as giving up mutual vengeance, is a condition for getting back together and for mutual acknowledgment. As Cavell puts it, these films "leads to acknowledgement; to the reconciliation of a genuine forgiveness; a reconciliation so profound as to require the metamor-phosis of death and revival" (*PH*, 19). Small wonder, then, that Cavell regards the comedies of remarriage to be heirs to Shakespeare's romances, for all the basic ingredients are indeed anticipated in *The Winter's Tale*: revenge, reconciliation, mutual acknowledgment, forgiveness, and metamorphosis from death to life.

Apart from conceiving acknowledgment, reconciliation, and forgiveness as related, we have gained little information as to how Cavell more substantially understands forgiveness. Further reflections are added in *The Pursuit of Happiness*, for example when Cavell understands the working of forgiveness as "putting the past into the past and clearing the future for a new start," but immediately after, Cavell also points to a further aspect: "I have at various junctures characterized this forgiving, the condition of remarriage, as the foregoing of revenge" (*PH*, 261). Indeed, these two dimensions—the temporal dimension and the foregoing of revenge—are widely recognized as belonging to the concept of forgiveness. For Arendt and other philosophers, the temporal dimension means that in forgiving the victim unbinds the wrongdoer from his or her enchainment to the past misdeeds—it puts "the past into the past." Arendt regards Jesus's teaching of forgiveness as outlining what real miracles are about: it not only puts an end to the reactive and compulsory stance toward the past, but it opens the presence for something truly new—as if allegorizing the miracle of our natality.[6] The second dimension, that of forgoing revenge, also echoes an insight of forgiveness that dates back at least to Joseph Butler's classical sermons on the topic: to forgive someone requires one to forswear both revenge and the excessive feeling of resentment.[7] Cavell's original contribution to the understanding of forgiveness may, however, be linked to how he perceives the internal connection between the temporal dimension and the forswearing of revenge.

When discussing forgiveness in his readings of the Hollywood comedies, Cavell alternates between Kierkegaard's and Nietzsche's perspectives in his typical manner. Surprisingly, Cavell chooses Nietzsche as his guide to understanding forgiveness—surprisingly, because Nietzsche holds that forgiveness is available only for those who do not have the strength to confront their noble enemy. "[N]ot being able to avenge one's self, is called not wishing to avenge one's self, perhaps even forgiveness," Nietzsche states, before aiming unmistakably at Christianity: "They also talk of the 'love of their enemies' and sweat thereby."[8] But it is always possible to make use of fruitful aspects of Nietzsche's thinking, even where it conflicts with his overarching project. As Nietzsche sees it, vengeance is tied up with temporality: the irreversibility of time, the inexorable "It was" that cannot be altered by the will, appears as an insult. And from that insult grows the wish for revenge in the sense of the will's reluctance toward the passing of time as such.[9] As Cavell points out, Leontes's revenge on life also takes the form of revenge on time, but for Leontes's part it is directed not so much at "It was" of the past as at "It will be." At least in the first part of the play (acts 1 to 4), it is not past failures, remorse, or guilt that torture Leontes, but rather the perception of the future as in itself an issue of the present that inexorably brings along further fecundity beyond control (*DK*, 211).

Nietzsche has not only unmasked the deep-seated desire for revenge, but has also suggested the overcoming of it—which brings me to the crux of Cavell's attraction to Nietzsche. By what he calls three spiritual metamorphoses, Nietzsche captures the decisive succeeding steps inherent to the plot of the comedies of remarriage. First, the spirit must become a camel in order to be weight-bearing—that is, it must endure the marriage with respect and awe. Then it must become a lion, with its "No" in order to create freedom for itself, reflected in the films' state of divorce. The transference to this state might be caused by disappointment on the female part, but it quickly proceeds to a state of mutual vengeance. Finally, the spirit must become a child: the child is the figure of the "sacred Yes," the new beginning promised at the end of the films.[10] For Cavell, Nietzsche's figure of the child captures forgiveness insofar as he ties the overcoming of past and the overcoming of revenge together, and thus establishes a new start, as Arendt will have it —or in Cavell's words, the "winning of a new beginning, a new creation, an innocence, by changes that effect or constitute the overcoming of revenge" (PH, 261).

Such metamorphoses bring about a new perception of time, as Nietzsche encapsulates in the affirmation of the eternal return of the same. Following Cavell, such a perception of time does not lead away from the ordinary toward the grand or sublime, even as "eternal" seems to suggest such; rather, Cavell thinks of Nietzsche as recasting Kierkegaard's sense of repetition—in Cavell's inflection, the repetition of the ordinary or, as he sometimes prefers, the diurnal. In a passage where Cavell reflects on his willingness to call the films "diurnal comedy," he writes:

> The title registers, to my mind, the two most impressive affirmations known to me of the task of human experience, the acceptance of human relatedness, as the acceptance of repetition. Kierkegaard's study called *Repetition*, which is the study of the possibility of marriage; and Nietzsche's Eternal Return, the call for which he puts by saying it is high time, a heightening or ascension of time; this is literally *Hochzeit*, German for marriage, with time itself as the ring. As redemption by suffering does not depend on something that has already happened, so redemption by happiness does not depend on something that has yet to happen; both depend on a faith in something that is always happening, day by day. (PH, 241)

In Cavell's suggestion, both Kierkegaard's and Nietzsche's perspectives highlight how time ties together remarriage and the everyday. The description of past and future versus the present clearly echoes Nietzsche's temporality but also Kierkegaard's account of recollection and hope versus repetition at the introduction of *Repetition*.[11] Furthermore, *Repetition* certainly refers to a young man's love relation to a woman. But Cavell's suggestion that the book is a study of marriage seems at first sight misleading, since the young man is redeemed from his despair precisely at the moment he learns that the woman in question is married to another. However, Cavell might still be right, for even though the young man finds meaning in Job's wailing and eventual surrender before God, the man is ultimately unable to make the second move, from the resignation and back into the ordinary, where everything is regained. Yet, precisely this double movement is the transcendent or religious sense of repetition.

In a related passage, alluding to the wedding at Cana (John 2:1–12), Kierkegaard writes that faith does not stop with "turning water into wine—it goes further and turns wine into water," which suggests to me an incorporation of the religious within the ordinary, as discussed in chapter 2.[12] If the young man portrayed in *Repetition* had been capable of conducting such a repetition, however, he would presumably have married the girl. As if providing a clue to this interpretation, I note that Cavell chose a sentence from Kierkegaard's journals as the epitaph to *Pursuits of Happiness:* "Had I had faith I should have remained with Regine." Repetition, understood in this religious sense, does not return you to the same, but the same altered—holding true for reunion as well as the return to the ordinary, both emblematized in Cavell's notion of remarriage. Only after the realization of the unavoidable separation is remarriage possible.[13]

However, the returning to the diurnal would demand both a confession and a request for forgiveness. As the forgiveness comes to pass within the comedy of remarriage, it is a matter not so much of an individual act or state of mind as of an unfulfilled project—as part of the quest for moral perfectionism, as Cavell comes to speak of it. It is perhaps for this reason that Cavell at this place invokes his favorite quotation from Luther: "All our life should be baptism" (*PH*, 239). This time it is regarded as neither a motto of romantic poetry (cf. *MWM*, 229) nor a promise of a yet-unattained self and society, as perhaps in *Senses of Walden*, but as expressing the will to return to and pursue marriage, unsponsored by a civil institution or sacramental status. Such displacement of the constitution of marriage also means a return to the ordinary as the locale for a continued life together, where forgiveness of the major and minor divorces that constitute domestic life becomes a repeated step that must continually be made anew. To regard forgiveness as integral to the diurnal is in keeping with the central temporal dimensions inherent to the concept of forgiveness: divorcing from the past, gaining a new start, striving for a yet-unattained state. Whether in Nietzsche's or Kierkegaard's sense, forgiveness is never over and done with, but is an unfulfilled promise to be pursued day by day. Forgiveness regarded as internal to the quest for the ordinary implies a particular stance toward the ordinary that Cavell understands as a "devotion to repetition, to dailiness" (*PH*, 241).

It is possible, however, that Cavell too hastily conflates Nietzsche's sense and the Christian sense of the temporality of forgiveness in terms of repetition and remarriage. For according to Heidegger, to whom Cavell's reading is indebted, Nietzsche's suggested mode to will back "It was" has a competing account—the Christian account. In the latter, Heidegger notes, "It was" can be taken back in repentance, which takes place in the awaiting of God's forgiveness of sins. Where this forgiveness is grasped in faith a new start is granted, and thereby an altered relation to the past comes into being. In Heidegger's reading, such repentance smacks too much of Nietzsche's *ressentiment* directed against being as such—it is just another version of the will to nothing.[14] But there are reasons to believe that the Christian outlook is as eager to refute the very same will to nothingness as Nietzsche, for it is precisely in terms of the will's inclination toward nothing that Augustine conceives of the Fall: the will becomes inclined toward that which lacks being.[15] Since sin is what Christian life is supposed to counter with the aid of divine grace, divine forgiveness might be thought of as initiating a change of the will's direction. With that changed direction, the perception of time also undergoes transformation, where the returning of days can be seen, not as a prolonged chain, but as a standing opportunity. According to Kierkegaard's double movement, the ordinary is thus received back.

The Economy of Forgiveness

This latter reflection on forgiveness as internal to the everyday, emblematically expressed in remarriage, suggests that forgiveness comes to expression at crucial junctures of Cavell's thought. Still, it is clear that there are limits to how long Cavell's remarks on the topic can be stretched. Cavell does not discuss, for instance, the vexed question of the possibility of a radically one-sided, unconditional forgiveness, but certain indications follow from what he says. However, important voices in the contemporary debate such as Derrida claim that forgiveness only qualifies as such if it is unconditional, indeed only if it forgives the unforgivable. As if he were commenting on Cavell's position, Derrida discards the tempering of forgiveness with mutual understanding, common language, and reconciliation: "ordinary forgiveness . . . is anything but forgiveness."[16]

To understand Derrida's position, it is necessary to keep in mind that he elaborates his ideas in clear polemic against what he sees as political misuse of forgiveness (forgiveness as a strategic means of stabilization of transnational relations, of bringing exchange into normal order, as a therapeutic means, etc.). But it is also necessary to realize how Derrida's thinking deals with the impact of economic logic. The clue to the importance of such a connection can be traced in the semantic link that exists in many languages between forgiveness and gift. Speaking of the gift, Derrida attests to its undeniable connection with economics, not least the figure of the circle, as in circular exchange. Semantically, economy includes

> the values of law (*nomos*) and of home (*oikos*, home, property, family, the hearth, the fire indoors). *Nomos* does not only signify the law in general, but also the law of distribution (*nemein*), the law of sharing or partition, the law as partition (*moira*), the given as assigned part, participation.[17]

This way of connecting the homely—let us say, the domestic and the ordinary—and the law of distributing, sharing, and participation to the logic of the gift parallels how a certain use of economic vocabulary strikes Cavell. In his early book on Thoreau's *Walden,* Cavell offered a lengthy account of how economic terms pervaded Thoreau's prose; but of more importance is how Cavell considers such vocabulary to be crucial for understanding the development in *The Winter's Tale.* According to his reading, the play contains two regions: first, that of telling and retelling, which amounts to counting and recounting, hence to its preoccupation with computation and business and the exchange of money (*DK,* 199–200); and second, that of breeding and issuing, interpreting relatedness as indebtedness, exchange of gifts, reciprocation, and the desire for getting even in terms of the annihilation of debt (*DK,* 210–211). And more generally, the whole play follows the economic trajectory from loss to gain.

Put aside these promising parallels for the moment in order to turn to Derrida's understanding of the gift. The decisive point for Derrida is how the gift presupposes and, at the same time, radically disrupts the economic logic of exchange: the gift, in its pure sense, qualifies as such to the extent that it defies exchange, reciprocity, return, and debt. While these economic terms make up the conditions of possibility of the gift, they simultaneously designate the conditions of its impossibility.[18] Against this background, the claim that only the unforgivable can be forgiven begins to make sense. Even though it is widely held that forgiveness requires some kind of reciprocity (e.g., that forgiveness is granted on the condition that it is asked for, that the guilty shows repentance, and that he or she has been changed), Derrida is resolute in thinking that forgiveness resists any exchange. It must be impossible: in its radical purity it must be "excessive, hyperbolic, mad."[19] Even if Cavell at times expresses his suspicion that Derrida takes part in the flight from the ordinary, Derrida does emphatically not detach his notion of forgiveness from speech, history, politics, and the law. For forgiveness is not only impossible, it is also an *aporia:*

> if our idea of forgiveness falls into ruin as soon as it is deprived of its pole of absolute reference, namely its unconditional purity, it remains nonetheless inseparable from what is heterogeneous to

it, namely the order of conditions, repentance, transformation, as many things as allow it to inscribe itself in history, law, politics, existence itself.[20]

Derrida not only insists on this aporetic position, but, furthermore, shows that precisely the undecidability of such a position is what calls on responsibility: "It is between these two poles, *irreconcilable but indissociable,* that decisions and responsibilities are to be taken."[21]

Let me return to the parallelism, or better, inverted parallelism, of Derrida's and Cavell's invocations of economic logic. For Derrida, both the gift and forgiveness instantiate impossibilities that breach the economy of reciprocity and exchange. While forgiveness must be inscribed in institutions and in history, it keeps its secret in reserve—it cannot be exhausted by them. In this sense, forgiveness conveys a dimension that points beyond the economic logic. Even though Cavell does not discuss unconditional forgiveness, and although he obviously regards forgiveness on par with reconciliation and a return to the domestic, he still can draw on economic logic, sometimes speaking of forgiveness in terms of gifts (*PDT,* 153). Nonetheless, Cavell draws a conclusion nearly the opposite of Derrida's. The gift of forgiveness, as Cavell sees it, does not disrupt the economic exchange; on the contrary, forgiveness is the offer that opens the possibility of a new stance *within* that economy—from revenge on it toward acceptance of participating in the exchange of life. In one sense, this perhaps places Cavell closer to John Millbank's theological alternative reading of the gift: The act of giving and of forgiving always takes place within a generous exchange of gifts always already at work. By receiving the divine gift of forgiveness, which emerges from God's initiative, one is enabled to return the gift, not by reciprocating God but by forgiving the other.[22] Cavell does not invoke the theological perspective, but suggests a primordial reception of the gift of life and, more importantly, affirms how forgiveness reinstalls us in an established social interchange of gifts.

This economic logic captures what Leontes cannot tolerate: "The literal, that is economic, ideas of paying back and of getting even allow us to see and formulate what revenge Leontes requires and why the revenge he imagines necessary for his rest only increases the necessity for it" (*DK,* 211). In Leontes's case, an overcoming of revenge in forgiveness does not mean bringing the exchange to a halt—which is indeed what Leontes wants—but placing ourselves within such an exchange, acknowledging receiving and giving as the conditions of our finite lives. The turn that is opened up by forgiveness—in terms of a divorce from the past, a change in relinquishing the grudge against "It was" together with an affirmation of "It will be"—simultaneously means a return to the diurnal, emblematized in the resurrection scene as remarriage. In this way, forgiveness implies an opportunity to re-enter the relations that are at the heart of human existence—

the relations to the other, to the world, and, according to the theological perspective, to the creator of life—and thereby to gain a new relation to oneself. For, as Cavell has pointed out, to accept one's relations as entailing both separateness and participation means that one has to accept oneself as indebted.

Metaphysical forgiveness reverts the narcissistic and isolating tendency to regard oneself as an exemption; it might take the form of accepting oneself as part of a common humanity. Cavell argues that Hermione's forgiveness happens in the absence of sufficient expiation; "as if nothing but a recognition of common humanity is sufficient to achieve this virtue, as if each instance of forgiveness constitutes in small a forgiveness for being human, a forgiveness of the human race" (*CHA,* 120). Taken in this register, elevated from particular misdeeds or faults beyond excuses, the question is what kind of guilt that forgiveness is supposed to absolve us from. In some reflections on forgiveness provided by a reading of Levinas, Derrida suggests that there is indeed a sense of guilt for being human—this is more accurately a survivor's guilt. The guiltiness for being alive stems from my substitution of the other and the other's death in Levinas's sense, and this radically questions my right to be.[23] Without pursuing Derrida's suggestions further, I note that survivor's guilt also surfaces in Cavell's reading of Coleridge's "The Rime of the Ancient Mariner," but this time with a focus on a particular blend of contempt and guilt. For as the poem goes, when the mariner survives the crew of the ship—"so many men, so beautiful"—he starts to despise other creatures along with himself: "And a thousand slimy things / Lived on; and so did I." Cavell glosses it thus:

> Then this for me means that he despises and envies his own being alive, as survivors may do. It is when, thereupon, he sees the snakes in a different light, in moonlight, that he accepts his participation as a being living with whatever is alive—accepts animals of the slime as also his others—that is, accepts the fact, or you may say the gift, of life. This begins his recovery from the death-in-life of inexpressible guilt. (*IQO,* 61)

The possibility of such acceptance, which I surmise is not optional to Derrida and Levinas, is what Cavell's forgiveness of being human amounts to. Redeemed from survivor's guilt, the mariner starts to see the creatures of the world in a new light, himself included. He is not removed from the circulation or economic exchange, but returned to it—as to life.

Passivity and the Difficulty of Forgiveness

As I noted above, Cavell points out that for Leontes to be forgiven, he must allow himself to be forgiven, accept it, whereupon Cavell asks, "Has Leontes accomplished this?" (*DK,* 220). If we leave aside the happy outcome of Shakespeare's play, Cavell touches on the general question concerning the conditions for accepting forgiveness in general. Taken in such a way, this suggests that receiving forgiveness might be difficult, and the obvious question follows: why? Perhaps the key to understanding such difficulty is suggested by a parallel formulation, referred to at the beginning of this chapter: "Leontes's acceptance of forgiveness for his unforgiveable actions requires an achievement of something I am prepared to call a passiveness beyond passiveness" (*PDT,* 153). What motives can there be for avoiding passivity? Why not receive and respond in gratitude or praise?

A similar question is raised in Cavell's reading of *King Lear:* what can move the king to avoid acknowledgment and love? *King Lear* is preoccupied with eyes and looking, and one reason for that might be the centrality of shame to the play. As shame is a reaction to being exposed to the other's gaze, the most immediate reaction to shame is to hide, as Cavell correctly observes. Hence, when Lear avoids love, particularly Cordelia's love, it is because he cannot really acknowledge her in fear of the self-revelation doing so implies. Speaking of Lear's spiritual twin, Gloucester, Cavell writes: "But if the failure to recognize others is a failure to let others recognize you, a fear of what is revealed to them, an avoidance of their eyes, then it is exactly shame which is the cause of his withholding of recognition" (*DK,* 49). Shame causes Lear to use his power and wealth to hide and thus prevent himself from being exposed to the world. Indeed, power and wealth are, in his own eyes, what makes him lovable, and when he ends up bereft of earthly glory, he consequently feels unworthy of love. "He cannot bear love when he has no reason to be loved, perhaps because of the helplessness, the passiveness, which that implies, which some take for impotence" (*DK,* 61). This shame of the passivity, the unworthiness of being loved for no other reason than being the one he is, runs so deep that the eventual redemption offered by Cordelia will, in Cavell's interpretation, subtly be avoided. His vision of their going to jail together perpetuates the fantasy of escaping being seen—it becomes just another occasion for unacknowledged love, hidden from the world (*DK,* 69).

Passivity, not least in its religious inflections, is one of the ambiguous themes in Cavell. For Cavell, Nietzsche's criticism of Christianity concerns a certain depiction of activity: "In particular, the problem seems to be that human action is everywhere disguised as human suffering: this is what acceptance of the Will to Power is to overcome" (*CR,* 352). At issue here is probably a reproach for regarding acting as something one suffers, something done to one, perhaps in contrast to a free and autonomous action. Putting aside the question of the adequacy of the perception of Christianity, such an interpretation draws close to Lear's understanding of passivity as helplessness and impotence, and hence it might easily turn into a pretext to withdraw from acting. In a note on Descartes's way of linking finitude and human dependence to the idea of God, Cavell reinforces the Nietzschean critique: "Nietzsche reinterpreted such an interpretation of dependence as an excuse for our passiveness, or self-punishment, our fear of autonomy, hence as a cover for our vengefulness, from which follows the killing of God" (IQO, 37–38). In this one sentence, Cavell in effect sums up Nietzsche's onslaught on Christianity, and the passivity in question seems to refer to the inverted will to power, inverted inward in fear of activity, only to be turned outward as spiritual revenge.[24] Ironically, perhaps, Nietzsche's critique of forgiveness also seems to fit into such an excuse for passiveness.

Nevertheless, such a summary of Nietzsche cannot be taken as expressing Cavell's exhaustive view of passivity, for, as discussions of it in earlier chapters have made evident, passivity is also something that he seeks to acknowledge and preserve. For instance, Cavell surely gives passivity its due weight within the concept of acknowledgment: in the acceptance of being addressed by a separate other, in the reception of the world beneath knowledge of it, and in the underscoring of language as heritage. In his later works, passivity and receptivity are also regarded as integral to his concept of thinking, and, of course, passivity pertains to what he has to say on forgiveness and acceptance of indebtedness.[25]

In two analyses of passivity related to Cavell's thinking and, in particular, to Cavell's notion of action, Timothy Gould regards one of Cavell's standing contributions to be that of countering the metaphysical repression of passivity, or more precisely, the metaphysical unwillingness to take into account the intimate and complex relation between passivity and activity. In the same vein as Cavell above, Gould notes how Pauline and Lutheran doctrine of justification by faith alone has affirmed that metaphysical tradition in making all actions appear essentially equal and powerless with regard to God.[26] However, as Gould discerns a significant theological resonance to Cavell's saying that the "self is concealed in assertion and action" (MWM, 72), he can surprisingly claim that the justification by faith positively expresses Cavell's central stake:

> One may hear in this concern an echo of the Christian or, more precisely, Lutheran condemnation of mere action as a means for altering the self's relation to God. Nowadays, our activities are designed to circumvent the need for acknowledgement, hence to shelter us from our awful truths. . . . But if this side of Cavell continues a certain strategy of passiveness, . . . it is through Nietzsche, I imagine, that Cavell would first have taken up the idea that most of what is called "action" (and not just by philosophers) is in fact a disguise for our passivity.[27]

This passage seems to read Luther and Nietzsche in light of each other. If one also senses an ambivalent stance toward Luther here, it is due to Nietzsche's suspicion of how passivity flows into a reactive *ressentiment;* but Luther is also cherished for emphasizing—in a way unparalleled by Nietzsche—the affirmation of passivity, as countering false activity as concealing our relation to God and to ourselves. In this reading, Luther and Nietzsche are in agreement insofar as they regard actions as the most common way to hide the truth, however differently that truth is conceived. Moreover, Gould's point seems to be that passivity is inscribed in all activity:

> And like grace, whether in the Christian's vision or in Chaplin's, it is not attained by the unaided will and its deeds. (The beauty of human action may be a consequence of such grace.) Only with a willingness for passivity—which goes beyond patience and the willingness to take our lumps—will the incessant round of human activity and action make the kind of sense we want it to make.[28]

This quotation again dwells on the connection between the importance of accepting passivity and the reception of grace, even if it could be pointed out that, whereas Chaplin's grace is achieved through his actions, Christian grace is not attained at all and only received, or so at least in the Lutheran tradition. Its theological inflection is arguably tapped from one of the most powerful veins of our cultural inheritance in which passivity's primacy vis-à-vis activity is preserved. As Gould here suggests, grace is not without inherent connection to action, for indeed beautiful as well as good actions can flow from the reception of grace.

Let me pursue these clues beyond Gould and Cavell and further into the suggested theological terrain. Luther's celebrated "The Disputation Concerning Man" culminates in the following formulation: "Paul . . . briefly sums up the definition of man, saying 'Man is justified by faith.'"[29] Justification essentially discerns persons from their works, in both action and speech, but it goes further: it not only argues that there is always more to a person than what is expressed in speech and actions, but also claims that the person's humanity is essentially not defined by such capabilities at all. The upshot is that our humanity is received from beyond ourselves, or as Eberhard Jüngel writes: "The Christian faith thus stands and falls with the fact that it dares to see the person, despite the incontestable connection between person and act, as more than simply an agent: namely as a human self who lives from God's recognition." Cavell would probably not be ready to follow these implications of passivity; still, Jüngel expounds the implications of the Lutheran anthropology in a way that arguably extends Gould's suggestions. Jüngel continues:

In order to become acquainted with oneself as such a person, as one gifted with oneself, the steadfastly active and working "I," the achiever, must be *elementally interrupted* in his or her being-active. . . . by which we are transposed out of our *activities* into a very lively, very intensive, indeed highly *creative passivity.*[30]

Justification or forgiveness of sins is thus a divine, unconditional forgiveness that brings forth a recognition as the person as something distinct from activity, a recognition, however, that is supposed to flow into creative passivity. To fully accept the passivity at the person's core does not mean that it turns into an excuse for inactivity or, worse, spiritual revenge; it rather signals a new start. As the justification depends on the event of the cross, it is particularly the resurrection that brings the new start into full expression: it is a turning of death to life, that is, a *creatio ex nihilo.*

But the question I have raised is why acceptance of forgiveness seems to be difficult. The consequence of Cavell's reading of *King Lear* is that there are human motives for refusing being acknowledged and loved, according to a sense of shame. Shame involves a sense of unworthiness on the most fundamental level: being unworthy of receiving the gift of life. Even if much theological ink has been spilled in convincing us of our sinful self-occupation and pride, it is still pertinent to say, as Tillich argued more than a half century ago, that our unwillingness to accept forgiveness or grace is not due to too much self-love, but to too little. Achievements and false activity become compensations for the unbearable sense of being small or for our attempts to distract the attention away from ourselves. From shame and self-loathing stems the feeling of not deserving forgiveness or grace; or where skeptical defense has been established, grace presents itself as an insulting reminder of one's passivity and is therefore better avoided. For Tillich, the justification takes on full importance at this impasse. The Pauline-Lutheran doctrine of justification by faith means, following Tillich, to "accept oneself as accepted in spite of being unacceptable."[31] We might call such acceptance both acknowledgment and divine forgiveness. But can we accept total acceptance? If we can, it requires at least a minimal trust, what Luther calls faith—not as an intellectual effort, but something like trust in a promise, as Cavell has pointed out (*DK,* 95). But will Cavell grant such faith?

In expanding on the theme of passivity and forgiveness, I have reached a theological outlook that transcends Cavell's suggestions. One might ask if this is a matter not only of arriving at conclusions Cavell has not drawn, but of moving in the opposite direction from him—for instance, with the idea that humanity is received from beyond itself. There are undeniable tensions here, expounded in Cavell's elaboration of Emerson's allusion to Descartes. For Descartes's *cogito ergo sum* leads to the questionable conclusion that I might exist only when actually thinking, from which Descartes takes recourse in God as the guarantor and author of my being. Emerson, in Cavell's reading, affirms Descartes insofar as "I am a being who to exist must say I exist, or must acknowledge my existence—claim it, stake it, enact it" (*IQO*, 109). Although this does not mean that I must literally create myself, as from dust and breath, as Cavell admits, it will still comprise Descartes's perception of God's enactment. The upshot of Emerson's allusion is that I can fail to think and thus declare my existence—I can fail to exist, whether depicted as fallen into conformity or as living our skepticism. But there are ways to regain humanity, and Cavell believes that the key to do so is in our own hands. But Christianity considers it otherwise. It seems that we are finally reaching the juncture where the paths part.

The Last Question: Self-redemption or Divine Redemption?

In this book I have tried to elaborate the analogies and overlappings between Cavell's philosophy and his religious perspective, either expressed philosophically or theologically. If such an undertaking might be deemed risky, it is because of Cavell's own repeated resistance toward certain Christian depictions of the human state as helpless, fixed, awaiting supernatural aid, pursuing untimely theologizing, and the like. This resistance has been emphasized by his commentators and has often been taken as Cavell's prevalent attitude. Especially in chapter 1 but also in the subsequent chapters, I have tried to oppose such interpretations—not because they are wrong (indeed, they touch on an undeniable dimension of Cavell's thought), but because I think they reveal only half of the story. It has been worthwhile to bring out *both* dimensions of Cavell's ambiguous attitude toward religion—both its dismissive and its affirmative dimensions. Accordingly, I hope that my way of expanding on Cavell's suggestions, notes, and hints has proved a possible way to extend his conversation with religion and theology—sometimes posed as arguments, sometimes as competitions and sometimes dismissive, but also often encouraging. Since my interest lies in countering the impression of Cavell as hostile to religion as such, my efforts run the danger of overemphasizing the other side of the story, as if he were providing a philosophical preparation or afterthought to lived religion or theological principles. But there are certainly dividing lines that Cavell will not cross.

The real question at stake concerns redemption and how it is to be conceived. The concepts of redemption and of recovery turn up already in *Senses of Walden* from 1972, but they reach fruition in Cavell's reading of romantic texts during the 1980s. The question at hand is, what can redemption and recovery possibly mean in Cavell's philosophical context? He asks himself, "But in all philosophical seriousness, recovery from what? Philosophy cannot say sin. Let us speak of a recovery from skepticism. This means, as said, from a drive to the inhumane" (*IQO*, 26). The impossibility of using the word "sin" to refer to the state we need redemption from has by commentators been taken differently as the decisive sign of Cavell's renunciation of theology in favor of a deified reason, or conversely, to be meant to invite us to ponder the strangeness of that statement, only to find philosophy inexorably entangled in theological questions.[1] It seems to me that the quotation is meant to draw attention to the distinction between philosophy and theology, not as the obstruction of exchange, but as constitutive of whatever exchange there can be between them. Moreover, the fact that both sin and skepticism reflect the drive to the inhumane suggests that they are interpretations of each other. The central problem then becomes how to carry out the redemption from sin and skepticism.

In romanticism, Cavell finds a recognition that both loss and gain as well as death and life are carried within one's self, which Cavell takes to articulate the way that both skepticism and acknowledgment are rival drives in each of us. The redemption under discussion is no doubt a redemption of philosophy. Guided by his understanding of romanticism, Cavell, however, thinks that philosophy cannot achieve such redemption by its own efforts. Still, he turns resolutely not to religion, but to poetry. What concerns Cavell is "redemption of genuine philosophy, where the preservation of poetry and philosophy by one another presents itself as the necessity of recovering or replacing religion" (IQO, 43). Thus, if the state of loss and alienation is a matter where philosophy can usefully learn from religion, this is decisively not true as far as redemption is concerned: while philosophy must be open to its other, this other is resolutely not religion, but poetry.

Philosophy and poetry stand under no obligation besides its own writing, and writing, Cavell consequently states, "is accordingly a kind of self-redemption" (IQO, 62). Redemptive writing and reading is one of the ways by which English romanticism is preserved and extended in the American transcendentalism of Thoreau and Emerson, deepening the sense of the need for marrying philosophy and literature.[2] But the loosening of redemption from its religious source sheds light back onto Cavell's hesitation toward a Christological reading of the resurrection scene in The Winter's Tale. It is not primarily Christ's resurrection that makes forgiveness among humans possible; forgiveness is rather Leontes's and Hermione's mutual achievement: "The final scene of The Winter's Tale interprets this creation as their creation by one another. Each awakens, each was stone" (DK, 220). At stake in this play is not the writer's or reader's own self-redemption, as in romantic poetry, but redemption by way of the human other— but in any case, not by appealing to anything beyond finite resources.

Such re-interpretation of redemption, of course, is hard to reconcile with Christian faith. Richard Eldridge takes this point further: "There is very little sense of original sin in Cavell's writing, very little sense of the need for grace and forgiveness."[3] As it stands, such an account is problematic, provided the way Cavell's skeptic can be seen as mirroring the doctrine of original sin, as elaborated in chapter 4; and according to my interpretation put forward in chapter 7, forgiveness cannot be regarded as insignificant to Cavell's central concerns. Nonetheless, from what Cavell explicitly says about redemption as self-redemption, Eldridge seems right when he insists that Cavell's thought has a certain Pelagian orientation, understood as an emphatic trust in human achievements—as if Cavell believes that his writing can bring about "both the return of the world and his own salvation."[4] But is such Pelagian self-redemption a sufficient response to the state of loss in which Cavell thinks we are floundering? William Desmond has powerfully argued that, according to the romantic depiction, if we are half-alive and half-dead, we cannot be in a position to resurrect ourselves. What, then, about the other, who in our state of modernity is supposed to bear "the weight of God" (*CR*, 470)?—is the human other in the position of a redeemer? If the other is under the same spell as I am, neither is it within the other's capacity to redeem us from this state.[5] Desmond thinks that this draws us toward the conclusion that the other cannot bear the weight of the redeeming God. Even if Desmond thinks that Cavell at times crosses the line to a theological understanding of redemption without admitting it, he still regards Cavell's overall refusal of divine redemption as locking philosophy itself up into the state of sin. But despite that—or perhaps precisely because of that—philosophy cannot help urging redemption:

> philosophy will continue the sickness because it can only name self-redemption, even though fitfully, as if in a dream or a fever, images seem to come to it, insurgently, of *being redeemed,* as of *being loved* . . . But then what "promise of redemption" can be here, since it seems evident that this ailment of the human cannot heal itself; it can only betray its symptoms; and many ways of betraying these symptoms are themselves betrayals of the promise of redemption.[6]

I agree with Desmond that finite humanity, drastically at odds with its own conditions, needs another remedy than what Cavell will offer. And indeed, seen from a religious point of view, self-redemption is not only insufficient, it also leads in the wrong direction: it begins to resemble a refusal of the infinite other by putting trust in one's own efforts in its place.[7]

Thus, if the inescapability of skepticism arguably cannot be redeemed without falling victim to the deification of human works, one might also ask what is entailed by the promised future, to which such redemption is supposed to open up. Emersonian perfectionism no doubt aspires to a constant movement forward, toward the next, the eventual, the unattained but attainable state of the self. We are called to strive for a constant move away from the shameful state in which we find ourselves, toward a life in more accordance with our hearts' desires. But essentially, such movement forward has no determined direction and no fixed goal, as Cavell finds reflected in Emerson's aphorism "Around each circle another may be drawn" (*PDT*, 121). But then the motivation for changes and turns seems to become self-referential. One might want to understand why change is worth undertaking in the first place. If change is undertaken in pursuit of happiness, or toward a more satisfying self-conception and conduct of life, one must then ask: more satisfying according to what? It seems that we only lapse back into the self's endless occupation with itself, caught in its own circle. How are we to measure such aspired states? There are essentially no answers to this—or, more congenially, the answers must be found by each of us, in each step we take. It is against a similar unwillingness to let go of itself that Mulhall claims that Cavell fails to fully interrogate "the ego's maddened and maddening desire to believe itself at the centre of things."[8]

At the end of the previous chapter, I raised the question of passivity. Cavell's reluctance to support the radical sense of passivity implied in justification bears directly on the self's position in the world. The Reformation's radical stress on grace alone at the expense of works can be thought of as a wishful escape from the responsibilities that go with the vulnerability of human speech and action. But, as Gould suggested, it can equally be taken as a way to undo the false activity that masks passivity of the self. If Cavell's reliance on Emersonian perfectionism grants the subjectivity its identity by its power to declare itself, it puts the self at the center of things, where its identity relies on its own achievements. I think justification by faith is meant not to render human activity indifferent, but to redirect it: if the self's ultimate identity is dependent not on its active achievements but rather on a gift of justification granted from beyond itself, then it is truly set free to orient its activity away from self-securing strategies and toward the world and others in it. Forgiveness is inextricably linked to such justification because it unties us from our former speech and deeds and opens us up for new beginnings. And even more profoundly, justification means the decentering of the self: its deepest identity no longer stands and falls with its own works, for the self receives itself as a gif.

According to the Christian outlook advocated by Jürgen Moltmann, faith fundamentally entails hope, a hope that is in turn tied to a promise of a future—not any future, but a future that is prefigured in the resurrection of the crucified Christ. Eschatology, the doctrine of the last things, is accordingly not an appendix to theology, as it is sometimes regarded, but the very nerve of theology as such. Since, according to Moltmann, this promise is given to humanity from beyond ourselves and since it directs our hopes to a future not invented by us, the purpose of change and forwardness does not risk lapsing back into the self's various strategies for self-realization. On the contrary, it provides a perspective from which one can take finitude into account, critically work on the present state, encouraged by the direction indicated by the promise.[9]

However, one should not too hastily dismiss Cavell for lacking any such direction, for one thing, chapter 3 emphasizes the promise as integral to his thinking; for another, there are places where Cavell draws explicitly on an eschatological horizon. Cavell most unequivocally turns to eschatology in his reading of the final scene in Ibsen's *A Doll's House*. In the scene where Nora is about to leave Torvald and her children, Torvald thinks at first she is merely going to sleep, whereas Nora is in fact swiftly changing her clothes and preparing to depart. Nora cannot stand what has become of their marriage; for her to stay would take a miracle—a change of their marriage, a redemption of it. Cavell is stricken by the dreamlike parallel to Paul's first letter to the Corinthians:

> Behold! I show you a mystery; We shall not all sleep, but we shall all be changed, in a moment, in a twinkling of an eye, at the last trump: for the trumpet shall sound, and the dead shall be raised incorruptible, and we shall be changed. For this corruptible must put on incorruption and the mortal must put on immortality. (1 Cor. 15:51–53)

Ibsen's references to sleep, a swift change of clothes, and redemption are indeed striking. In quoting Paul, Cavell appears to be reopening the eschatological horizon, but only apparently. For the passage is immediately juxtaposed by quoting Marx, for whom redemption is revolution, a change within our reach that presupposes that criticism of religion must be brought to completion. In Cavell's hands, Ibsen—like Emerson—proposes a distinctively secularized version of Christian ideas:

> I might put the point of invoking the passage from Corinthians by claiming that Ibsen, in secularizing it, indeed domesticating it, is announcing that the task before humanity is no longer for the mortal to put on immortality, but rather for the pre-mortal (the songbird and the doll, for example, . . .) to put on mortality, to become responsible for their lives of finitude, to become intelligible to themselves and to each other. (*CW*, 263)

The reference to Marx along with the secularizing of eschatology brings Cavell in proximity to such thinkers as Ernst Bloch, particularly in terms of the latter's appeal to the principle of hope. If both Cavell and Bloch appreciate the significance of the religious tradition, they nevertheless find it important to oppose tendencies entailed in it—not least its tendency to reify mythological images of the future to come. Although perfectionism's future-directedness surely implies a sense of transcendence, it is important to Cavell that according to his Emersonian perfectionism, there is no sense given to the idea of a final, perfected state that we are to pursue (*PDT*, 121). At the very least, religious ideas of a particular perfected state depart from what philosophy can attain. "Presumably a religious perfectionism may find that things can happen otherwise. The idea of the self as on (or lost with respect to) a path, as a direction to a fixed goal, needs its own study" (*CHU*, xxxiv). In the Christian tradition, there is surely no shortage of detailed, reified accounts of the awaited kingdom, but it is doubtful that such accounts play any decisive role in contemporary theological reflection. Moltmann criticizes Bloch for making his case too easy for himself by attacking a caricature rather than theology at its best. In his reply to Bloch, Moltmann insists that, although eschatology is not void or without direction, it is certainly not fixed. On the contrary, with regard to eschatology, theology keeps the iconoclasm intact. The hiddenness of God and the hiddenness of the human destination are preserved in the suspended future.[10]

It is inextricable to Moltmann's project to see how the future horizon works back into the everyday. From the perspective of the promise, there is, nevertheless, an undeniable conflict between the way things are and the future to which the promise aspires. Such a conflict is also central to Cavell because it is central to Emerson's and Nietzsche's aversion of the state of conformity: the perspective of the coming man must necessarily present itself in contradiction to the present (*PDT*, 117). Moltmann's theology is meant to counter resignation, melancholy, or what Cavell calls disappointment, and inspire the constant return to the everyday as always on its way forward. Even if revelation has often been conceived in terms of (Greek) epiphanies, with their emphasis on the eternal as coming to light in the present, the Hebrew understanding of revelation, Moltmann argues, is of the God who comes with promises, just as the presence of Christ is essentially connected to his expected advent. Cavell seems at one place to be onto exactly this, as he writes, "Christianity is something that in its very presence is to be expected, that exists only in expectation, say faith" (*DK*, 21). But such expectation puts a particular pressure on the present, as a place of exile, perhaps, or in any case a state from which one must be ready to leave and move on. Moltmann writes:

> The God of the exodus and of the resurrection "is" not the eternal presence, but he promises his presence and nearness to him who follows the path on which he is sent into the future. YHWH, as the name of the God who first of all promises his presence and kingdom and makes them prospects for the future, is a God "with future as his essential nature," a God of promise and of leaving the present to face the future.[11]

Cavell certainly also wants to preserve the importance of leaving or of departure as involved in the promise of redemption. One of the quotations from Emerson's "Self-Reliance" that Cavell returns to most frequently turns on exactly this: "I shun father and mother, wife and brother, when my genius calls me. I would write on the lintels of the doorpost, *Whim*."[12] The localization of the "whim" suggests to Cavell that Emerson alludes to the Jewish mezuzah, which is a small piece with inscriptions from Deuteronomy affixed to a door frame. The whim, which in Emerson's lingo is not only a sudden, passing idea, but the call of one's own genius, is put precisely in the place of a the mezuzah. Of course, this is meant to appear as mocking and blasphemous, but, as Cavell comments, it is perhaps only a small blasphemy compared to the fact that "God is mostly taken in the place of a whim" (SW, 155). Emerson is alluding to the biblical sense of departure, in part by invoking Exodus, of which the mezuzah is a reminder, in part by Emerson's allusion to Jesus's demand that his followers abandon their families and follow him. There are, however, significant differences at stake: in Emerson's case, the departure is commanded by no one but yourself, your genius; in the New Testament, you follow a divine call. "To say, 'Follow me and you will be saved,' you must be sure you are of God. But to say, 'Follow in yourself what I follow in mine and you will be saved,' you merely have to be sure you are following yourself" (SW, 160).

And this is where the ways finally part: either humanity is capable of self-redemption, following its own genius, or else such self-redemption must appear as works in the Pauline sense, which only conceals our passiveness and the need for an initiative beyond human reach. But must perfectionism necessarily reject the latter? Also, such a passivity must turn into what Jüngel calls creative passivity, for which human autonomy indeed matters, whether morally, politically, or psychologically; for Moltmann, the reception of the given promise grants direction and inspiration to the constant work on the self and the ordinary as they stand. Is not this what Cavell also means when he refers to the father tongue— the ability to speak responsibly for oneself—as developed out of the reception of a prior mother tongue, even depicting the transference from the latter to the former in the figure of rebirth and baptism (SW, 15–17)? Perhaps it could mean something compatible with that, but not as long as "Following yourself!" is undertaken at the expense of "Follow me!"

NOTES

Introduction

1. Terry Eagleton, *Reason, Faith, and Revolution: Reflections on the God Debate* (New Haven, Conn.: Yale University Press, 2009), 140.

2. Stephen Mulhall, *Stanley Cavell: Philosophy's Recounting of the Ordinary* (Oxford: Oxford University Press, 1994), 286.

3. In this book, I follow Cavell's tendency to use the term "religion" when referring to religious practice within the scope of the Jewish and especially the Christian inheritance. This term overlaps with "Christianity," which I use where there are more particular Christian ideas and perceptions at play. I use the word "theology" to refer to the reflective and normative discourse of the validity of Christian doctrines and traditions, as well as the interrogation of theology's own conditions as an academic discipline.

4. Giovanna Borradori, *The American Philosopher: Conversations with Quine, Davidson, Putnam, Nozick, Danto, Rorty, Cavell, MacIntyre, and Kuhn*, trans. R. Crocitto (Chicago: University of Chicago Press, 1994), 136.

5. Ibid.

6. Writing about this position, Peter Dula aptly speaks of the "strangeness of the space Cavell inhabits." *Cavell, Companionship, and Christian Theology* (Oxford: Oxford University Press, 2011), 157.

7. Such a position is held by Richard Eldridge, "Romantic Rebirth in a Secular Age: Cavell's Aversive Exertions," *Journal of Religion* 71 (1991): 410–418; Simon Critchley, *Very Little . . . Almost Nothing* (London: Routledge, 1997), 118–138; Asja Szafraniec, "Inheriting the Wound: Religion and Philosophy in Stanley Cavell," in *Religion Beyond a Concept*, ed. H. de Vries (New York: Fordham University Press, 2007), 368–379; Ludger H. Viefhues-Bailey, *Beyond the Philosopher's Fear: A Cavellian Reading of Gender, Origin and Religion in Modern Skepticism* (Aldershot: Ashgate, 2007). This latter work stands out from the rest since it also suggests a reinvention of religion beyond Christianity.

8. Mulhall, *Stanley Cavell*, ch. 12; Judith E. Tonning, "Acknowledging a Hidden God: A Theological Critique of Stanley Cavell on Scepticism," *Heythrop Journal* 48 (2007): 384–405.

9. Fergus Kerr, *Immortal Longings: Versions of Transcending Humanity* (Notre Dame, Ind.: University of Notre Dame Press, 1997), 123–131; William Desmond, "A Second Primavera: Cavell, German Philosophy, and Romanticism," in *Stanley Cavell*, ed. R. Eldridge (Cambridge: Cambridge University Press, 2003), 143–171; Timothy Gould, review of *Stanley Cavell: Philosophy's Recounting of the Ordinary*, by Stephen Mulhall, *Journal of Aesthetics and Art Criticism* 56 (1998): 83–85; Dula, *Cavell, Companionship, and*

Christian Theology; Mark D. Jordan, "The Modernity of Christian Theology *or* Writing Kierkegaard Again for the First Time," *Modern Theology* 27 (2011): 442–451; and Graham Ward, "Philosophy as Tragedy *or* What Words Won't Give," *Modern Theology* 27 (2011): 478–496; Hent de Vries, "Stanley Cavell on St. Paul," *MLN: Modern Language Notes* 126 (2011): 979–993.

10. Paul Ricoeur, *The Conflict of Interpretations: Essays in Hermeneutics,* ed. D. Ihde, trans. K. McLaughlin et al. (London: Continuum, 2004), 437.

11. Martin Heidegger, "Phenomenology and Theology," in *Pathmarks,* trans. W. Mc-Neill (Cambridge: Cambridge University Press, 1998).

12. Jürgen Habermas, "Religion in the Public Sphere," *European Journal of Philosophy* 14 (2006): 16.

13. Martin Heidegger, *Being and Time,* trans. J. Macquarrie and E. Robinson (Oxford: Blackwell, 1962), 16, 423.

14. For a further discussion of the criteria's status, see Steven G. Affeldt, "The Ground of Mutuality: Criteria, Judgment, and Intelligibility in Stephen Mulhall and Stanley Cavell," *European Journal of Philosophy* 6 (1998): 1–31; Stephen Mulhall, "Stanley Cavell's Vision of the Normativity of Language: Grammar, Criteria and Rules," in *Stanley Cavell,* ed. Eldridge, 79–106.

15. For the phenomenologists' "reduction," see Richard Kearney, "The Epiphanies of the Everyday: Toward a Micro-Eschatology," in *After God: Richard Kearney and the Religious Turn in Continental Philosophy,* ed. J. Panteleimon Manoussakis (New York: Fordham University Press, 2006).

16. I note that Hillary Putnam therefore is able to include his Jewish philosophers, particularly Buber and Levinas, among perfectionist writers; *Jewish Philosophy as a Guide to Life* (Bloomington: Indiana University Press, 2008), 59, 72. This motivates further readings of Levinas through Cavell's lenses, something I attempt in chapter 6.

17. Richard Eldridge, introduction: Between Acknowledgment and Avoidance, in *Stanley Cavell,* ed. Eldridge, 4–5.

1. Modernism and Religion

1. Tonning's quotation stops at "our possible freedom from it," while Mulhall includes the next sentence; Tonning, "Acknowledging a Hidden God," 395; Mulhall, *Stanley Cavell,* 289.

2. Mulhall, *Stanley Cavell,* 289; Tonning, "Acknowledging a Hidden God," 396. Fergus Kerr includes the reference, but does not make much out of it; *Immortal Longings: Versions of Transcending Humanity* (Notre Dame, Ind.: University of Notre Dame Press, 1997), 127–128.

3. Mulhall, *Stanley Cavell,* 293–294.

4. Charles Taylor, *The Sources of the Self: The Making of the Modern Identity* (Cambridge: Cambridge University Press, 1989), 211–226.

5. Mulhall, *Stanley Cavell,* 305.

6. Critchley, *Very Little . . . Almost Nothing,* 134.

7. Ibid., 179.

8. The much-repeated phrase in Cavell's work of being "condemned to meaning" seems to be borrowed from Maurice Merleau-Ponty's *Phenomenology of Perception*, trans. C. Smith (London: Routledge, 1962), xix.

9. Martha C. Nussbaum's interpretation of Becket also emphasizes his essentially Christian horizon. From her own perspective, however, there is no question of transforming Christianity—Christianity is what must be overcome, particularly its interpretation of finitude "suffused with a sense of *guilt* and *disgust*"; *Love's Knowledge: Essays on Philosophy and Literature* (Oxford: Oxford University Press, 1990), 309. Certainly, Cavell frequently comments on Christianity's interpretation of finitude and guilt, but this interpretation arguably leaves its possible future open, as I explore in chapter 4.

10. Symptomatically, this important "conclusion" is omitted from Critchley's reading of Cavell's essay on Beckett. *Very Little . . . Almost Nothing*, 176–180.

11. Ludwig Wittgenstein, *Culture and Value*, ed. G. H. von Wright and H. Nyman, trans. P. Winch (Chicago: University of Chicago Press, 1980), 64.

12. Cf. *PI*, § 90; Immanuel Kant, *Critique of Pure Reason*, trans. N. K. Smith (London: Macmillan Press, 1929), A56, B81.

13. Cf. Ludwig Wittgenstein, *Tractatus logico-philosophicus*, trans. D. F. Pears and B. F. McGuinness (New York: Routledge, 2001), § 6.521.

14. Richard Rorty, "Response to Putnam," in *Rorty and His Critics*, ed. R. B. Brandom (Oxford: Blackwell, 2000), 90. Cf. Gordon C. F. Bearn, "Sounding Serious: Cavell and Derrida," *Presentations* 63 (1998): 83–86.

15. For the dialectic of aesthetic modernism vis-à-vis culture, see Michael Fried, "Three American Painters: Noland, Olitski, Stella," in *Art and Objecthood: Essays and Reviews* (Chicago: University of Chicago Press, 1998), 217–219.

16. Stephen Cavell, "The *Investigations'* Everyday Aesthetics of Itself," in *The Cavell Reader*, ed. S. Mulhall (Oxford: Blackwell, 1996), 373.

17. For Kierkegaard, contrary to Cavell's modernist rendering of him, there is ultimately no possible publicly assessable license for being an apostle, and this follows grammatically or dialectically from the kind of authority in question: an authority essentially issued from the qualitatively other. Hence, the authority cannot be proven without being leveled to "the same"—to think otherwise is to confuse aesthetic genius and apostleship. *The Book on Adler*, trans. H. V. and E. H. Hong, Kierkegaard's Writings, 24 (Princeton, N.J.: Princeton University Press, 1998), 177–182.

18. Cf. Clement Greenberg, "Modernist Painting," in *The Collected Essays and Criticism: Modernism with a Vengeance, 1957–1969*, vol. 4, ed. J. O'Brian (Chicago: University of Chicago Press, 1993), 85–86.

19. Jordan, "Modernity of Christian Theology," 445.

20. Quoted from Dula, *Cavell, Companionship, and Christian Theology*, 172.

21. Jean-François Lyotard, *The Postmodern Condition: A Report on Knowledge*, trans. B. Gennington and B. Massumi (Manchester: Manchester University Press, 1984), 10, 41.

22. Cf. John Caputo, *On Religion* (London: Routledge, 2001), 56–66.

23. Charles Taylor, *A Secular Age* (Cambridge, Mass.: Belknap Press of Harvard University Press, 2008), 25.

24. Ibid., 569–574.

25. Ibid., 549.

26. Maurice Merleau-Ponty, *In Praise of Philosophy*, trans. J. Wild and J. M. Edie (Evanston, Ill.: Northwestern University Press, 1962), 44.

27. Stanley Cavell, *Cavell on Film*, ed. W. Rothman (New York: SUNY, 2005), 92.

28. Ibid., 340.

2. The Ordinary Sublime

1. Jean-François Lyotard focuses on the "unpresentable" and "the event"; "What Is Postmodernism?," in *Postmodern Condition*, 81. Jacques Derrida understands the sublime as the very dividing line or passage between the limited and the unlimited, the presentable and the unpresentable; *The Truth in Painting*, trans. G. Bennington and I. McLeod (Chicago: University of Chicago Press, 1987), 143–144. For a critical account, see Richard Kearney, *Strangers, Gods and Monsters: Interpreting Otherness* (Routledge: London, 2003), 88–100, 107.

2. Cavell, *Cavell on Film*, 377.

3. Kant, *The Critique of the Power of Judgment*, trans. P. Gayer and E. Matthews (Cambridge: Cambridge University Press, 2001), 128–130.

4. Cf. *PI*, §§ 38, 94.

5. Cavell thinks David Pole advocates such an interpretation of Wittgenstein. *MWM*, 47–48.

6. Cf. Cora Diamond, *The Realistic Spirit: Wittgenstein, Philosophy, and the Mind* (Cambridge, Mass. MIT Press, 1991), 27–28.

7. Cavell has elsewhere argued how the apparent extraordinariness of Beckett's drama is indeed enacted ordinariness, and that the ordinary surface of Chekhov's drama is designed to awaken the sense of extraordinariness. *MWM*, 117–119; *IQO*, 167.

8. Diamond, *Realistic Spirit*, 20.

9. This, of course, is Diamond's way of rendering Wittgenstein's recommendation to "don't think, but look." *PI*, § 66.

10. Ted Hughes, "Six Young Men," in *Collected Poems* (New York: Farrar, Straus Giroux, 2003), 46.

11. The presence and absence in photographs in general is one of the major occupations of Cavell's investigation of the medium of film in *WV*, ch. 2–4, as Diamond is surely aware of. Mulhall has brought this point out in *The Wounded Animal: J. M. Coetzee and the Difficulty of Reality in Literature and Philosophy* (Princeton, N.J.: Princeton University Press, 2009), 91–93.

12. Traditionally, and exemplarily in Kant, the concept of the sublime has been tied to horror, absence, and violence, in contrast to beauty and harmony. John Milbank has fruitfully argued for a marriage of both these poles as elements within a broader conception of the sublime; "Sublimity: The Modern Transcendent," in *Transcendence: Philosophy, Literature, and Theology Approach to the Beyond*, ed. R. Schwartz (New York: Routledge, 2004).

13. According to Diamond and Cavell, such agonizing isolation is what J. M. Coetzee's *Elisabeth Castello* is about; *PAL*, 47, 111–112. I have omitted Diamond's dis-

cussion of Coetzee here, because her treatment of our relation to animals needs further elaboration than this framework allows. Cavell also picks up on this theme in "A Touch of Words," in *Seeing Wittgenstein Anew*, ed. W. Day and V. J. Krebs (Cambridge: Cambridge University Press, 2010). See also Stephen Mulhall, *Wounded Animal*, ch. 5.

14. Affeldt has worked out the passive and the active ignorance in "On the Difficulty of Seeing Aspects and the 'Therapeutic' Reading of Wittgenstein," in *Seeing Wittgenstein Anew*, 273–274.

15. Heidegger, *Being and Time*, 95–102, 163–169. For an analysis along these lines, see my *Phenomenology and the Holy: Religious Experience after Husserl* (London: SCM Press, 2010), ch. 6. Cf. *IQO*, 32.

16. Blaise Pascal, *Pensées*, trans. A. J. Krailsheimer (London: Penguin Books, 1966), 516.

17. Timothy Gould, "Where the Action Is: Cavell and the Skeptic's Activity," in *The Senses of Stanley Cavell*, ed. R. Fleming and M. Payne (London: Bucknell University Press, 1989), 96.

18. I have borrowed "embrace" from Ronald L. Hall, *The Human Embrace: The Love of Philosophy and the Philosophy of Love* (University Park: Pennsylvania State University Press, 2000).

19. Charles Taylor has pointed out how Kant and the post-Kantian romantic sense of the sublime was taken as humanizing—celebrating human spontaneity and freedom—in opposition to the prevailing "detached reason" of the Enlightenment; *Secular Age*, 338–343.

20. For more on Freud's concept of the uncanny and its relevance for the sacred, see my *In Between: The Holy Beyond Modern Dichotomies*, trans. B. McNeill (Göttingen: Vandenhoeck & Ruprecht, 2011), 94–100.

21. James Noggle, "The Wittgensteinian Sublime," *New Literary History* 27 (1996): 614.

22. Ibid., 616.

23. Ibid.

24. Kierkegaard, *Fear and Trembling*, in *Fear and Trembling/Repetition*, trans. H. V. and E. H. Hong, Kierkegaard's Writings, 6 (Princeton, N.J.: Princeton University Press, 1983), 38, 41.

25. Hall, *Human Embrace*, 213.

26. Ibid., 2.

27. Jacques Derrida, *Gift of Death*, trans. D. Wills (Chicago: University of Chicago Press, 1995), ch. 3.

28. Kierkegaard, *Repetition*, in *Fear and Trembling/Repetition*, 132.

29. Cavell, "The *Investigations*' Everyday Aesthetic of Itself," 382.

3. Acknowledging God

1. Cavell, "Responses," *Modern Theology* 27 (2011): 525.

2. Norman Malcolm, "The Privacy of Experience," in *Epistemology: New Essays in the Theory of Knowledge*, ed. A. Stoll (London: Harper & Row, 1967), 129–158.

3. For the distinction between first- and third-person perspective with regard to Cavell's "acknowledgement," see Stephen Mulhall, *Wittgenstein's Private Language Argument* (Oxford: Oxford University Press, 2007), 44–45.

4. Tonning, "Acknowledging a Hidden God," 394.

5. Ibid., 397.

6. Ibid., 398.

7. Ibid., 397.

8. For acknowledgment and separation, see *IQO*, 172, 178.

9. Tonning, "Acknowledging a Hidden God," 297.

10. James Conant has detected similar misinterpretations of Cavell's position versus the skeptical position, in "On Bruns, on Cavell," *Critical Inquiry* 17 (1991): 616–634.

11. "Confessions" can here be taken in its double meaning: "confession," as Henry Chadwick explains, carries the meaning "of confession as praise as well as of confession as acknowledgment of faults." See his introduction, in Augustine, *Confessions*, trans. H. Chadwick (Oxford: Oxford University Press, 1991), ix. For a more elaborate account, see Helmut Kuhn, "Die Bekenntnisse des heilige Augustin als literarisches Werk," *Stimmen der Zeit* (1968): 225–226.

12. Cf. C. Taylor, *Sources of the Self,* 129–136.

13. Augustine, *Confessions*, trans. H. Chadwick (Oxford: Oxford University Press, 1991), 8.7.28.

14. Ibid., 1.7.13.

15. One might ask oneself: Is this "falling asleep" an allusion to Socrates's symposium or to Christ in Gethsemane, or, given Augustine, is Cavell perhaps alluding to both?

16. Augustine, *Confessions* 8.12.28.

17. Ibid., 10.33.50, 5.2.2.

18. For an alternative account of the problem of beginning in Augustine, see Charles T. Mathews, "Book One: The Presumptuousness of Autography and the Paradox of Beginning," in *A Reader's Companion to Augustine's Confessions,* ed. K. Paffenroth and R. P. Kennedy (London: Westminster John Knox Press, 2003), 7–11.

19. For a penetrating reading of these passages (one that, however, does not emphasize their theological implications), see Timothy Gould, *Hearing Things: Voice and Method in the Writing of Stanley Cavell* (Chicago: University of Chicago Press 1998), 68–84.

20. Augustine, *Confessions* 10.3.3.

21. Richard Eldridge has drawn attention to the relation between Augustine and Wittgenstein on this point; *Leading a Human Life: Wittgenstein, Intentionality, and Romanticism* (Chicago: University of Chicago Press, 1997), 130–131.

22. Stephen Mulhall, *Inheritance and Originality: Wittgenstein, Heidegger, Kierkegaard* (Oxford: Oxford University Press, 2001), 50.

23. In his analytical approach, Alvin Plantinga undertakes an investigation of the relation between other minds and God (paying critical attention to contributions of

Wittgensteinians) in order to assess whether this can establish rational grounds for belief in God. Even though Plantinga argues that such a strategy fails as a convincing anti-skeptical argument, one's belief in both other's minds and God are still rational. *God and Other Minds: A Study of the Rational Justification of Belief in God* (London: Cornell University Press, 1969), 271.

24. Sarah Beckwith, *Shakespeare and the Grammar of Forgiveness* (Ithaca, N.Y.: Cornell University Press, 2011), 2–5; Beckwith spells out the argument in her chapter 2.

25. Martin Luther, *The Babylonian Captivity of the Church*, in *Luther's Works*, vol. 36, ed. A. Ross Wentz and H. T. Lehmann, trans. A. T. W. Steinhäuser, F. C. Ahrens, and A. Ross Wentz (Philadelphia, Pa.: Fortress Press, 1975), 40.

26. Oswald Bayer, *Martin Luthers Theologie. Eine Vergegenwärtigung* (Tübingen: Mohr, 2004), 46–48.

27. Cavell derives his lessons of promise here from Nietzsche, who asks whether the human problem stems from exactly the ability to promise, which in Cavell's thought involves the problem of inheriting and bequeathing language as the problem of the self; *PoP*, 183.

28. Cf. Luther, *Babylonian Captivity*, 70.

29. Critchley speaks of "Cavell's weak messianism" in *Very Little . . . Almost Nothing*, 130.

30. Luther, *Babylonian Captivity*, 58.

31. Paul Ricoeur, *Hermeneutics and the Human Sciences: Essays on Language, Actions and Interpretation*, ed. and trans. J. B. Thompson (Cambridge: Cambridge University Press, 1981), 99–100.

32. Cf. Dagfinn Dybvig, "Kingdom and Exile: A Study in Stanley Cavell's Philosophical Modernism and Its Dilemmas," PhD diss., NTNU: Norges Teknisk-Naturvitenskaplige Universitet, 2007, 160–164.

33. Cavell, "Responses," 525.

34. Martin Luther, *The Freedom of a Christian*, in *Luther's Works*, vol. 31, ed. H. J. Grimm and H. T. Lehmann, trans. W. A. Lambert (Philadelphia, Pa.: Fortress Press, 1971), 344.

35. Viefhues-Bailey, *Beyond the Philosopher's Fear*, 156.

36. Cavell, "Responses," 525.

37. Conant's influential reading of *Tractatus* does indeed invite silence—as the end of nonsense, religious nonsense included. Despite his invocation of Kierkegaard, it is hard to see that his reading preserves the religious sense that, no doubt, was an abiding impulse in Wittgenstein's intellectual life. James Conant, "Must We Show What We Cannot Say?," in *The Senses of Stanley Cavell*, ed. R. Fleming and M. Payne (London: Bucknell University Press, 1989), 242–270.

4. Skepticism, Finitude, and Sin

1. Kerr, *Immortal Longings*, 120. In this far-reaching study of human finitude in theology and philosophy, Kerr employs Cavell's passage quoted above (*MWM*, 61) as his starting point. Ibid., vii–viii.

2. Martin Luther, *Lectures on Genesis 1–5,* in *Luther's Works,* vol. 1, ed. J. Pelican, trans. G. V. Schick (St. Louis, Mo.: Concordia Publishing House, 1958), 147–149.

3. Paul Tillich, *The Dynamics of Faith* (London: Allen & Unwin, 1957), 16.

4. Ibid., 22.

5. Karl Barth, *Evangelical Theology: An Introduction,* trans. G. Foley (London: Weidenfeld, 1963), 124.

6. Ibid., 144.

7. Tillich, *Dynamics of Faith,* 19.

8. Kant, *Critique of Pure Reason,* A vii.

9. Ibid., A398, B354.

10. Ibid., B307, A255, B311.

11. Interestingly, Philip R. Shields also characterizes Wittgenstein's philosophy as restless and, furthermore, likens it to Augustine's state before his heart found rest in God; see *Logic and Sin in the Writings of Ludwig Wittgenstein* (Chicago: University of Chicago Press, 1993), 106. Paul Ricoeur captures the same phenomenon by speaking of the "non-coincidence" of the human with itself; see *Fallible Man,* trans. C. A. Kelby (New York: Fordham University Press, 1986), 1.

12. This is not to deny that Emerson's "fall" is problematic seen from a Christian view. Emerson's concern, as Cavell expounds it, is with sin as conformity and with the self-recovery from conformity in terms of self-creation; *IQO,* 111–112.

13. Stephen Mulhall, *Philosophical Myths of the Fall* (Princeton, N.J.: Princeton University Press, 2005), 6.

14. Cf. Ricoeur, *Fallible Man,* 144–145.

15. I note that Cavell here speaks of the Fall in terms of knowledge, in accordance with the tradition from Kant and Hegel. But he also suggests that Eden, prior to the Fall, might present itself as a temptation to deny that we know, as a cover story or excuse for a certain repression. For when the fruit is eaten, fear is launched, which is fear of nakedness, which seems to be read as everything Cavell takes to be implied in knowledge or, at its root, acknowledgment: exposure to the other, to being known, separation and the vulnerability of knowledge; *IQO,* 29.

16. Paul Tillich, *Systematic Theology II* (London: SCM Press, 1978), 34, 67.

17. Augustine, *The City of God against the Pagans,* trans. P. Levine (Cambridge, Mass.: Harvard University Press, 1966), 12.1–3, 14.3, 14.13. For Augustine, the possibility of a fallen will stems from its creation from nothing. For the distinction between finitude and sin, see also John Macquarrie, *Principles of Christian Theology* (London: SCM Press, 1977), 264–265.

18. Rudolf Bultmann, *Theology of the New Testament,* trans. K. Gropel (Waco, Tex.: Baylor University Press, 2007), 251.

19. Jacques Lacan, *The Ethics of Psychoanalysis 1959–1960,* trans. J. A. Miller (London: Routledge 1992), 102–103. Alternatively, a Girard-inspired reading takes as its premise mimetic desire, in which desire is formed by imitating what another person desires. Such desire results in rivalry to attain the same desired objects. Along these lines, James Allison has suggested that although God's prohibitions in

Eden are initially good, the serpent suggests that the prohibition should be taken as a sign of God's possessive desire for his own fruits—thus, the humans imitate the possessive desire and end up in rivalry with God. James Allison, *The Joy of Being Wrong: Original Sin through Easter Eyes* (New York: Crossroad Publishing Company, 1998), 149, 246.

20. Tillich, *Systematic Theology II*, 52.

21. Ricoeur, *Symbolism of Evil*, trans. E. Buchanan (Boston: Beacon Press, 1967), 253.

22. Tillich, *Systematic Theology II*, 49–50.

23. Shame, Cavell points out, is a more primitive reaction than guilt. It is not related to deeds, but to identity: who we are in the eyes of the other. *DK*, 49.

24. I borrow this formulation from Mulhall, *Philosophical Myths of the Fall*, 94.

25. Cf. Tillich, *Systematic Theology II*, 67.

26. Kearney, *Strangers, Gods and Monsters*, 118.

27. A similar thought is accounted for by Julia Kristeva, *Strangers to Ourselves*, trans. L. S. Roudiez (New York: Columbia, 1994), 191–192.

5. The Tragic Dimension of the Ordinary

1. Cf. Kevin Taylor and Giles Waller, introduction, in *Christian Theology and Tragedy: Theologians, Tragic Literature and Tragic Theory*, ed. K. Taylor and G. Waller (Farnham: Ashgate, 2011), 1–5.

2. In "Must We Mean What We Say?," Cavell attempts to elaborate the "must" in opposition to semantic theories and pragmatics, calling it a "categorical declarative." *MWM*, 31.

3. Anthony J. Cascardi, "'Disowning Knowledge': Cavell on Shakespeare," in *Stanley Cavell*, ed. R. Eldridge (Cambridge: Cambridge University Press), 190.

4. I have elsewhere given Derrida and Cavell's criticism of him more space; see "On Morality of Speech: Cavell's Critique of Derrida," *Continental Philosophy Review* 44 (2011): 81–101.

5. Jacques Derrida, *Of Grammatology*, trans. G. C. Spivak (Baltimore, Md.: Johns Hopkins University Press, 1997), 6–8, 18–20.

6. A problem with Cavell's reply, as Roger V. Bell Jr. notes, is that those essays were not published at the time Austin wrote *HDTW*; *Sounding the Abyss: Readings Between Cavell and Derrida* (Lanham, Md.: Lexington Books, 2004), 201. However, since Austin most probably had elaborated the themes already, and since the essay was readily accessible to Derrida, it remains an immanent critique of Derrida's own demand for careful and scholarly reading.

7. J. L. Austin, "A Plea for Excuses," in *Philosophical Papers* (Oxford: Clarendon Press, 1961), 124.

8. Ibid., 125.

9. Szafraniec, "Inheriting the Wound," 171–172.

10. Espen Hammer, *Stanley Cavell: Skepticism, Subjectivity, and the Ordinary* (Cambridge: Polity Press, 2002), 162–163.

11. Stanley Cavell, "Foreword to *The Scandal of the Speaking Body*," in Shoshana Felman, *The Scandal of the Speaking Body: Don Juan with J. L. Austin, or Seduction in Two Languages*, trans. C. Porter (Stanford, Calif.: Stanford University Press, 2002), xii.

12. Austin, "Plea for Excuses," 124.

13. Cavell thinks that such asymmetries between actions and speech potentially have grave consequences for Austin's theory of performatives: "hence [the asymmetry of speech and acts] releases the grounding thought . . . into the open again." *PoP*, 105.

14. The centrality of the question "why" for intentionality is a lesson Cavell learned from G. E. M. Anscombe's classical *Intention* (Cambridge, Mass.: Harvard University Press, 2000), 9–10.

15. Bernhard Williams, "Moral Luck" in *Moral Luck: Philosophical Papers 1973–1980* (Cambridge: Cambridge University Press, 1981), 30 n2.

16. Ibid., 24.

17. Ibid., 25.

18. Robert B. Pippin, "Recognition and Reconciliation: Actualized Agency in Hegel's Jena Phenomenology," *Internationales Jahrbuch des Deutschen Idealismus* 2 (2004): 261.

19. Allen Speight, *Hegel, Literature and the Problem of Agency* (Cambridge: Cambridge University Press, 2001), 48–49.

20. Ibid., 56.

21. Ibid., 60.

22. Hent de Vries has written an illuminating essay on these regions of Cavell's thought. But he takes the uncontrollable dimensions of words to imply that we "must not (fully and exclusively or transparently) mean what we say." I think such a way of putting it is not completely pertinent, since the redeeming of words is meant to call attention to the fact that we are answerable for them, and hence that the entire point is precisely how we must mean what we say and learn what we meant. "Must We (NOT) Mean What We Say? Seriousness and Sincerity in the Work of J. L. Austin and Stanley Cavell," in *The Rhetoric of Sincerity*, ed. E. van Alphen, M. Bal, and C. Smith (Stanford, Calif.: Stanford University Press, 2009), 106.

23. Jacques Lacan, *Écrits: A Selection*, trans. A. Sheridan (Routledge: London, 2001), 1–8.

24. Bell, on the contrary, thinks that the return of words is precisely what Derrida is after. But again, I fear Derrida lacks the specific sense of responsibility attached to the self that Cavell wants to affirm. *Sounding the Abyss*, 212.

25. Mulhall, *Philosophical Myths of the Fall*, 56.

26. Augustine, *Confessions*, 1.9.14. Interestingly, Wittgenstein used this quote as the epigraph to his *Philosophical Remarks*, ed. R. Rhees, trans. R. Hargreaves and R. White (Oxford: Blackwell, 1975).

27. Ricoeur, *Conflict of Interpretations*, 282.

28. Arendt's development of how the meaning of speech and deeds unfolds through history is similar to how I developed intentions. Hannah Arendt, *The Human Condition* (Chicago: University of Chicago Press, 1998), 190–191, 233, 236. Michael Lambek has elaborated the conjunction of Arendt and Cavell on this topic; "Toward an Ethics of the

Act," in *Ordinary Ethics: Anthropology, Language, and Action,* ed. M. Lambek (New York: Fordham University Press, 2010), 50–53.

29. For all his reservations with regard to the hope that goes with the Judeo-Christian vision, George Steiner does not hesitate to find original sin—entailing homelessness, alienation, and guilt—to be "the nucleus (*Ur-grund*)" that makes up the "background noise" of Greek tragedy. "'Tragedy,' Reconsidered," in *Rethinking Tragedy,* ed. R. Felski (Baltimore, Md.: Johns Hopkins University Press, 2008), 30–31.

30. Søren Kierkegaard, *Either/Or: Part I,* trans. H. V. Hong, E. H. Hong. Kierkegaard's Writings, 3. (Princeton, N.J.: Princeton University Press, 1987), 148.

31. Ibid., 150.

32. Ibid., 144–148.

33. Stephen Mulhall, introduction, in *The Cavell Reader,* ed. S. Mulhall (London: Blackwell, 1996), 17. Emphasis added.

34. Ricoeur, *Conflict of Interpretations,* 428.

35. Arendt, *Human Condition,* 237.

6. The Other and Violence

1. For Cavell and Levinas on acknowledgment, see Michael Morgan, *Discovering Levinas* (Cambridge: Cambridge University Press 2007), 76–78.

2. Simon Critchley, *The Ethics of Deconstruction: Derrida and Levinas* (Edinburgh: Edinburgh University Press, 1999), 287. Cf. Morgan, *Discovering Levinas,* 85–88.

3. As an exception, Paul Standish has provided some comments in "Education for Grown-ups, a Religion for Adults: Scepticism and Alterity in Cavell and Levinas," *Ethics and Education* 2 (2007): 88.

4. Robert Bernasconi, "Skepticism in the Face of Philosophy," in *Re-Reading Levinas,* ed. R. Bernasconi and S. Critchley (Bloomington: Indiana University Press, 1991), 153. Bernasconi has also argued convincingly that Levinas's sympathetic account of skepticism can be seen as a response to Derrida's critical question: how can his philosophy at once be philosophy—hence true to its *logos*—and yet bear witness to what falls beyond it? Cf. Jacques Derrida, *Writing and Difference,* trans. A. Bass (London: Routledge, 1978), 136–146.

5. Cavell has noted a similar thought in Emerson and Heidegger, where knowledge tends to take objects violently into possession. *NYUA,* 86.

6. Emmanuel Levinas, "Is Ontology Fundamental?," in *Entre Nous: On Thinking-of-the-Other,* trans. M. B. Smith and B. Harsav (New York: Columbia University Press, 1998), 9.

7. Emmanuel Levinas, "Philosophy and the Idea of Infinity," in *Collected Philosophical Papers,* trans. A. Lingis (Pittsburgh, Pa.: Duquesne University Press, 1987), 49.

8. Emmanuel Levinas, "The Trace of the Other," in *Deconstruction in Context,* ed. M. Taylor (Chicago: University of Chicago Press, 1986), 356.

9. One might ask if Cavell's insistence on the concrete, particular other runs counter to, and can be read as a criticism of, Levinas's rather generic other.

10. Emmanuel Levinas, "Freedom and Command," in *Collected Philosophical Papers,* 19.

11. Despite his own reservations, Levinas's thought has deep affinity to psycho-analysis. For a discussion of the literature on this topic, see Stine Holte, "Meaning and Crisis: Emmanuel Levinas and the Difficult Meaning of the Ethical," diss., University of Oslo, 2011, 107–127.

12. Cavell comments on the depressive position, in which the child is capable of conceiving whole objects (not just split parts), and is overwhelmed with guilt and feels the urge to mend; *PAT,* 148. Cavell is right to detect something similar in Levinas: at some point the face will put my justification for being in question, making me ashamed of harboring a murderer in me; "Philosophy and the Idea of Infinity," 58. To both Klein and Levinas, such a depressive position is decisive for establishing responsibility at the center of subjectivity.

13. Melanie Klein, "A Contribution to the Psychogenesis of the Manic-Depressive States," in *Love, Guilt and Reparation and Other Works 1921–1945* (London: Vintage Classics, 1997), 277.

14. Levinas, "Freedom and Command," 18.

15. Ibid., 19. Cf. Jill Robbins, *Altered Readings: Levinas and Literature* (Chicago: University of Chicago Press, 1999), 67–68.

16. Levinas, "Freedom and Command," 19.

17. Ibid.

18. Melanie Klein, "Envy and Gratitude," in *Envy and Gratitude and Other Works 1946–1963* (London: Vintage Classics, 1997), 189.

19. De Vries has studied their mutual attraction to Descartes; see "From 'Ghost in the Machine' to 'Spiritual Automaton': Philosophical Meditation in Wittgenstein, Cavell, and Levinas," *International Journal of Philosophy of Religion* 60 (2006): 86–91.

20. To Espen Hammer, Cavell appears to depart unequivocally from Levinas when it comes to religion, because Hammer thinks that Cavell advocates a liberal tradition that is flatly opposed to religion's appeal to authority. But upon closer reading of the quotation above, Cavell betrays the same hesitation, perhaps ambivalence as we have seen before; he does not straightforwardly say that it is incompatible with his own "responsibilities"—he writes that he *does not know* whether they are his. Hammer, *Stanley Cavell,* 146.

21. Viefhues-Bailey, *Beyond the Philosopher's Fear,* 51.

22. Emmanuel Levinas, "God and Philosophy," in *Collected Philosophical Papers,* 59.

23. Cf. Rudolf Bernet, "The Traumatized Subject," *Research in Phenomenology* 30 (2000): 162–168.

24. Viefhues-Bailey, *Beyond the Philosopher's Fear,* 151.

25. Emmanuel Levinas, "A Man-God?," in *Entre Nous,* 57.

26. Ibid., 60.

27. Cf. Dula, *Cavell, Companionship, and Christian Theology,* 158, 220.

28. This corresponds to the recent tendency to stress the weakness of God, as in Gianni Vattimo's proposed "weak thought" in *Belief,* trans. L. D'Isanto and D. Webb (Stanford, Calif.: Stanford University Press, 1999); or, following a deconstructive approach, John D. Caputo, *The Weakness of God: A Theology of the Event* (Bloomington: Indiana University Press, 2006).

29. Maurice Merleau-Ponty, *Signs,* trans. R. C. McCleary (Evanston, Ill.: Northwestern University Press, 1964), 71.

30. René Girard, *Things Hidden Since the Foundation of the World,* trans. S. Bann and M. Metteer (London: Continuum, 1987), 180–181.

31. Ibid., 216.

7. Forgiveness and Passivity

1. Charles S. Griswold, *Forgiveness: A Philosophical Exploration* (Cambridge: Cambridge University Press, 2007), 34.

2. Friedrich Nietzsche, *The Genealogy of Morals,* trans. H. B. Samuel (New York: Dover Publications, 2003), 16–17.

3. Rene Girard invests interest in the play for similar reasons. *The Winter's Tale* Shakespeare's most explicit about what Girard regards as his recurring motive: mimetic violence and scapegoating. In this play, Shakespeare reveals the awful fact, essentially modeled on the Gospels' account, namely that such sacrifice of the scapegoat is only a temporary and illusory solution that rests on a false projection of rivalry and violence. *A Theater of Envy: William Shakespeare* (South Bend, Ind.: St. Augustine's Press, 2004), 339–342.

4. Beckwith thinks that the full implication of forgiveness demands that Shakespeare's scene must be regarded as both art and religion, or more specifically, "of religion working through the agencies of theatrical art." *Shakespeare and the Grammar of Forgiveness,* 138.

5. Hammer, *Stanley Cavell,* 111.

6. Arendt, *Human Condition,* 247.

7. Joseph Butler, *Fifteen Sermons Preached at Rolls Chapel* (London: J. & J. Botham, 1726), 157–158. Resentment does, however, not take into account the full implications of Nietzsche's *ressentiment.*

8. Nietzsche, *Genealogy of Morals,* 27.

9. Nietzsche, *Thus Spoke Zarathustra,* ed. R. Pippin, trans. A. D. Caro (Cambridge: Cambridge University Press, 2006), 111–112.

10. Ibid., 16–17.

11. Kierkegaard, *Repetition,* 131–132.

12. Kierkegaard, *Fear and Trembling,* 37. Cf. *Repetition,* 185–187.

13. Cf. Hall, *Human Embrace,* 151–152.

14. Martin Heidegger, *What Is Called Thinking?,* trans. J. G. Grey (New York: Harper & Row, 1994), 105.

15. Augustine, *City of God,* 12.3.

16. Jacques Derrida, *On Cosmopolitanism and Forgiveness,* trans. M. Dooley and M. Hughes (London: Routledge, 2001), 49.

17. Jacques Derrida, *Given Time: I. Counterfeit Money,* trans. P. Kamuf (Chicago: University of Chicago Press, 1992), 6.

18. Ibid., 12.

19. Derrida, *On Cosmopolitanism and Forgiveness,* 39.

20. Ibid., 44.

21. Ibid., 45.

22. Still, Millbank argues that the whole exchange is initiated from God in an act of grace that exceeds any economy, but that makes economy possible in the first place. Millbank also reflects on *The Winter's Tale*, where the source of Leontes's refusal is conceived as a lack of trust and the destructive demand of security. *Being Reconciled: Ontology and Pardon* (London: Routledge, 2003), 57, 145–152

23. Jacques Derrida, *Acts of Religion*, ed. G. Anidjer (New York: Routledge, 2002), 383–384.

24. Jan Olav Henriksen has criticized Nietzsche for underestimating subjectivity's dependence upon otherness, in "Feeling of Absolute Dependence or Will to Power? Schleiermacher vs. Nietzsche on the Conditions for Religious Subjectivity," *Neue Zeitschrift für Systematische Theologie und Religionsphilosophie* 45 (2003), 319–323.

25. Cf. Mulhall, *Stanley Cavell*, 293.

26. Along this line, Beckwith reads Reformation theology (a bit one-sidedly, I find) as a form of skeptical solution to the troubling uncertainties of human capabilities. *Shakespeare and the Grammar of Forgiveness*, 43–49.

27. Gould, "Where the Action Is," 98.

28. Timothy Gould, "The Names of Action," in *Stanley Cavell*, ed. R. Eldridge (Cambridge: Cambridge University Press, 2003), 77.

29. Martin Luther, "The Disputation Concerning Man," in *Luther's Works*, vol. 34, ed. and trans. L. W. Spitz (Philadelphia, Pa.: Fortress Press, 1972), 139.

30. Eberhard Jüngel, *Theological Essays II*, ed. J. B. Webster, trans. A. Neufeldt-Fast and J. B. Webster (Edinburgh: T. & T. Clark, 1995), 238.

31. Paul Tillich, *The Courage to Be* (New Haven, Conn.: Yale University Press, 2000), 164.

Conclusion

1. For the former, see Mulhall, *Stanley Cavell*, 311; for the latter, see Dula, *Cavell, Companionship, and Christian Theology*, 156.

2. Cavell can also speak of redemptive reading in a more psychoanalytic way, with particular attention to how being read by a text compares with transference, *TS*, 52. For the way redemptive reading still trades on the religious sense of that notion, see William Day, "A Soteriology of Reading: Cavell's Excerpts from Memory," in *Stanley Cavell: Philosophy, Literature and Criticism*, ed. J. Loxley and A. Taylor (Manchester: Manchester University Press, 2012).

3. Eldridge, "Romantic Rebirth in a Secular Age," 417.

4. Ibid.

5. Desmond, "Second *Primavera*," 158.

6. Ibid., 160.

7. In his Heideggerian reading of Paul and his Pauline reading of *Being and Time*, Simon Critchley has similarly argued in favor of human weakness, impotence, and sinfulness, and correspondingly, for the need for a redeeming love beyond its own demands. *The Faith of the Faithless: Experiments in Political Theology* (London: Verso, 2012), 188–194, 206.

8. Mulhall, *Stanley Cavell*, 311. The Christian alternative that Mulhall proposes is a rather extreme self-sacrifice found in Simon Weil's writing.

9. Jürgen Moltmann, *Theology of Hope: On the Ground and Implications of a Christian Eschatology*, trans. J. W. Leitsch (London: SCM Press, 1967), 15–17.

10. Jürgen Moltmann, "'Das Prinzip Hoffnung' und die 'Theologie der Hoffnung,'" in *Theologie der Hoffnung* (Gütersloh: Güterslohe Verlagshaus, 1997), 331–334.

11. Moltmann, *Theology of Hope*, 30.

12. Cited at various junctures, such as *SW*, 137, 154; *CHU*, 136; *IQO*, 114; and *CW*, 30.

BIBLIOGRAPHY

Affeldt, Steven. "The Ground of Mutuality: Criteria, Judgment, and Intelligibility in Stephen Mulhall and Stanley Cavell." *European Journal of Philosophy* 6 (1998): 1–31.
———. "On the Difficulty of Seeing Aspects and the 'Therapeutic' Reading of Wittgenstein." In *Seeing Wittgenstein Anew*, ed. W. Day and V. J. Krebs. Cambridge: Cambridge University Press, 2010.
Allison, James. *The Joy of Being Wrong: Original Sin through Easter Eyes*. New York: Crossroad Publishing Company, 1998.
Anscombe, G. E. M. *Intention*. Cambridge, Mass.: Harvard University Press, 2000.
Arendt, Hannah. *The Human Condition*. Chicago: University of Chicago Press, 1998.
Augustine. *The City of God against the Pagans*. Trans. P. Levine. Cambridge, Mass.: Harvard University Press, 1966.
———. *Confessions*. Trans. H. Chadwick. Oxford: Oxford University Press, 1991.
Austin, J. L. *How to Do Things with Words*. 2nd ed. Ed. J. O. Urmson and M. Sbisa. Cambridge, Mass.: Harvard University Press, 1975.
———. "A Plea for Excuses." In *Philosophical Papers*. Oxford: Clarendon Press, 1961.
Barth, Karl. *Evangelical Theology: An Introduction*. Trans. G. Foley. London: Weidenfeld, 1963.
Bayer, Oswald. *Martin Luthers Theologie. Eine Vergegenwärtigung*. Tübingen: Mohr, 2004.
Bearn, Gordon C. F. "Sounding Serious: Cavell and Derrida." *Presentations* 63 (1998): 65–92.
Beckwith, Sarah. *Shakespeare and the Grammar of Forgiveness*. Ithaca, N.Y.: Cornell University Press, 2011.
Bell, Roger B., Jr. *Sounding the Abyss: Readings between Cavell and Derrida*. Lanham: Lexington Books, 2004.
Bernasconi, Robert. "Skepticism in the Face of Philosophy." In *Re-Reading Levinas*, ed. R. Bernasconi and S. Critchley. Bloomington: Indiana University Press, 1991.
Bernet, Rudolf. "The Traumatized Subject." *Research in Phenomenology* 30 (2000): 160–179.
Borradori, Giovanna. *The American Philosopher: Conversations with Quine, Davidson, Putnam, Nozick, Danto, Rorty, Cavell, MacIntyre, and Kuhn*. Trans. R. Crocitto. Chicago: University of Chicago Press, 1994.
Bultmann, Rudolf. *Theology of the New Testament*. Trans. K. Gropel. Waco, Tex.: Baylor University Press, 2007.
Butler, Joseph. *Fifteen Sermons Preached at Rolls Chapel*. London: J. & J. Botham, 1726.
Caputo, John. *On Religion*. London: Routledge, 2001.

———. *The Weakness of God: A Theology of the Event*. Bloomington: Indiana University Press, 2006.

Cascardi, Anthony J. "'Disowning Knowledge': Cavell on Shakespeare." In *Stanley Cavell*, ed. R. Eldridge. Cambridge: Cambridge University Press, 2003.

Cavell, Stanley. *Cavell on Film*. Ed. W. Rothman. New York: SUNY Press, 2005.

———. *Cities of Words: Pedagogical Letters on a Register of the Moral Life*. Cambridge, Mass.: Belknap Press of Harvard University Press, 2004.

———. *The Claim of Reason: Wittgenstein, Skepticism, Morality, and Tragedy*. New York: Oxford University Press, 1979.

———. *Conditions Handsome and Unhandsome: The Constitution of Emersonian Perfectionism*. Chicago: University of Chicago Press, 1990.

———. *Contesting Tears: The Hollywood Melodrama of the Unknown Woman*. Chicago: University of Chicago Press, 1996.

———. *Disowning Knowledge in Seven Plays of Shakespeare*. Updated ed. Cambridge: Cambridge University Press, 2003.

———. "Foreword to *The Scandal of the Speaking Body*." In Shoshana Felman, *The Scandal of the Speaking Body: Don Juan with J. L. Austin, or Seduction in Two Languages*, trans. C. Porter. Stanford, Calif.: Stanford University Press, 2002.

———. "The *Investigations'* Everyday Aesthetics of Itself." In *The Cavell Reader*. Ed. S. Mulhall. Oxford: Blackwell, 1996.

———. *In Quest of the Ordinary: Lines of Skepticism and Romanticism*. Chicago: University of Chicago Press, 1988.

———. *Little Did I Know: Excerpts from Memory*. Stanford, Calif.: Stanford University Press, 2010.

———. *Must We Mean What We Say? A Book of Essays*. Cambridge: Cambridge University Press, 1976.

———. *Philosophical Passages: Wittgenstein, Emerson, Austin, Derrida*. Cambridge, Mass.: Blackwell, 1995.

———. *Philosophy the Day after Tomorrow*. Cambridge, Mass.: Belknap Press of Harvard University Press, 2005.

———. *A Pitch of Philosophy: Autobiographical Exercises*. Cambridge, Mass. Harvard University Press, 1994.

———. *Pursuits of Happiness: The Hollywood Comedy of Remarriage*. Cambridge, Mass.: Harvard University Press, 1981.

———. "Responses." *Modern Theology* 27 (2011): 517–525.

———. *Senses of Walden*. Expanded ed. Chicago: University of Chicago Press, 1981.

———. *Themes Out of School*. San Francisco: North Point Press, 1984.

———. *This New Yet Unapproachable America: Lectures after Emerson after Wittgenstein*. Albuquerque, N.M.: Living Batch Press, 1989.

———. "A Touch of Words." In *Seeing Wittgenstein Anew*, ed. W. Day and V. J. Krebs. Cambridge: Cambridge University Press, 2010.

———. *The World Viewed*. Enlarged ed. Cambridge, Mass.: Harvard University Press, 1979.

Cavell, Stanley, Cora Diamond, John McDowell, Ian Hacking, and Cary Wolfe. *Philosophy and Animal Life*. New York: Columbia University Press, 2008.

Chadwick, Henry. Introduction to *Confessions*, by Augustine. Trans. H. Chadwick. Oxford: Oxford University Press, 1991.

Conant, James. "Must We Show What We Cannot Say?" In *The Senses of Stanley Cavell*, ed. R. Fleming and M. Payne. London: Bucknell University Press, 1989.

———. "On Bruns, on Cavell." *Critical Inquiry* 17 (1991): 616–634.

Critchley, Simon. *The Ethics of Deconstruction: Derrida and Levinas*. Edinburgh: Edinburgh University Press, 1999.

———. *The Faith of the Faithless: Experiments in Political Theology*. London: Verso, 2012.

———. *Very Little . . . Almost Nothing*. London: Routledge, 1997.

Dahl, Espen. *In Between: The Holy Beyond Modern Dichotomies*. Trans. B. McNeill. Göttingen: Vandenhoeck & Ruprecht, 2011.

———. "On Morality of Speech: Cavell's Critique of Derrida." *Continental Philosophy Review* 44 (2011): 81–101.

———. *Phenomenology and the Holy: Religious Experience after Husserl*. London: SCM Press, 2010.

Day, William. "A Soteriology of Reading: Cavell's Excerpts from Memory." In *Stanley Cavell: Philosophy, Literature and Criticism*, ed. J. Loxley and A. Taylor. Manchester: Manchester University Press, 2012.

Derrida, Jacques. *Acts of Religion*. Ed. G. Anidjer. New York: Routledge, 2002.

———. *Gift of Death*. Trans. D. Wills. Chicago: University of Chicago Press, 1995.

———. *Given Time: I. Counterfeit Money*. Trans. P. Kamuf. Chicago: University of Chicago Press, 1992.

———. *Limited Inc*. Trans. S. Weber. Evanston, Ill.: Northwestern University Press, 2008.

———. *Of Grammatology*. Trans. G. C. Spivak. Baltimore, Md.: Johns Hopkins University Press, 1997.

———. *On Cosmopolitanism and Forgiveness*. Trans. M. Dooley and M. Hughes. London: Routledge, 2001.

———. *The Truth in Painting*. Trans. G. Bennington and I. McLeod. Chicago: University of Chicago Press, 1987.

———. *Writing and Difference*. Trans. A. Bass. London: Routledge, 1978.

Desmond, William. "A Second *Primavera*: Cavell, German Philosophy, and Romanticism." In *Stanley Cavell*, ed. R. Eldridge. Cambridge: Cambridge University Press, 2003.

de Vries, Hent. "From 'Ghost in the Machine' to 'Spiritual Automaton': Philosophical Meditation in Wittgenstein, Cavell, and Levinas." *International Journal of Philosophy of Religion* 60 (2006): 77–97.

———. "Must We (NOT) Mean What We Say? Seriousness and Sincerity in the Work of J. L. Austin and Stanley Cavell." In *The Rhetoric of Sincerity*, ed. E. van Alphen, M. Bal, and C. Smith. Stanford, Calif.: Stanford University Press, 2009.

———. "Stanley Cavell on St. Paul." *MLN: Modern Language Notes* 126 (2011): 979–993.

Diamond, Cora. "The Difficulty of Reality and the Difficulty of Philosophy." In Cavell
    et al., *Philosophy and Animal Life*. New York: Columbia University Press, 2008.
———. *The Realistic Spirit: Wittgenstein, Philosophy, and the Mind*. Cambridge, Mass.:
    MIT Press, 1991.
Dula, Peter. *Cavell, Companionship, and Christian Theology*. Oxford: Oxford University
    Press, 2011.
Dybvig, Dagfinn. "Kingdom and Exile: A Study in Stanley Cavell's Philosophical Mod-
    ernism and Its Dilemmas." PhD diss., NTNU: Norges Teknisk-Naturvitenskaplige
    Universitet, 2007.
Eagleton, Terry. *Reason, Faith, and Revolution: Reflections on the God Debate*. New Haven,
    Conn.: Yale University Press, 2009.
Eldridge, Richard. "Introduction: Between Acknowledgment and Avoidance." In
    Stanley Cavell, ed. R. Eldridge. Cambridge: Cambridge University Press, 2003.
———. *Leading a Human Life: Wittgenstein, Intentionality, and Romanticism*. Chicago:
    University of Chicago Press, 1997.
———. "Romantic Rebirth in a Secular Age: Cavell's Aversive Exertions." *Journal of
    Religion* 71 (1991): 410–418.
Fried, Michael. "Three American Painters: Noland, Olitski, Stella." In *Art and Object-
    hood: Essays and Reviews*. Chicago: University of Chicago Press, 1998.
Girard, René. *A Theater of Envy: William Shakespeare*. South Bend, Ind.: St. Augustine's
    Press, 2004
———. *Things Hidden since the Foundation of the World*. Trans. S. Bann and M. Metteer.
    London: Continuum, 1987.
Gould, Timothy. *Hearing Things: Voice and Method in the Writing of Stanley Cavell*. Chi-
    cago: University of Chicago Press 1998.
———."The Names of Action." In *Stanley Cavell*, ed. R. Eldridge. Cambridge: Cam-
    bridge University Press, 2003.
———. Review of *Stanley Cavell: Philosophy's Recounting of the Ordinary*, by Stephen Mul-
    hall. *Journal of Aesthetics and Art Criticism* 56 (1998): 83–85.
———. "Where the Action Is: Cavell and the Skeptic's Activity." In *The Senses of Stanley
    Cavell*. Ed. R. Fleming and M. Payne. London: Bucknell University Press, 1989.
Greenberg, Clement. "Modernist Painting." In *The Collected Essays and Criticism: Mod-
    ernism with a Vengeance: 1957–1969*, vol. 4. Ed. J. O'Brian. Chicago: University of
    Chicago Press, 1993.
Griswold, Charles S. *Forgiveness: A Philosophical Exploration*. Cambridge: Cambridge
    University Press, 2007.
Habermas, Jürgen. "Religion in the Public Sphere." *European Journal of Philosophy* 14
    (2006): 1–25.
Hall, Ronald L. *The Human Embrace: The Love of Philosophy and the Philosophy of Love*.
    University Park: Pennsylvania State University Press, 2000.
Hammer, Espen. *Stanley Cavell: Skepticism, Subjectivity, and the Ordinary*. Cambridge:
    Polity Press, 2002.
Heidegger, Martin. *Being and Time*. Trans. J. Macquarrie and E. Robinson. Oxford:
    Blackwell, 1962.

————. "Phenomenology and Theology." In *Pathmarks,* trans. W. McNeill. Cambridge: Cambridge University Press, 1998.

————. *What Is Called Thinking?* Trans. J. G. Grey. New York: Harper & Row, 1994.

Henriksen, Jan Olav. "Feeling of Absolute Dependence or Will to Power? Schleiermacher vs. Nietzsche on the Conditions for Religious Subjectivity." *Neue Zeitschrift für Systematische Theologie und Religionsphilosophie* 45 (2003): 319–323.

Holte, Stine. "Meaning and Crisis: Emmanuel Levinas and the Difficult Meaning of the Ethical." PhD diss., University of Oslo, 2011.

Jordan, Mark D. "The Modernity of Christian Theology *or* Writing Kierkegaard Again for the First Time." *Modern Theology* 27 (2011): 442–451.

Jüngel, Eberhard. *Theological Essays II.* Ed. J. B. Webster. Trans. A. Neufeldt-Fast and J. B. Webster. Edinburgh: T & T. Clark, 1995.

Kant, Immanuel. *The Critique of the Power of Judgment.* Trans. P. Gayer and E. Matthews. Cambridge: Cambridge University Press, 2001.

————. *Critique of Pure Reason.* Trans. N. K. Smith. London: Macmillan Press, 1929.

Kearney, Richard. "The Epiphanies of the Everyday: Toward a Micro-Eschatology." In *After God: Richard Kearney and the Religious Turn in Continental Philosophy,* ed. J. Panteleimon Manoussakis. New York: Fordham University Press, 2006.

————. *Strangers, Gods and Monsters: Interpreting Otherness.* Routledge: London, 2003.

Kerr, Fergus. *Immortal Longings: Versions of Transcending Humanity.* Notre Dame, Ind.: University of Notre Dame Press, 1997.

Kierkegaard, Søren. *The Book on Adler.* Trans. H. V. and E. H. Hong. Kierkegaard's Writings, 24. Princeton, N.J.: Princeton University Press, 1998.

————. *Either/Or: Part I.* Trans. H. V. Hong and E. H. Hong. Kierkegaard's Writings, 3. Princeton, N.J.: Princeton University Press, 1987.

————. *Fear and Trembling.* In *Fear and Trembling/Repetition.* Trans. H. V. and E. H. Hong. Kierkegaard's Writings, 6. Princeton, N.J.: Princeton University Press, 1983.

————. *Repetition.* In *Fear and Trembling/Repetition.* Trans. H. V. and E. H. Hong. Kierkegaard's Writings, 6. Princeton, N.J.: Princeton University Press, 1983.

Klein, Melanie. "A Contribution to the Psychogenesis of the Manic-Depressive States." In *Love, Guilt and Reparation and Other Works 1921–1945.* London: Vintage Classics, 1997.

————. "Envy and Gratitude." In *Envy and Gratitude and Other Works 1946–1963.* London: Vintage Classics, 1997.

Kristeva, Julia. *Strangers to Ourselves.* Trans. L. S. Roudiez. New York: Columbia University Press, 1994.

Kuhn, Helmut. "Die Bekenntnisse des heilige Augustin als literarisches Werk." *Stimmen der Zeit* (1968): 223–238.

Lacan, Jacques. *Écrits: A Selection.* Trans. A. Sheridan. London: Routledge, 2001.

————. *The Ethics of Psychoanalysis 1959–1960.* Trans. J. A. Miller. London: Routledge, 1992.

Lambek, Michael. "Toward an Ethics of the Act." In *Ordinary Ethics: Anthropology, Language, and Action,* ed. M. Lambek. New York: Fordham University Press, 2010.

Levinas, Emmanuel. "Freedom and Command." In *Collected Philosophical Papers*, trans. A. Lingis. Pittsburgh, Pa.: Duquesne University Press, 1987.

———. "God and Philosophy." In *Collected Philosophical Papers*, trans. A. Lingis. Pittsburgh, Pa.: Duquesne University Press, 1987.

———. "Is Ontology Fundamental?" In *Entre Nous: On Thinking-of-the-Other*, trans. M. B. Smith and B. Harsav. New York: Columbia University Press, 1998.

———. "A Man-God?" In *Entre Nous: On Thinking-of-the-Other*, trans. M. B. Smith and B. Harsav. New York: Columbia University Press, 1998.

———. *Otherwise than Being or Beyond Essence*. Trans. A. Lingis. Pittsburgh, Pa.: Duquesne University Press, 1998.

———. "Philosophy and the Idea of Infinity." In *Collected Philosophical Papers*, trans. A. Lingis. Pittsburgh, Pa.: Duquesne University Press, 1987.

———. *Totality and Infinity: An Essay on Exteriority*. Trans. A. Lingis. Pittsburgh, Pa.: Duquesne University Press, 1969.

———. "The Trace of the Other." In *Deconstruction in Context*, ed. M. Taylor. Chicago: University of Chicago Press, 1986.

Luther, Martin. *The Babylonian Captivity of the Church*. In *Luther's Works*, vol. 36, ed. A. Ross Wentz and H. T. Lehmann, trans. A. T. W. Steinhäuser, F. C. Ahrens, and A. Ross Wentz. Philadelphia, Pa.: Fortress Press, 1975.

———. "The Disputation Concerning Man." In *Luther's Works*, vol. 34, ed. and trans. L. W. Spitz. Philadelphia, Pa.: Fortress Press, 1972.

———. *The Freedom of a Christian*. In *Luther's Works*, vol. 31, ed. H. J. Grimm and H. T. Lehmann, trans. W. A. Lambert. Philadelphia, Pa.: Fortress Press, 1971.

———. *Lectures on Genesis 1–5*. In *Luther's Works*, vol. 1, ed. J. Pelican, trans. G. V. Schick. St. Louis, Mo.: Concordia Publishing House, 1958.

Lyotard, Jean-François. *The Postmodern Condition: A Report on Knowledge*. Trans. B. Gennington and B. Massumi. Manchester: Manchester University Press, 1984.

Macquarrie, John. *Principles of Christian Theology*. London: SCM Press, 1977.

Malcolm, Norman. "The Privacy of Experience." In *Epistemology: New Essays in the Theory of Knowledge*. Ed. A. Stoll. London: Harper & Row, 1967.

Mathews, Charles T. "Book One: The Presumptuousness of Autography and the Paradox of Beginning." In *A Reader's Companion to Augustine's Confessions*, ed. K. Paffenroth and R. P. Kennedy. London: Westminster John Knox Press, 2003.

Merleau-Ponty, Maurice. *In Praise of Philosophy*. Trans. J. Wild and J. M. Edie. Evanston, Ill.: Northwestern University Press, 1962.

———. *Phenomenology of Perception*. Trans. C. Smith. London: Routledge, 1962.

———. *Signs*. Trans. R. C. McCleary. Evanston, Ill.: Northwestern University Press, 1964.

Millbank, John. *Being Reconciled: Ontology and Pardon*. London: Routledge, 2003.

———. "Sublimity: The Modern Transcendent." In *Transcendence: Philosophy, Literature, and Theology Approach to the Beyond*, ed. R. Schwartz. New York: Routledge, 2004.

Moltmann, Jürgen. "'Das Prinzip Hoffnung' und die 'Theologie der Hoffnung.'" In *Theologie der Hoffnung*. Gütersloh: Güterslohe Verlagshaus, 1997.

————. *Theology of Hope: On the Ground and Implications of a Christian Eschatology.* Trans. J. W. Leitsch. London: SCM Press, 1967.

Morgan, Michael. *Discovering Levinas.* Cambridge: Cambridge University Press 2007.

Mulhall, Stephen. *Inheritance and Originality: Wittgenstein, Heidegger, Kierkegaard.* Oxford: Oxford University Press, 2001.

————. "Introduction." In *The Cavell Reader,* ed. S. Mulhall. London: Blackwell, 1996.

————. *Philosophical Myths of the Fall.* Princeton, N.J.: Princeton University Press, 2005.

————. *Stanley Cavell: Philosophy's Recounting of the Ordinary.* Oxford: Oxford University Press, 1994.

————. "Stanley Cavell's Vision of the Normativity of Language: Grammar, Criteria and Rules." In *Stanley Cavell,* ed. R. Eldridge. Cambridge: Cambridge University Press, 2003.

————. *Wittgenstein's Private Language Argument.* Oxford: Oxford University Press, 2007.

————. *The Wounded Animal: J. M. Coetzee and the Difficulty of Reality in Literature and Philosophy.* Princeton, N.J.: Princeton University Press, 2009.

Nietzsche, Friedrich. *The Genealogy of Morals.* Trans. H. B. Samuel. New York: Dover Publications, 2003.

————. *Thus Spoke Zarathustra.* Ed. R. Pippin. Trans. A. D. Caro. Cambridge: Cambridge University Press, 2006.

Noggle, James. "The Wittgensteinian Sublime." *New Literary History* 27 (1996): 605–619.

Nussbaum, Martha C. *Love's Knowledge: Essays on Philosophy and Literature.* Oxford: Oxford University Press, 1990.

Pascal, Blaise. *Pensées.* Trans. A. J. Krailsheimer. London: Penguin Books, 1966.

Pippin, Robert B. "Recognition and Reconciliation: Actualized Agency in Hegel's Jena Phenomenology." *Internationales Jahrbuch des Deutschen Idealismus* 2 (2004): 241–267.

Plantinga, Alvin. *God and Other Minds: A Study of the Rational Justification of Belief in God.* London: Cornell University Press, 1969.

Putnam, Hillary. *Jewish Philosophy as a Guide to Life.* Bloomington: Indiana University Press, 2008.

Ricoeur, Paul. *The Conflict of Interpretations: Essays in Hermeneutics.* Ed. D. Ihde. Trans K. McLaughlin et al. London: Continuum, 2004.

————. *Fallible Man.* Trans. C. A. Kelby. New York: Fordham University Press, 1986.

————. *Hermeneutics and the Human Sciences: Essays on Language, Actions and Interpretation.* Ed. and trans. J. B. Thompson. Cambridge: Cambridge University Press, 1981

————. *Symbolism of Evil.* Trans. E. Buchanan. Boston: Beacon Press, 1967.

Robbins, Jill. *Altered Readings: Levinas and Literature.* Chicago: University of Chicago Press, 1999.

Rorty, Richard. "Response to Putnam." In *Rorty and His Critics,* ed. R. B. Brandom. Oxford: Blackwell, 2000.

Shields, Phillip R. *Logic and Sin in the Writings of Ludwig Wittgenstein.* Chicago: University of Chicago Press, 1993.

Speight, Allen. *Hegel, Literature and the Problem of Agency.* Cambridge: Cambridge University Press, 2001.

Standish, Paul. "Education for Grown-ups, a Religion for Adults: Scepticism and Alterity in Cavell and Levinas." *Ethics and Education* 2 (2007): 73–91.

Steiner, George. "'Tragedy,' Reconsidered." In *Rethinking Tragedy*, ed. R. Felski. Baltimore, Md.: Johns Hopkins University Press, 2008.

Szafraniec, Asja. "Inheriting the Wound: Religion and Philosophy in Stanley Cavell." In *Religion Beyond a Concept*, ed. H. de Vries. New York: Fordham University Press, 2007.

Taylor, Charles. *A Secular Age*. Cambridge, Mass.: Belknap Press of Harvard University Press, 2008.

———. *The Sources of the Self: The Making of the Modern Identity*. Cambridge: Cambridge University Press, 1989.

Taylor, Kevin, and Giles Waller. "Introduction." In *Christian Theology and Tragedy: Theologians, Tragic Literature and Tragic Theory*, ed. K. Taylor and G. Waller. Farnham: Ashgate, 2011.

Tillich, Paul. *The Courage to Be*. New Haven, Conn.: Yale University Press, 2000.

———. *The Dynamics of Faith*. London: Allen & Unwin, 1957.

———. *Systematic Theology II*. London: SCM Press, 1978.

Tonning, Judith E. "Acknowledging a Hidden God: A Theological Critique of Stanley Cavell on Scepticism." *Heythrop Journal* 48 (2007): 384–405.

Vattimo, Gianni. *Belief*. Trans. L. D'Isanto and D. Webb. Stanford, Calif.: Stanford University Press, 1999.

Viefhues-Bailey, Ludger H. *Beyond the Philosopher's Fear: A Cavellian Reading of Gender, Origin and Religion in Modern Skepticism*. Aldershot: Ashgate, 2007.

Ward, Graham. "Philosophy as Tragedy or What Words Won't Give." *Modern Theology* 27 (2011): 478–496.

Williams, Bernhard. "Moral Luck." In *Moral Luck: Philosophical Papers 1973–1980*. Cambridge: Cambridge University Press, 1981.

Wittgenstein, Ludwig. *Culture and Value*. Ed. G. H. von Wright and H. Nyman. Trans. P. Winch. Chicago: University of Chicago Press, 1980.

———. *Philosophical Investigations*. Trans. G. E. M. Anscombe, P. M. S. Hacker, and J. Schulte. Oxford: Wiley-Blackwell, 2009.

———. *Philosophical Remarks*. Ed. R. Rhees. Trans. R. Hargreaves and R. White. Oxford: Blackwell, 1975.

———. *Tractatus logico-philosophicus*. Trans. D. F. Pears and B. F. McGuinness. New York: Routledge, 2001.

INDEX

acknowledgment, 1, 3, 13, 14, 16, 18, 39, 42, 44, 45, 47–51, 53, 56, 60, 63–64, 65, 100, 115, 119, 121, 123, 125, 127, 133, 135, 136, 137, 140, 154n15; avoidance of, 50, 82, 134; failure of, 49, 79, 107; first-person, 54, 59; implications of, 49, 50; and knowledge, 53, 54, 60, 66; of limitation, 66, 70; mutual, 78, 126; and separation, 52–53, 66; third-person, 59. *See also under* God; other, the; self

actions, human, 19, 73, 83, 85–86, 91–94, 122, 126, 134, 135–136; consequences of, 81, 85, 86, 90, 96, 99–100, 101; indebtedness of, 86–87; and speech, 82, 91–93, 100, 136, 142, 156n13, 156n28; and suffering, 98; violent, 110

activity, 41, 60, 111, 134, 137; false, 42, 136, 137, 142; fear of, 135; hyperactivity, 110; and passivity, 19, 42, 135–136

Adam, 73–74, 76, 78–79, 97. *See also* Eden; Fall, the

aesthetic, the, 12, 14, 29, 33, 34–35, 43, 46, 65, 99, 149n17

alienation, 3, 24, 40, 43, 68, 72, 76, 78, 140, 157n29; self-alienation, 56

alterity, 37, 102, 105, 106, 108

ambivalence, 31, 68, 71. *See also* sublime: ambivalence of

art, 4, 16, 22, 26–29, 30, 47, 52, 59, 65, 91, 159n4; artists, 16, 28, 52, 92; criteria for, 27; genuineness of, 27

atheism, 3, 5, 22, 31

Augustine, 1, 12, 14, 47, 55–59, 64, 72, 74, 97, 130, 152n15, 152n21, 154n11, 154n17

Austin, J. L., 1, 7, 8, 10–11, 14, 35, 39, 61, 82–91, 93–96, 121, 155n6, 156n13

authority, 5, 27, 31, 90, 94, 149n17, 158n20; divine, 29; genuineness of, 28; philosophical, 8, 58

autonomy, fear of, 135; human, 3, 31, 92, 106, 145

avoidance, 18, 123, 134. *See also* acknowledgment: avoidance of

baptism, 61–63, 129, 145

Barth, Karl, 7, 58, 67–68

beauty, 23, 37–38, 102, 136, 150n12

Beckett, Samuel, 20–22, 149n10, 150n7

Beckwith, Sarah, 60, 153n24, 159n4, 160n26

Bible, 1, 61, 74, 118, 145; New Testament, 38, 145; Old Testament, 2, 89, 99. *See also* Adam; Eden; Eve; Genesis

birth, 13, 62–63, 97

body, human, 11, 17, 37, 38, 49, 54, 85, 108, 117; mind-body dualism, 116

catharsis, 43, 120

certainty, 9, 48–49, 51, 58, 61, 67, 77–78, 103, 108, 111, 123

change, 12, 24, 44, 46, 58, 62–63, 76, 80, 82, 120, 121, 130, 132, 141, 142; inner, 59, 63; possibility of, 100; promise of, 63, 64; sensibility of, 13

Christianity, 2–3, 16–21, 22–23, 24, 26, 30, 31, 80, 88, 89, 99, 100, 101, 107, 116, 117, 127, 130, 135–136, 138, 139, 140, 143, 144, 147n7, 149n9, 154n12, 161n8; Christian inheritance, 3, 147n3; Christian outlook, 2, 17, 18, 81, 97, 130, 142; Christian theology, 4, 15, 29, 114; Christian tradition, 4, 87, 144, 147n3; criticism of, 17, 20, 134. *See also* Judeo-Christian tradition

Coleridge, Samuel Taylor, 73, 74, 133
community, 36, 39, 52, 55, 65, 92; sense of,
    30, 65
confession, 2, 3, 14, 47, 48, 54–56, 57–60,
    62, 64, 80, 100–101, 126, 129, 152n11;
    consequences of, 58–59
conformity, 44, 138, 144, 154n12
consequences, 4, 56, 91, 92, 93, 100, 118,
    119, 121, 136; moral, 4; of the un-
    remarkable, 56. *See also under* ac-
    tions; confession; words
conservatism, 8, 12
creation, by God, 51, 68, 78, 124
Critchley, Simon, 20, 103, 149n10, 153n29,
    160n7
criteria, 10, 13, 27, 33, 34, 35, 39, 41, 50, 57,
    58, 67, 72–73, 76, 78, 85–86, 88, 94,
    123–124; limits of, 42, 43; public, 48
criticism, 29, 57; philosophical, 57; of re-
    ligion, 26, 143. *See also* Christianity:
    criticism of
Crucifixion, the, 54, 117, 142
culture, 4–5, 18, 61, 116; criteria for, 57; cul-
    tural inheritance, 136; modernist, 19
cynicism, 32, 68

death, 11, 37, 61, 62, 73, 75, 76, 125, 126,
    133, 137, 140. *See also* God: death of
deflection, 41–42, 44, 110
denial, 9, 13, 41, 50, 72, 76, 80, 91, 96, 105,
    110, 111, 116, 118; of the human, 17–
    18, 68, 73. *See also* skepticism: and
    denial
dependence, 51, 77, 78, 79, 124, 126, 135.
    See also other, the: dependence on
depressive position, 110, 122, 158n12
Derrida, Jacques, 7, 14, 30, 45, 82–85, 90,
    92, 93–97, 106, 121, 130, 131–133,
    150n1, 155n4, 155n6, 156n24, 157n4
Descartes, René, 41, 54, 64, 107, 113–115,
    116, 135, 137–138, 158n19
desire, 39, 52, 56, 70, 75–76, 78, 79, 108,
    120, 122, 123, 141, 154n19
despair, 10, 21, 68, 70, 89, 124
destiny, 81, 90, 97–98, 100, 102; and re-
    sponsibility, 97–99. *See also* words:
    destiny of

Diamond, Cora, 33, 35, 36–39, 41, 43–44,
    45, 46, 150n9, 150n11, 150n13
dogma, 32, 58; dogmatics, 57; dogma-
    tism, 70
doubt, 52, 67–68, 77, 108
Dula, Peter, 29, 147n6

Eden, 73, 154n15, 154n19
Eldridge, Richard, 140, 147n7, 152n21
Emerson, Ralph Waldo, 2, 6, 10–12, 13, 29,
    37, 71, 111, 137–138, 140, 141–142, 143,
    144–145, 154n12, 157n5
emptiness, 11, 24, 74, 75
epiphany, 102, 106
epistemology, 46, 48, 49–50, 51, 52, 60, 64,
    78, 103, 107, 115, 123
eschatology, 62–63, 142–144
ethics, 4, 14, 33, 43, 75, 87, 99, 103, 106, 110,
    111, 112–113, 114, 115
Euripides, 84, 85, 87
Eve, 73–74, 76, 78–79. *See also* Fall, the
everyday, the, 7–8, 11, 12, 13, 35, 37, 39, 41,
    42, 45, 62, 128, 130, 144. *See also* ordi-
    nary, the
evidence, 41, 49, 50, 55, 58, 108, 110, 123;
    empirical, 25
evil, 97, 101
exclusions, 83–85
exile, 3, 42, 57, 144; self-exile, 62. *See also*
    words: exile of
existence, human, 5, 64, 67, 71, 73, 79, 96,
    132
Exodus, 2, 62, 144, 145
extraordinary, the, 33, 36, 39, 46, 102–103

face, 105, 106–108, 109–110, 117, 158n12;
    ambiguity of, 106; denial of, 105; du-
    ality of, 110; ignorance of, 112; inde-
    pendence of, 107; negation of, 107; of
    the other, 50, 64, 102, 106, 110–112;
    and violence, 105, 109–110
faith, 1, 5, 14, 25, 26, 31, 44–45, 47, 53, 57,
    58, 61, 62, 63, 68, 79, 117, 128, 129,
    130, 135, 136, 140, 142, 144; ambi-
    guity toward, 22; and knowledge, 60,
    64, 70; and reason, 7. *See also* justifi-
    cation: by faith

Fall, the, 67, 70, 71, 73, 74, 76, 77, 78, 130, 154n15
fallibility, 73, 85, 87, 96
familiarity, 10, 11, 34, 37, 40, 43
fate, 14, 72, 82, 97
fear, 77, 80, 135, 154n15
film, 1, 4, 5, 14, 37, 79, 126, 128, 150n11
finitude, 3, 44, 67, 69, 70, 74, 75, 76, 121, 132, 141; acceptance of, 118; denial of, 76; of resources, 114, 115, 140. *See also* infinite, the; other, the: finitude of
forgiveness, 14, 36, 60, 101, 120, 121, 125, 126–127, 128, 129–130, 131–135, 140, 142, 159n4; acceptance of, 15, 122, 134, 137; genuineness of, 126; possibility of, 101
foundation, 35, 65; biblical, 61; metaphysical, 25, 58
freedom, 17, 62, 81, 82, 99, 128, 151n19
Freud, Sigmund, 43, 55, 59, 79, 84, 99, 111
future, the, 12, 24, 61, 62–63, 92, 94, 97, 98, 99, 100, 127, 128, 141, 142, 143, 144, 149n9

Genesis, 67, 74, 78, 125
gestures, 81, 91–92, 97, 103
gifts, 45; exchange of, 124, 131, 132; and forgiveness, 130, 132; from God, 51; indebtedness of, 125; of life, 111, 124, 125, 132, 133, 137; possibility of, 131
Girard, René, 118–120, 154n19, 159n3
God, 1, 5, 14, 16, 21–22, 23, 29, 30, 51, 52, 54, 55–56, 57, 59, 60–61, 63, 66, 70, 74, 76, 78, 98–99, 116–119, 129, 130, 132, 135, 136, 138, 141, 144–145, 152n23, 154n11, 154n19, 160n22; acknowledgment of, 51, 53, 54, 59, 60, 61, 63, 79; death of, 3, 19, 21, 23, 54, 64, 118; dependence on, 51, 79; existence of, 113, 114; humans' relation to, 47, 51, 52–54, 60, 64–65, 68, 69, 70, 79, 113, 135–136; idea of, 64, 103, 113, 114, 115, 135; judgments of, 22; possibility of, 31; separation from, 53, 72; trust in, 67. *See also* other, the: and God; self, the: relation to God

Gould, Timothy, 42, 135–136, 142
grace, 17, 29, 46, 51, 120, 130, 136, 137, 140, 142, 160n22
guilt, 81, 97, 98–99, 101, 110, 122, 127, 133, 149n9, 155n23, 157n29, 158n12

Heidegger, Martin, 5–6, 7, 12, 40, 71, 130, 157n5, 160n7
hope, 21, 81, 101, 128, 142–143, 157n29; false, 22, 62
horror, 34, 37, 42, 80, 150n12
Hughes, Ted, 37, 38
human condition, 8, 9, 19, 45, 59, 66, 67, 71, 73, 75, 76, 118
human nature, 17
humanity, 14, 18, 30, 34, 51, 68, 76, 80, 116, 133, 136, 137, 138; denial of, 73, 80; of God, 118; of the other, 116; and sin, 97. *See also* inhumanity
humiliation, 116, 118
humility, 8, 59, 116

identity, 85, 95, 100, 124, 142, 155n23; conceptual, 72; divine, 118; human, 80, 95, 101, 112, 114, 142; moral, 20; of self, 112, 142
ignorance, 40, 41, 112; passive, 40, 151n14
illusion, 12, 13, 22, 23, 43, 44, 70
immanence, 30–31, 119, 155n6
impotence, 86, 115, 123, 134–135, 160n7; of God, 118
incarnation, 116, 117, 118
indebtedness, 124, 125, 131, 133; acceptance of, 135. *See also* actions: indebtedness of
infinite, the, 35, 38, 44, 67, 75–76, 114–115, 117. *See also* finitude
inheritance, 63, 81, 136; Christian, 3, 147n3; philosophical, 6, 82. *See also* language: inheritance of; past, the: inheritance of; theology: inherited
inhumanity, 9, 17, 30, 68, 79–80, 139–140
instability, 31, 69, 104; of everyday speech and acts, 34
intention, 14, 20, 81, 82, 83, 87, 90–94, 95, 96, 98, 156n28; consequences of, 93,

100; inevitability of, 90, 91; intentionality, 84, 89, 156n14
intimacy, 39, 58, 101; of existence, 74; between humanity and God, 113; with
the world, 11, 71
isolation, 39, 49, 52, 65, 78, 113, 114, 122,
150n13
iterability, 83, 95–96

James, William, 31, 60
jealousy, 98, 108–109, 110, 111, 123
Jesus Christ, 2, 17, 54, 98, 116–119, 125,
142, 144, 152n15. See also resurrection: of Christ
Judaism, 2–3, 98, 99, 116, 145, 147n3,
148n16
Judeo-Christian tradition, 4, 75, 98, 99,
123, 157n29
judgments, 22, 68, 72, 93; moral, 92Jüngel,
Eberhard, 136, 145
justification, 28, 68, 84, 86, 87, 92, 119, 121,
137, 158n12; by faith, 67, 135, 136,
137, 142

Kierkegaard, Søren, 1, 7, 11, 12, 14, 16, 19,
21, 23–25, 26, 27, 32, 44–45, 98–99,
127, 128–129, 130, 149n17, 153n37
Klein, Melanie, 109–111, 122, 158n12
knowledge, 8, 9, 11, 35, 48, 49, 50, 51, 52,
53, 54–55, 60, 62, 64, 66, 69–70, 72, 75,
77, 79, 86, 103, 106–108, 111, 123, 135,
154n15; failure of, 68; finitude of, 70;
God's, 69–70, 76; possessive, 110–111,
157n5; possibility of, 68, 69, 71, 105;
self-knowledge, 14, 55–57, 59, 64, 100

Lacan, Jacques, 75, 95
language, 7, 10, 14, 20, 21, 23, 26, 28, 33,
34, 35, 39, 56, 61, 76, 85, 86, 104, 123,
153n27; bonds of, 72, 89; common,
78, 90, 130; criteria for, 78; inheritance of, 23, 57, 62, 94, 135, 153n27;
language games, 9, 23, 29, 30, 35, 38–
39, 43, 75, 105; private, 47, 87; responsibility for, 24, 62, 72, 90, 94, 95, 145;
trust in, 96. See also ordinary language; speech; utterances; words

Levinas, Emmanuel, 2, 7, 14, 102–110, 111,
112–117, 118, 122, 133, 148n16, 157n4,
157n9, 158nn11–12, 158n20
limitations, human, 9, 53, 66, 70–71, 75
literature, 5, 11, 75, 116, 140
loss, 12, 13, 57, 131, 140–141; possibility of,
45; of the self, 57, 62
love, 22, 23, 58, 119, 128, 134, 160n7; of
God, 56; self-love, 137
luck: extrinsic, 93; intrinsic, 93; moral,
92, 95
Luther, Martin, 1, 13, 30, 47, 60–62, 63–65,
67, 68, 99, 113, 129, 136, 137
Lyotard, Jean-François, 29, 45, 150n1

marriage, 78–79, 125, 126, 128–129; remarriage, 14, 121–122, 123, 125, 126–127,
128, 129–130, 132
Marx, Karl, 26, 143
meaning, 5, 20, 72, 81, 82, 83, 86, 87, 88, 89,
90, 91, 93, 96–97, 98, 99, 101, 106, 111,
129, 149n8; criteria for, 10, 18; possibility of, 104. See also words: meaning of
meaninglessness, 21–22, 73
Merleau-Ponty, Maurice, 32, 118, 149n8
messianism, 116, 117, 153n29
metaphysics, 3, 8, 9, 10, 11, 16, 17, 24,
25, 29, 34, 35, 43, 44, 46, 51–53, 58,
60–61, 70, 82, 84, 88, 89, 90, 91, 93,
95, 97, 103, 112, 114, 115, 122, 124,
135
Millbank, John, 132, 160n22
Milton, John, 1, 12, 79
miracles, 38, 46, 117, 118, 127, 143
modernism, 1, 16, 19, 26, 27, 28, 29, 31, 33,
65; postmodernism, 27, 29–30
Moltmann, Jürgen, 142, 144, 145
Mulhall, Stephen, 20, 59, 73, 97, 100, 142,
148n1, 150n11, 155n24
murder, 106–109, 110, 118
myths, 4, 73, 143; of the Fall, 67, 73–74

Nietzsche, Friedrich, 2, 7, 14, 16–19, 21,
31, 46, 75, 99, 122, 123, 126, 127–128,
129–130, 134–136, 144, 153n27, 159n7,
160n24

nihilism, 17, 41, 51, 109, 123, 124, 125–126
Noggle, James, 43–44, 45

ordinary, the, 1, 7–8, 10–14, 20, 26, 30, 33–36, 39–41, 42–43, 44, 45, 46, 59, 81, 88, 89, 97, 102–103, 104, 118, 128, 129, 131, 145, 150n7; achievements of, 22, 25; attentiveness to, 11, 56; finitude of, 74; instability of, 104; return to, 129, 130. See also ordinary language
ordinary language, 8, 9, 10, 24, 33, 34–35, 48, 55, 59, 61, 64, 71, 72, 82, 83, 96; ordinary language philosophy, 1, 8–9, 10, 18, 19, 20, 33, 43, 48, 55–56, 59, 61, 78, 90, 92, 93
other, the, 14, 39, 41, 48–51, 52, 53, 54, 64, 65, 66, 79, 104, 110–111, 113, 114, 119, 132, 141, 154n15, 155n23; acknowledgment of, 49, 50, 60, 80, 82, 102, 107, 114; annihilation of, 106, 107, 108, 112; denial of, 105, 110; dependence on, 78, 112, 160n24; finitude of, 60, 64, 80, 113–114, 117, 118; and God, 113–114; humanity of, 116; indebtedness to, 124; otherness, 34, 41, 66, 80, 106, 107, 109, 121, 124, 160n24; one's relation to, 77–79, 102, 103, 106, 108, 112, 113, 115, 117–118, 133; recognition of, 50, 55, 64, 108, 109, 116, 134; skepticism toward, 77, 107; and violence, 103, 107

pain, 47–49, 55, 85–86, 98, 99; criteria for, 50
paranoia, 110, 116; paranoid-schizoid position, 109–110, 122
partiality, 3, 78, 79
Pascal, Blaise, 1, 12, 13, 42, 54
passivity, 14, 17, 19, 40, 41–42, 44, 45, 111, 114, 115, 117, 122, 124, 134–137, 142, 145, 151n14; acceptance of, 112
past, the, 21, 28, 99, 100, 127, 129, 130, 132; inheritance of, 27, 97–98
Paul, Saint, 17, 39, 63, 73, 75, 76, 97, 118, 135, 136, 137, 143, 145, 160n7
Pelagianism, 72, 81, 97, 141

perception, 8, 10, 11, 37, 89, 95, 99, 103, 147n3; self-perception, 41, 104; sense, 9, 41, 52
perfectionism, 13, 32, 78, 145, 148n16; Emersonian, 12–13, 141, 142, 143; moral, 8, 12–13, 18, 63, 129
perspective: first-person, 48, 49, 59; third-person, 48, 49
phenomenology, 11, 40, 102, 116
photography, 37, 38, 39, 43, 150n11
poetry, 27, 39, 70, 140; romantic, 1, 10, 11, 129, 140
possession, 45, 62, 64, 70, 75–76, 106, 107, 108–109, 110–112, 157n5
praise, 2, 51, 134, 152n11
prohibitions, 106; God's, 74, 154n19
promises, 47, 60, 61–64, 87, 88–91, 128, 129, 137, 141, 142, 144, 145, 153n27; God's, 22, 61, 144; trust in, 47, 61, 137
prophecy, 4, 19, 39, 46, 63
Protestantism, 4, 28–29, 52, 64, 67, 80, 115; Protestant theology, 4, 15, 67, 80

reality, 16, 36, 41–42, 45, 52, 75, 86, 90, 113; difficulty of, 36–37, 38, 44
receptivity, 51, 56, 66, 112, 135
reciprocity, 61, 124, 131–132
recognition. See acknowledgment
recovery, 12, 101, 124, 125, 133, 139–140, 154n12
redemption, 2, 3, 15, 17, 21, 22, 62, 74, 117, 128, 134, 139–141, 143; promise of, 62, 141, 144; self-redemption, 118, 140–141, 145
reflexivity, 28, 56; self-reflexivity, 29
Reformation, 20, 30, 52, 60, 61, 65, 75, 113, 142, 160n26; post-Reformation, 20
rejection, 3, 9, 40, 112, 119, 123, 125; acceptance of, 117. See also skepticism: skeptical rejection
repetition, 45, 59, 95, 128–130
resignation, 44–45, 67, 129, 144
responsibility, 10, 12, 14, 22, 23, 25, 45, 53, 64, 74, 81–82, 84–85, 86–87, 91, 92, 93–94, 97–101, 102, 105, 112, 113, 114, 117, 119, 121, 132, 142, 143, 156n24, 158n12; ambiguity of, 98; avoidance

of, 29, 87, 115; delimits of, 86, 121; denial of, 96; moral, 50, 96; personal,
52, 53, 55, 94, 96, 97. *See also* language: responsibility for
resurrection, 22, 61, 62, 125, 132, 140, 141;
of Christ, 62, 117, 125, 137, 140, 142,
144
return, 2, 12, 43–46, 62, 128–130, 131, 132,
141, 144. *See also* words: return of
revelation, 5, 24–25, 29, 33, 50, 53, 55, 118,
144; of God, 116–117; self-revelation,
49, 50, 54, 80, 134
revenge, 100, 109, 122, 124, 126–128, 132;
against life, 125–126, 127; spiritual,
123, 135, 137
Ricoeur, Paul, 5, 62, 75, 97, 100, 154n11
risk, 25, 35, 39, 103
romanticism, 8, 10–11, 34, 69, 71, 140; English, 20, 140

sacrament, 58, 60, 61, 88, 89–90, 129
salvation, 25, 100, 141
scapegoat, the, 80, 118–120, 159n3
secularity, 5–6, 14, 19, 30–31, 67, 72, 79, 88;
secularization, 16, 30–31, 113, 143
self, the, 3, 12, 20, 50, 57, 59, 62, 63, 73, 95,
96, 106, 141, 142–143, 145, 153n27,
156n24; acknowledgment of, 52, 57,
100; relation to God, 47, 64, 135; identity of, 112, 142; selfhood, 12, 55
sensibility, 13, 34, 35; aesthetic, 46; contemporary, 2
separation, 3, 7, 52, 53, 64, 66, 78, 82, 102,
107, 124, 126, 129, 154n15; acceptance
of, 79, 125, 135; certainty of, 108; fear
of, 77; and participation, 78, 79; separateness, 6, 41, 42, 49, 51, 53, 72–
73, 74, 76, 77–79, 102, 103, 106, 108,
109–110, 111, 112, 117, 118, 124, 125,
133, 135
Shakespeare, William, 1, 5–6, 14, 50, 53, 60,
82, 121–123, 124, 126, 134, 159nn3–
4; *King Lear*, 50, 100, 117, 118, 119–120,
134, 137; *Othello*, 53, 77–78, 108, 111–
112, 115, 123; *The Winter's Tale*, 122–
123, 126, 131, 140, 159n3, 160n22
shame, 76, 134, 137, 155n23

silence, 21–22, 25, 39, 56, 64, 86, 153n37
sin, 3, 6, 9, 14, 17, 51, 53, 62, 66–67, 68–
69, 71–72, 75, 80, 97–99, 101, 102, 118,
130, 139–141, 154n12; and finitude,
74, 76; original, 14, 17, 18, 68, 69, 72,
80, 81, 97–98, 140, 157n29; responsibility for, 74, 81; wages of, 74, 76
sincerity, 85–86, 88, 89
skepticism, 1, 3, 9, 10, 11–12, 13, 14, 18,
30, 34, 40–41, 43–44, 47, 48–49, 50–
53, 64–65, 66–68, 70, 72–73, 75, 76–
78, 80, 85–86, 88, 89, 97, 103–105, 107–
109, 111–112, 114, 115, 121, 122, 123,
137, 138, 139–140, 141, 152n10, 157n4,
160n26; and deflection, 41, 42, 44;
and denial, 10, 79, 105, 108; inevitability of, 104; of other minds, 47, 82,
85, 109; and philosophy, 43, 105; refuting of, 25, 43, 48, 66, 104–105; and
sin, 6, 14, 66–69, 101, 140; skeptical
rejection, 25, 104–105; and sublime,
41, 42; and violence, 14, 101, 102, 105,
116
soul, 54, 56, 58, 59, 63, 117
speech, 25, 32, 36, 39, 48, 61, 62, 73, 81, 85,
89, 90, 91, 94, 106, 110, 131, 142; intelligible, 41; justice of, 96; ordinary,
34, 82; speech acts, 39, 61, 82, 83, 84,
87, 90. *See also* actions, human: and
speech
Speight, Allan, 93, 94, 95, 98
spirit, 45, 63, 128; realistic, 36
strangers, 3, 79
subjectivity, 52, 82, 112, 117, 142, 158n12,
160n24; ethical, 112; modern, 9, 16
sublime, 11, 35–37, 44–45, 76, 128, 150n1,
150n12, 151n19; ambiguity of, 39,
42, 43; ambivalence of, 34, 39; ignorance of, 40, 41; ordinary, 14, 33, 36,
38, 39, 40, 41, 42–44, 45–46, 102; possibility of, 45. *See also* skepticism: and
sublime
substitution, 112, 116, 117, 133

Taylor, Charles, 20, 30–31, 151n19
temporality, 12, 62, 92, 97, 98, 104, 106,
127, 128, 129–130

theater, 119–120, 125
theology, 2, 3–6, 14, 22, 26, 33, 47, 50, 51, 53, 54, 57, 58, 60, 63, 66, 67, 73, 75, 79, 115, 117, 132–133, 135, 136, 137, 139–140, 141, 142, 144, 147n3, 160n26; inherited, 5, 20, 62; limitations of, 28; and philosophy, 5–7, 13, 15, 53, 139, 153n1; theologians, 2, 68. *See also* Christianity: Christian theology; Protestantism: Protestant theology
Thoreau, Henry David, 2, 10, 11, 12, 13, 37, 45, 62–63, 131, 140
Tillich, Paul, 7, 67–68, 72, 137
Tonning, Judith E., 50–54, 148n1
totality, 35, 70, 76, 82
trace, 106, 113, 114, 117; and the face, 110, 117; and the other, 113, 114
tradition, 26–27, 52, 54, 58; Augustinian, 81; break with, 27; Greek, 82; Jewish, 2; Judeo-Christian, 98; Lutheran, 136; metaphysical, 82, 103, 115, 135; philosophical, 7, 102, 104, 111; religious, 143; theological, 54. *See also* Christianity: Christian tradition
tragedy, 50, 76, 81, 82, 85, 87, 88–90, 91–92, 93, 95, 97, 100–101, 121; Greek, 98, 101, 157n29; possibility of, 86
tragic, the, 81, 84, 86–89, 93, 96, 97, 98–99, 100, 101; tragic dimension, 14, 81, 101
transcendence, 9, 18, 31, 46, 66, 69–70, 103, 106, 117, 118, 119, 129, 143; of the face, 105, 110
transfiguration, 2, 13, 22
trauma, 102, 112, 114–115
trust, 67, 96, 137, 141, 160n22. *See also* promises: trust in
truth, 5, 18, 26, 57, 59, 66, 68, 86, 89, 135, 136; criteria for, 58; skeptical, 104, 112

uncertainty, 67, 103
understanding, 36, 69, 93; mutual, 36, 130; self-understanding, 19, 27
utterances, 2, 23, 31, 36, 48–49, 61, 81, 83, 84, 85–86, 87, 88, 89, 91, 92, 95, 100, 123; passionate, 39, 43. *See also* language; speech; words

vengeance. *See* revenge
Viefhues-Bailey, Ludger H., 114, 115
violence, 14, 101, 102–103, 105–106, 109–111, 112, 113, 115–117, 150n12; consequences of, 119; mimetic, 118, 159n3
voice, 32, 82, 93–95, 96; of correction, 58, 59, 63; of temptation, 58, 59, 63

will, the, 72, 127, 129, 130; will to nothing, 130; will to power, 76, 123, 134
Wittgenstein, Ludwig, 1, 4, 7, 8, 9–13, 16, 20, 23–26, 27, 28, 29, 30, 31, 34–36, 38, 40, 41, 42, 43, 46, 47–48, 49, 55–58, 59, 63, 64, 66, 69, 70, 71, 85–86, 87, 90, 150n5, 150n9, 152n21, 152n23, 153n37, 154n11, 156n26
wonder, 38, 46, 51
words, 8, 9–10, 11, 14, 19, 21, 22, 26, 29, 35, 39, 40, 46, 55, 59, 61, 62, 63, 68, 71–72, 77, 82, 87–90, 91, 94–96, 100, 123, 125, 156n22; Christian, 20, 21, 23, 24, 31, 89; consequences of, 20, 24, 48, 101; destiny of, 95, 96, 98; exile of, 24, 30; meaning of, 19–21, 23–24, 25–26, 31, 48, 72, 77, 89, 90–91, 95, 98, 156n28; ordinary, 21, 46, 48, 81; religious, 20, 23, 25, 31, 32; return of, 3, 24, 25, 30, 31, 94, 95–96, 101, 156n24; word as bond, 87, 88–89, 93. *See also* language; speech; utterances
writing, 62, 82–83, 93–94, 95, 140

ESPEN DAHL is associate professor of systematic theology at the University of Tromsø. He is author of *The Holy and Phenomenology: Religious Experience after Husserl* and *In Between: The Holy Beyond Modern Dichotomies*, along with several articles on ordinary language philosophy, phenomenology, and the philosophy of religion.